The
Fast Forward MBA
Pocket Reference

THE FAST FORWARD MBA SERIES

The Fast Forward MBA Series provides time-pressed business professionals and students with concise, one-stop information to help them solve business problems and make smart, informed business decisions. All of the volumes, written by industry leaders, contain "tough ideas made easy." The published books in this series are:

The Fast Forward MBA in Business (0-471-14660-9)
by Virginia O'Brien

The Fast Forward MBA in Finance (0-471-10930-4)
by John Tracy

The Fast Forward MBA in Marketing (0-471-16616-2)
by Dallas Murphy

The
Fast Forward MBA
Pocket Reference

PAUL A. ARGENTI

The Amos Tuck School of Business Administration
Dartmouth College

John Wiley & Sons, Inc.

New York • Chichester • Weinheim • Brisbane • Singapore • Toronto

This text is printed on acid-free paper.

Copyright © 1997 by Paul A. Argenti
Published by John Wiley & Sons, Inc.

This publication is designed to provide accurate and
authoritative information in regard to the subject matter
covered. It is sold with the understanding that the publisher
is not engaged in rendering legal, accounting, or other
professional services. If legal advice or other expert
assistance is required, the services of a competent
professional person should be sought.

Library of Congress Cataloging-in-Publication Data
Argenti, Paul A.
    The fast forward MBA pocket reference / Paul A. Argenti.
        p.   cm. — (The Fast forward MBA series)
    Includes bibliographical references and index.
    ISBN 0-471-14595-5 (alk. paper)
    1. Industrial management—Handbooks, manuals, etc.
    I. Title. II. Series.
    HD31.A6456   1997
    658—dc21   96-40006
                                                      CIP

Printed in the United States of America

10 9 8 7 6 5 4 3 2 1

For Julia and Lauren

Professor Paul A. Argenti has provided management and corporate communication consulting and training for over 75 corporations and nonprofit organizations in both the United States and abroad over the past 17 years. His clients cover a broad range, including Champion International, Warner-Lambert Corporation, the United States Information Agency, Sony, and Nokia.

Professor Argenti's work focuses on corporate communication issues, such as developing comprehensive communication strategies for organizations, products, or departments; enhancing media relations; creating links with government agencies; preparing for crises; creating a focused image and identity; and building better employee relations.

Professor Argenti has taught management and corporate communication starting in 1977 at the Harvard Business School, from 1979 to 1981 at the Columbia Business School, and since 1981 he has been a faculty member at Dartmouth's Tuck School. Professor Argenti has also taught as a visiting professor at the International University of Japan and the Helsinki School of Economics.

He published a textbook for Irwin in 1994 entitled *Corporate Communication* and is the editor of *The Portable MBA Desk Reference,* which was also published in 1994 through Wiley. He has written over 30 case studies and is the author of various articles for both academic and managerial journals. Professor Argenti also serves on the editorial board of *Management Communication Quarterly.*

Professor Argenti's department has been rated number one in the nation by *U.S. News & World Report.*

ACKNOWLEDGMENTS

Writing a book that takes an author beyond his own area of expertise leads inevitably to help from others. Professor James Seward from Tuck provided the raw material for the chapters on accounting and finance; Cathy Sirett, a grad student at Columbia, shaped the chapter on organizational behavior; Steve Lubrano, career-services director at Tuck, provided the material for the chapter on job search; Maura Harford, a writer and consultant from New York, was instrumental in creating the other chapters in the book; and Laura Turner, an undergraduate research assistant from Dartmouth, helped immeasurably with the development of key terms and references. But this book would have taken much longer to produce without the incessant cajoling of my most trusted research assistant here at Tuck, Mary Tatman. She made the book come together and deserves credit for what you hold in your hands. I would also like to thank Janet Coleman for signing the book at Wiley, Bob O'Sullivan for keeping me to deadlines, and Jim Childs for taking over the project in its final stages. Finally, Mary Hill, my administrative assistant, deserves credit for producing final copy and getting things where they needed to be throughout the project.

CONTENTS

INTRODUCTION

You know that the skills taught in MBA programs are essential to success in business today, but you can't afford either the tuition or the time away from your job. Or maybe you received an MBA several years ago and feel that some of the ideas and references you have in your notebooks are outdated.

This book is geared to those of you who want to learn more about the kinds of material covered in the top business schools without actually having to spend the time and money involved in attending an MBA program. Each chapter introduces you to the most important ideas from some of the most critical business school disciplines: accounting, communication, economics, entrepreneurship, finance, international business, marketing, organizational behavior, and strategy.

In addition, we have included a chapter on the job market. Most top business school programs put a heavy emphasis on helping students to get jobs, and this chapter reflects that emphasis.

Each chapter follows a similar format. Chapters start with *the basics* of each discipline. We have tried to provide you with the most current thinking culled from top experts in each field. The overview is not meant to be comprehensive, but rather to give readers the essence of a topic.

The basics are followed by *key concepts*—terms that you really need to know to understand each field. You will find all of the most important terms and ideas that people who work in these fields use and understand in this section of the book.

We also include an annotated list of *more readings* for each of the chapters. These are the most recent ideas that have shaped the thinking behind each discipline. Those of you who want more detailed information will benefit from this list of the best books, articles, and journals in each field.

In all, *The Fast Forward MBA Pocket Reference* should become an invaluable companion for you whether you just want to know a little bit about a topic or are seeking a more comprehensive look into a discipline. We hope that you will find the information useful and easy to use.

Paul A. Argenti
Hanover, New Hampshire

CHAPTER 1

Accounting

MANAGEMENT ACCOUNTING: DIFFERENT FROM FINANCIAL ACCOUNTING

Financial accounting is concerned with the reporting and communication of a business' economic information to *external* stockholders: shareholders, creditors (such as bankers and bondholders), regulators, and governmental tax authorities. Financial accounting information is intended to summarily convey the consequences of the decisions and process improvements made by managers and employees to the outside world. There are, of course, common rules that all businesses must follow in reporting their financial information. Financial accounting decisions are constrained by external regulatory authorities, such as the Financial Accounting Standards Board (FASB) and the Securities and Exchange Commission (SEC) in the United States, and by government tax agencies. As a consequence, financial accounting tends to be a rule-driven discipline, and students of financial accounting study the prescribed journal entries that generate a business' required financial statements. The benefit of such a process is that economic performance of many different businesses should be relatively easy to compare.

In contrast, management accounting attempts to provide economic and performance information to business insiders, such as employees, middle managers, and senior executives. Companies have significant discretion in the design of their management accounting systems. Thus, it is less rule-driven than financial accounting. Management accounting systems should be designed to provide information that assists an organization's employees in making value-enhancing decisions about its products, processes, and customers. For example, the information from a management accounting system should help employees understand how to improve the quality, lower the cost, and increase the responsiveness of their operations for customer needs. Therefore, management accounting students learn about the decision-making process and information needs of an organization, not about rules and journal entries. Table 1.1 provides a summary of the fundamental characteristics of financial and management accounting.

Based upon this brief overview, it seems sensible that the accounting process should start by determining an organization's information needs for internal purposes and then consider how to aggregate and present the economic impact of internal decisions for external constituencies. Historically, companies' accounting systems were primarily designed to meet the decision-making and control needs of internal management. During the past century, however, accounting for external constituencies became quite demanding because of external regulations (from the FASB and SEC) and shareholder and creditor expectations. Consequently, many organizations reduced their emphasis on developing information for internal purposes and began to emphasize external reporting as the higher priority. In this chapter, we will focus on both the production of information for internal purposes as well as its dissemination to outside interested parties. A sound accounting system is one that will provide accurate information for improved internal decision making and will create a concise representation of the business' operations to outside constituencies.

MANAGEMENT ACCOUNTING INFORMATION

The information produced by a management accounting system can include, for example, the expenses incurred in operating a department or the cost of providing a product, service, or activity. Management accounting information is one of the primary information sources for organizations. *Management accounting* produces information that helps workers, managers, and executives in organizations make better decisions. Traditionally, most management accounting information has been financial in nature. However, the areas of coverage in modern management accounting systems have increasingly expanded recently to encompass operational or physical (nonfinancial) information, such as quality and process times, as well.

TABLE 1.1 CHARACTERISTICS OF FINANCIAL AND MANAGERIAL ACCOUNTING

	Financial Accounting	Managerial Accounting
Audience	External: Stockholders, creditors, tax authorities	Internal: Workers, managers, executives
Purpose	Reports on past performance to external parties; contracts with owners and lenders	Informs internal decisions made by employees and managers; provides feedback and control on operating performance
Timeliness	Delayed, historical	Current, future-oriented
Restrictions	Regulated; rules driven by generally accepted accounting principles and government authorities	No regulations; systems and information determined by management to meet strategic and operational needs
Type of Information	Financial measurements only	Financial, plus operational and physical measurements on processes, technologies, suppliers, customers, and competitors
Nature of Information	Objective, auditable, reliable, consistent, precise	More subjective and judgmental; valid, relevant, accurate
Scope	Highly aggregate; reports on entire organization	Disaggregate; informs local decisions and actions

Measures and assessments of the *economic condition* of an organization—the cost and profitability of the business's products, services, customers, and activities—are available only from management accounting systems. Management accounting information also measures the *economic performance* of decentralized operating units, such as business units, subsidiaries, divisions, and departments. These measures of economic performance provide a link between the overall strategy of the hierarchical organization and the execution and implementation of the strategy by various operating entities. Management accounting information is also one of the primary means by which employees, middle managers, and executives receive *feedback* on their performance, thereby enabling each to learn from their past decisions and to improve performance.

Ultimately, organizations succeed and prosper by designing cost-efficient products and services that customers value. They produce these products and services and distribute them to customers with efficient operating processes. Finally, the organization's outputs are marketed and sold effectively to customers. Although an organization's management accounting information cannot by itself create success in these important activities, inadequate and inaccurate information from management accounting systems can lead a company and its decision makers to encounter severe operating and financial difficulties. An effective management accounting system creates considerable organizational value by providing timely and accurate information about the activities that are required for success in today's increasingly competitive environment.

FUNCTIONS OF MANAGEMENT ACCOUNTING

Management accounting information serves several functions, such as *operational control, product costing, customer costing,* and *management control.* Table 1.2 summarizes the important objective of each function.

The demand for management accounting information varies, depending on the level of the organization. At the line level, where raw materials or purchased parts are converted into finished products or where services are performed for customers, information is needed primarily to control and improve operational efficiency. That is, how can the organization provide a quality product at the lowest possible cost? Relevant information here is diffuse and frequent; it is more physical and operational than financial and economic. As we move higher in an organization, where supervisory work is performed and decisions about products, services, and customers are made, information may be received less frequently but is more aggregate and strategic. Information at this level is used primarily to convey a broad picture of the organization, to provide a

TABLE 1.2 FUNCTIONS OF MANAGEMENT ACCOUNTING INFORMATION

Operational Control	Provides feedback information about the efficiency of tasks performed.
Product and Customer Costing	Measures the costs of resources used to produce a product or service and to market and deliver the product/service to customers.
Management Control	Provides information on the performance of managers and operating units.

more complete assessment of the business, and to identify potential problem areas if some aspect of operations differs from expectations.

The information needs at higher organizational levels include summaries of transactions and events that occur at the individual employee or customer level. Here, more financial information is necessary so that managers can assess the profitability of events occurring at the operational level of the organization. At the highest level of the organization, the information is even more strategic and less frequent. A much larger percentage of the information is now financial, with only a few key operational variables or value drivers used to report on important success factors for the organization. Thus, management accounting information must be designed to provide what employees and managers need at each level of an organization.

CHANGING COMPETITIVE ENVIRONMENT

During the past two decades, the competitive environment for both manufacturing and service companies has become far more challenging and demanding. As a consequence, today's successful companies require better management accounting information. Information must be succinct and yet informative enough so that the proper actions and decisions can be taken on a timely basis. Let us explore the changes, both in competition and in the nature and type of the new requirements for management accounting information.

Deregulation of Service Companies

The deregulation of many industries in North America and Europe during the 1970s and 1980s has changed the competitive rules under which many service companies operate. Pricing, product mix, and geographic and competitive restrictions have gradually been virtually eliminated in the financial services industry. Transportation companies are now permitted to enter and exit markets and to establish the prices at which they offer their services to customers. Telecommunications companies, rather than having prices set by regulations to achieve allowable returns based on costs incurred and assets employed, now compete aggressively on price, quality, and service. Health care reimbursement is also shifting away from pure cost-plus recovery systems. Even government monopolies, such as the postal service, are today experiencing competition from private companies, such as Federal Express and UPS, that offer overnight delivery of letters and packages; from telecommunication companies that allow documents to be sent via facsimile transmission; and from new technologies that permit messages and documents to be transmitted on international electronic mail networks. Information to improve the quality, timeliness, and efficiency of the activities they perform and to accurately assess the cost and profitability of individual products, services, and customers has now become critical to the economic success of all these service organizations.

Manufacturing and Service Organizations in the Global Environment

Beginning in the mid-1970s, manufacturing companies in North America and Europe encountered severe competition from overseas companies that offered high-quality products at low prices. Global markets for raising and allocating capital, for acquiring and transporting raw materials, and for distributing finished goods allow the more efficient manufacturers, in whatever country they are located, to access markets throughout the world. It is no longer sufficient for a company to have cost and quality advantages against domestic competitors. A company survives and prospers only if its costs, quality, and product capabilities are as good as those of the best companies in the world.

Due to this enhanced competitive environment, the demands have become much greater for accurate, relevant information on a company's actual costs. This information is needed to:

- Assist engineers in the design of products.
- Identify where improvements in quality, efficiency, and speed are needed in manufacturing operations.
- Guide product-mix decisions.
- Choose among alternative suppliers.
- Negotiate about price, product features, quality, delivery, and service with customers.

Due to a variety of circumstances, however, companies' existing management accounting systems were inadequate for this more demanding environment.

Service companies' previously regulated and protected markets and operations provided no motivation for them to invest resources to develop accurate information on the costs of their products or the cost of serving individual customers. Thus, completely new systems had to be created to measure the cost and profitability of their product lines, market segments, and individual products and customers. New operational control systems also were required to improve the production cost, product quality, and process time reduction activities in these organizations.

Traditional systems that manufacturing companies had used for decades to measure product costs were now supplying highly distorted information, however.

These archaic systems failed to accurately assign the increasingly large indirect and support expenses that were now required to design, produce, market, sell, and deliver products and services that customers demanded. The errors introduced by costing systems that no longer reflected the economics of contemporary operations were causing incorrect decisions at all levels of the organization. Product engineers were designing automobiles and electronic instruments with too many options. While these designs greatly raised purchasing, materials handling, and manufacturing costs, customers were unwilling to pay high prices for products with features they did not want. Companies attempted to reach new market segments and new geographic regions, but the additional revenues from these initiatives failed to cover the incremental costs required to design, produce, deliver, sell, and service products for the new segments and regions.

Role for Activity-Based Cost (ABC) Systems

Activity-based costing (or ABC, as it is frequently called) is now being introduced in many manufacturing and service organizations to overcome the inability of traditional cost systems to accurately assign overhead costs. With many manufacturing companies now having overhead costs five or ten times as large as their direct labor costs, management accounting systems that allocate overhead based on direct labor may lead to large distortions in the costs assigned to an organization's products and customers.

ABC systems are designed to avoid arbitrary allocations and subsequent cost distortions by *assigning the costs of organizational resources to the activities being performed* by the resources. Then, activity costs are assigned to *the products, services, and customers that are creating the demand for or benefiting from the activities being performed.* Consequently, the cost of purchasing is assigned to the items being purchased, the cost of designing products is directly assigned to the new products being designed, and the cost of assisting customers is assigned to the individual customers.

Activity-Based Management (ABM)

Managerial decisions that are based on activity-based cost information are part of *activity-based management,* or ABM. ABM includes decisions to adjust pricing policies, change the product mix, and modify customer mix; to alter or even terminate supplier and customer relationships; and to improve the design and provision of products and services. Activity-based management also includes performing existing activities more efficiently and eliminating other organizational activities that do not create customer value. For example, companies can reengineer and improve their business processes and invest in new technologies that reduce the cost of providing activities demanded by the firm's customers.

Improvement of Operational Control Systems

The traditional product costing system was not the only management accounting system that became inadequate in the new competitive and technological environment. Operational control systems, with their detailed periodic summaries of financial performance, were slow in forwarding summary reports. Consequently, corrective actions were not taken on a timely basis. This information needed to be timely (available shortly after a process is finished) and disaggregated (reporting on the resources used for each individual job, not the sum of all resources used for all jobs performed during a month). The net result was that existing systems did not adequately identify the source(s) of favorable and unfavorable performance.

Monthly performance reports of many operating departments also had become filled with cost allocations, so that managers were being held accountable for performance that was neither under their control nor incurred by their operations. The costs of corporate- or factory-level resources, such as the heat and lighting in the building or the landscaping outside, were being allocated arbitrarily to individual departments, even though the departments were not directly responsible for these costs. Their incurrence could not be traced to the actions taken at the individual departments.

Changing the Nature of Work: From Controlling to Informing

Distorted and untimely information from management accounting systems was symptomatic of profound changes occurring in organizations. The nature of work was undergoing radical transformations. In the current climate of global competition that companies were now confronting, performance against historical standards was no longer adequate. *Continuous monitoring and improvement* of performance was necessary to remain competitive. *Continuous improvement* refers to ongoing processes by which employees problem solve and search for methods to reduce and eliminate costly waste, improve quality, and reduce product defects.

Managers came to realize that perhaps their best source of new ideas for continually improving performance would come from their employees, the individuals who were actually performing the work and who could see, firsthand, the defects that were occurring and the principal causes of these defects. Allowing employees to directly take corrective actions, without explicit authorization from middle managers and senior executives, has come to be known as *employee empowerment.* Companies practicing employee empowerment encourage their employees to solve problems and to devise new approaches for performing work and satisfying customers. To implement such improvements, however, the local operators could not be held strictly to inflexible, predetermined performance standards. Employees also needed information to identify the source and likely causes of defects and, subsequently, to observe quickly the consequences from attempts to fix the causes of the defects. In this *total quality* philosophy, employees became problem solvers. They were now part of the process that helped to find solutions for eliminating defective output, costly waste, and inefficient activities that do not add value to existing or potential customers. Thus, the role of employees changed from following standard operating procedures and monitoring the machines that were producing output to a role of quickly identifying problems as they arose, devising solutions for the problems, implementing the new approach, and ensuring that the identified problems had indeed been solved by these changes. In order to competently perform such a role, information was needed to *inform* about problem-solving activities, rather than to *control* employees against preset and potentially obsolete standards. *Management accounting information is thus shifting away from its traditional focus on controlling and prescribing the actions of employees. The information is now being used to inform and empower the employees to facilitate their continuous improvement activities.*

Role for Nonfinancial Information

Nonfinancial information about activities being performed has become critical to success in the modern organization. Employees must focus not just on reducing costs but also on how to improve quality, reduce operating-cycle times, and satisfy customer needs. For these new responsibilities, employees need performance data on activities, such as defects, rework, scrap, yields, on-time delivery, customer lead times, and returns. This type of information must be supplied frequently if employees, managers, and executives are to take effective action to improve performance. The exact nature of the data to be provided is driven from the organization's operational and strategic objectives that will make it more competitive in global markets.

Employee Empowerment: Sharing Financial Information

Among the myriad of new and interesting changes under way in providing relevant and timely information to assist employees in their quality and process improvement activities is an expanded role for financial information: quantities of inputs used, time required to complete a task, quality of work accomplished. Operating or nonfinancial information, of course, becomes even more important to employees as they participate in quality and process improvement activities.

Employees also benefit from the provision of cost and expense information about the resources they are using. For example, they can decide whether to bear the cost of replacing the tooling in a machine so that the output has more consistent quality. As employees modify and redesign processes, they should be concerned not only with improving cycle times, quality, yields, and productivity, but also with reducing the cost of completing work. For this purpose, innovative organizations are now sharing financial information with operators to enable them to:

- Identify the opportunities for significant cost reduction.
- Set priorities for improvement projects.
- Make trade-offs among alternative ways to improve operations.
- Evaluate proposed investments to improve operations.
- Assess the consequences of their improvement activities.

Thus, another new and important theme in management accounting is the role for *management accounting information to provide information to employees for their problem-solving and continuous improvement activities.* This approach stresses the use of financial and nonfinancial information to *inform* local decision making and deemphasize the traditional role for cost accounting information to *control* operator performance.

Measuring and Managing Activities

The concepts of activity-based cost systems, operational control systems, and expanded use of nonfinancial information for guiding employees' continuous improvement activities can be integrated by observing that activities constitute the central focus of an organization. *The measurement of activities is the key organizing principle for studying management accounting information.* Activities should be viewed as the method by which organizational resources and employees accomplish work and produce output. *Operational control information provides finan-*

cial and nonfinancial information on the cost, quality, and time required to perform activities. In turn, the operational control information is used to develop performance measures and targets that will signal how well individual activities are contributing to the overall collection of activities that are performed to satisfy customer needs. Activities also are the unit of measurement for cost information, leading naturally to the use of activity-based cost systems. *Activities are the link between organizational expenditures on productive inputs (people, equipment, materials and supplies, and energy) and the final products and services that are created and distributed to customers.*

BEHAVIORAL IMPLICATIONS OF MANAGEMENT ACCOUNTING INFORMATION

Thus far, we have focused on the role of management accounting information to *inform* the decisions and problem-solving activities of employees and managers. Information is never neutral, however. The actual process of measuring and informing affects the individuals involved and, consequently, their actions as well. As assessments are made on employees and, especially, on individuals and groups, the behavior of the individuals and groups is affected. People react to the measurements being made. They will focus their efforts and attention on those attributes or the behavior being measured and spend less attention on attributes and behavior that are not measured. In addition, if managers attempt to introduce or redesign cost and performance measurement systems, individuals accustomed to the previous systems may resist, perhaps even sabotaging the new system. These individuals have acquired expertise in the use (and occasional misuse) of the old system and will be concerned with whether their experience and expertise will be transferable to, and rewardable under, the new system. Employees also may feel some commitment to the decisions and actions that were taken based on the information the old system produced. But these decisions and actions may no longer seem valid under the information from a newly designed management accounting system.

Management accountants must understand and anticipate the reactions of individuals to information and measurements. The design and introduction of new measurements and systems must be accompanied by an analysis of the likely reactions to the innovations.

PRINCIPAL FINANCIAL STATEMENTS

The financial statements that constituencies external to a firm most frequently use appear in the firm's annual report to shareholders. The annual report to shareholders typically includes a letter from the firm's CEO or president summarizing operating and financial activities of the past year and assessing the firm's prospects for the coming year. The section of the annual report containing the financial statements includes the following:

1. Balance sheet
2. Income statement
3. Statement of cash flows
4. Notes to the financial statements, including various supporting schedules
5. Opinion of the independent certified public accountant

The Balance Sheet

The *balance sheet* is an accountant's snapshot of the firm's aggregate value on a particular date, as though the firm was momentarily frozen. The balance sheet has two sides: On the left are the assets and on the right the liabilities and stockholders' equity. The balance sheet states what the firm owns and how it is financed. The accounting definition that underlies the balance sheet is:

$$\text{Assets} \equiv \text{liabilities} + \text{stockholders' equity}$$

We have put a three-line equality in the balance equation to indicate that it must always hold, by definition. In fact, the stockholders' equity is *defined* to be the difference between the assets and the liabilities of the firm. In principle, equity is what the stockholders would retain after the firm discharged its other financial obligations.

Figure 1.1 gives the 19X2 and 19X1 balance sheet for a fictitious company, which we'll call the U.S. Generic Corporation. The assets in the balance sheet are listed in order by the length of time it normally takes a firm to convert them into cash. The asset side depends on the nature of the business and how management chooses to conduct it. Management makes decisions about cash versus marketable securities, credit versus cash sales, whether to make or buy commodities, whether to lease or purchase items, the types of business in which to engage, and so on. The liabilities and the stockholders' equity are listed in the order in which they must be paid.

The liabilities and stockholders' equity side reflects the types and proportions of financing, which depend on management's choice of capital structure, as between debt and equity and between current debt and long-term debt.

When analyzing a balance sheet, the financial manager should be aware of three concerns: accounting liquidity, debt versus equity, and value versus cost.

U.S. GENERIC CORPORATION
Balance Sheet 19X2 and 19X1
(in $ millions)

Assets	19X2	19X1
Current assets:		
Cash and equivalents	$ 420	$ 321
Accounts receivable	882	810
Inventories	807	840
Other	174	156
Total current assets	2,283	2,127
Fixed assets:		
Property, plant, and equipment	4,269	3,822
Less accumulated depreciation	(1,650)	(1,380)
Net property, plant, and equipment	2,619	2,442
Intangible assets and others	735	663
Total fixed assets	3,354	3,105
Total assets	$5,637	$5,232

Liabilities (debt) and Stockholders' Equity	19X2	19X1
Current liabilities:		
Accounts payable	$ 639	$ 591
Notes payable	150	159
Accrued expenses	669	615
Total current liabilities	1,458	1,365
Long-term liabilities:		
Deferred taxes	351	312
Long-term debt	1,413	1,374
Total long-term liabilities	1,764	1,686
Stockholders' equity:		
Preferred stock	117	117
Common stock ($1 par value)	165	96
Capital surplus	1,041	981
Accumulated retained earnings	1,170	1,041
Less treasury stock	(78)	(60)
Total equity	2,415	2,175
Total liability and stockholders' equity	$5,637	$5,226

FIGURE 1.1 *The balance sheet of the U.S. Generic Corporation.*

Accounting Liquidity

Accounting liquidity refers to the speed and certainty with which assets can be converted to cash. *Current assets* are the most liquid and include cash as well as those assets that the firm expects to convert into cash within a year. *Accounts receivable* are the amount of the firm's sales not yet collected from customers. This is generally due to the sale of merchandise on credit to customers. *Inventory* consists of raw materials to be used subsequently in production, work in process, and finished goods. *Fixed assets* are the least liquid class of asset. Tangible fixed assets include items such as property, plant, and equipment. These assets do not convert to cash from normal business activity, and they are not usually used to pay expenses, such as payroll. However, the activities they perform within the firm are designed to generate cash for the firm. For example, the construction of a new manufacturing plant is designed to increase productive capacity. Other fixed assets are not tangible. Intangible assets have no physical existence but can be very valuable. Examples of intangible assets are the value of a trademark, a brand name, or a patent.

The more liquid a firm's assets, the less likely the firm is to experience problems meeting short-term obligations. Thus, the probability that a firm will avoid financial distress can be linked to the firm's liquidity. However, liquid assets frequently have lower rates of return than fixed assets; for example, cash generates no income for the firm. A firm that invests more in liquid assets sacrifices an opportunity to invest that amount in more profitable investment projects. Thus, a firm's liquidity position often involves a trade-off between the likelihood of financial distress and the loss of foregone investment activities.

Debt versus Equity

Liabilities are obligations of the firm that require a payment of cash on specific dates in the future. Many liabilities involve legal contractual obligations to repay a predetermined amount and interest over a particular period. Thus, liabilities are debts and are frequently associated with nominally fixed cash burdens, known as *debt service*. Failure to repay on a timely basis places the firm in default. *Stockholders' equity* represents an ownership claim against the firm's assets. Generally speaking, when the firm borrows, it gives the bondholders a priority claim on the firm's cash flow stream. Bondholders can sue the firm if the firm defaults on its contractual obligation. This may lead the firm to declare bankruptcy. Stockholders' equity is the residual or remaining difference between the firm's assets and liabilities:

$$\text{Assets} - \text{liabilities} \equiv \text{stockholders' equity}$$

This is the stockholders' ownership share in the firm expressed in accounting terms. The accounting value of stockholders' equity increases when retained earnings are added or new shares are sold. The former occurs when the firm decides to retain part of its earnings instead of paying them out as dividends.

Value versus Cost

The accounting value of a firm's assets is frequently referred to as the *carrying value* or the *book value* of the assets. Under *generally accepted accounting principles (GAAP),* audited financial statements of firms in the United States report the value of the firm's assets at cost. Thus the terms *carrying value* and *book value* are misnomers in some ways. They specifically say "value," when in fact the accounting numbers are more representative of their cost. This may mislead readers of financial statements who mistakenly assume that the firm's assets are recorded at true market values. *Market value* is the value or price at which buyers and sellers are willing to trade the assets. Thus, it would only be a coincidence if the accounting value and market value of a firm were identical. In fact, management's job is to create a market value for the firm that exceeds the firm's cost.

Many constituencies use the balance sheet to extract financial information about the firm. A banker may look at a balance sheet to determine the firm's accounting liquidity and net working capital position. A supplier may be more interested in the size of accounts payable. This may indicate the general promptness of payments to its suppliers. Many users of financial statements, including managers and investors, want to know the value of the firm, not its cost. This is not found on the balance sheet. In fact, many of the true resources of the firm do not appear on the balance sheet: good management, proprietary assets, favorable economic conditions, and so on. These factors all add value to the firm, but will generally not appear as assets on the firm's balance sheet.

THE INCOME STATEMENT

The *income statement* measures performance over a specific period of time, usually reported on a quarterly and an annual basis. The accounting definition of income is:

$$\text{Revenue} - \text{expenses} \equiv \text{income}$$

If the balance sheet can be viewed as a snapshot, then the income statement is similar to a video recording of what activities the firm initiated between two snapshots. Figure 1.2 gives the income statement for the U.S. Generic Corporation for 19X2.

The income statement usually includes several important pieces of information. The *operations section* reports the firm's revenues and expenses from its principal business operations. Among other things, the *nonoperating section* of the income statement includes provision for all of the firm's financing costs, such as interest expense. Usually a second section reports as a separate item the amount of income taxes. The last item on the income statement is the *bottom line,* or *net income.* Net income is frequently expressed per share of outstanding common stock, that is, earnings per share.

When analyzing an income statement, the financial manager should keep in mind GAAP, noncash items, time, and costs.

Generally Accepted Accounting Principles

The matching principle of GAAP dictates that revenues be matched with expenses. Thus, income is reported when it is earned, or accrued, even though no cash flow has necessarily occurred (for example, when goods are sold for credit, sales and profits are reported). Revenue is reported on a firm's income statement when the earnings process is virtually completed and an exchange of goods or services has occurred. Therefore, items such as the unrealized appreciation in owning property will not be recognized as income on the firm's income statement. This provides an alternative for managers to smooth income by selling appreciated property at their discretion. For example, if the firm owns a subsidiary that has doubled in value, then in a year, when its earnings from other businesses are down, it can raise overall earnings by selling the subsidiary.

Noncash Items

The market value of assets depends upon their future incremental cash flows. However, cash flow is not reported on an income statement. This is due to the fact that there are several *noncash items* reported as expenses against revenues, but these items do not affect cash flow. The most important noncash item is *depreciation.* Depreciation represents an accountant's estimate of the cost of equipment used during that time period in the production process. For example, suppose an asset with a five-year life and no resale value is purchased for $5,000. The $5,000 cost must be expensed over the useful life of the asset, despite the fact that the firm actually incurs the full expense at the time of purchase. If straight-line depreciation is used, there will be five equal charges of $1,000 of depreciation expense

U.S. GENERIC CORPORATION
Income Statement
19X2
(in $ millions)

Total of operating revenues	$ 6,786
Cost of goods sold	(4,965)
Selling, general, and administrative expenses	(981)
Depreciation	(270)
Operating income	570
Other income	87
Earnings before interest and taxes	657
Interest expense	(147)
Pretax income	510
Taxes	(252)
Current: $213	
Deferred: $39	
Net income	$ 86

FIGURE 1.2 *The income statement of the U.S. Generic Corporation.*

each year. From a finance perspective, the cost of the asset is the actual negative cash flow incurred when the asset is acquired (that is, $5,000, *not* the accountant's smoothed $1,000-per-year depreciation expense). Depreciation does have a cash flow effect, however. This is due to the fact that depreciation is deductible for corporate income tax purposes.

Another common noncash expense is *deferred taxes*. Deferred taxes result from differences between accounting income and true taxable income. Notice that the accounting tax shown on the income statement for the U.S. Generic Corporation is $252 million. It can be broken down as current taxes and deferred taxes. The current tax portion is the amount actually sent to the tax authorities during the time period covered by the income statement (for example, the Internal Revenue Service). The deferred tax portion is not. However, if taxable income is less than accounting income in any given year, it will exceed accounting income in the future. Consequently, taxes that are not paid today must be paid at some point in the future; hence, they represent a liability of the firm. This liability shows up on the balance sheet of the firm as deferred tax liability. From the cash flow perspective, though, deferred tax is not a cash outflow.

Time and Costs

Think of future time as having two distinct parts, the *short run* and the *long run*. The short run is that period of time in which certain equipment, resources, and commitments of the firm are fixed. It is, however, long enough for the firm to vary its output by using more labor and raw materials. The short run is not a precise period of time that will be the same for all industries or even all firms within the same industry. However, all firms making decisions in the short run have some *fixed costs,* that is, costs that will not change because of the fixed commitments. Examples of fixed costs are interest payments, overhead expenses, and property taxes. Costs that are not fixed are variable. *Variable costs* change as the output of the firm changes. Some common examples of variable costs are those for raw materials and employee wages.

In the long run, all costs are variable. Financial accountants do not distinguish between variable costs and fixed costs. Instead, accounting costs usually fit into a classification that distinguishes product costs from period costs. *Product costs* are the total production costs incurred during some particular period and are reported on the income statement as cost of goods sold. *Production costs* would normally consist of items such as raw materials, direct labor, and manufacturing overhead. Both variable and fixed costs are included in product costs. Period costs are costs that are allocated to a time period. Those are usually referred to as *selling, general, and administrative expenses*. An example of a period cost would be the company CEO's salary.

NET WORKING CAPITAL

Net working capital is defined as current assets minus current liabilities. Net working capital is positive when current assets are greater than current liabilities. In this case, the cash that will become available from assets over the next year exceeds the cash that must be paid out. The net working capital of the U.S. Generic Corporation is $825 million in 19X2 and $756 million in 19X1:

	Current assets ($ millions)	–	Current liabilities ($ millions)	=	Net working capital ($ millions)
19X2	$2,283	–	$1,458	=	$825
19X1	$2,121	–	$1,365	=	$756

In addition to investing in fixed assets (i.e., capital spending), a firm can invest resources in net working capital. This incremental investment is called the *change in net working capital*. The change in net working capital in 19X2 is the difference between the net working capital in 19X2 and 19X1, that is, $825 million – $756 million = $69 million. The change in net working capital is usually positive in a growing firm. Hence, the difference must be financed with some long-term source of capital, such as debt or equity.

FINANCIAL CASH FLOW

Perhaps the most important item that can be extracted from financial statements is the firm's actual *cash flow*. The statement of cash flow helps to explain the change in accounting cash and equivalents, which for U.S. Generic is $99 million in 19X2. Notice in Figure 1.1 that cash and equivalents increase from $321 million in 19X1 to $420 million in 19X2. The market value of the firm increases as the firm generates financial cash flow.

Cash flow is not the same as net working capital. For example, increasing inventory requires a use of the firm's cash. Because both inventories and cash are current assets, this investment does not affect net working capital. In this situation, an increase in a particular net working capital account, such as inventory, decreases cash flow.

Similar to the relationship that the value of a firm's assets is equal to the value of the liabilities and the value of the equity, the cash flows from the firm's assets (that is, its operating activities), CF(A), must equal the cash flows to the firm's creditors, CF(B), and equity investors, CF(S):

$$CF(A) \equiv CF(B) + CF(S)$$

The first step in determining a firm's cash flow is to calculate the *cash flow from operations*. As can be seen in Figure 1.3, operating cash flow is the cash flow generated by business activities, including sales of goods and services. Operating cash flow reflects tax payments, but not financing, capital spending, or changes in net working capital.

	(*in $ millions*)
Earnings before interest and taxes	$657
Depreciation	270
Current taxes	(213)
Operating cash flow	$714

Another important component of cash flow involves *changes in fixed assets*. The net change in fixed assets equals sales of existing fixed assets minus the acquisition of new fixed assets. The result is the cash flow used for capital spending:

Acquisition of fixed assets	$594
Sales of fixed assets	(75)
Capital spending	$519

Cash flows are also used for making investments in net working capital. In the U.S. Generic Corporation in 19X2, *additions to net working capital* are:

Additions to net working capital	$594

Total cash flows generated by the firm's assets are the sum of:

U.S. GENERIC CORPORATION
Financial Cash Flow
19X2
(in $ millions)

Cash flow of the firm

Operating cash flow	$ 714
(Earnings before interest and taxes plus depreciation minus taxes)	
Capital spending	(519)
(Acquisitions of fixed assets minus sales of fixed assets)	
Additions to net working capital	(69)
Total	$ 126

Cash flow to investors in the firm

Debt	$ 108
(Interest plus retirement of debt minus long-term debt financing)	
Equity	18
(Dividends plus repurchase of equity minus new equity financing)	
Retained earnings: $129	
Total	$ 126

FIGURE 1.3 *Financial cash flow of the U.S. Generic Corporation.*

Operating cash flow	$714
Capital spending	(519)
Additions to net working capital	(69)
Total cash flow of the firm	$126

The total outflow of cash of the firm can be separated into cash flow paid to creditors and cash flows paid to stockholders. Creditors are paid an amount generally referred to as *debt service*. Debt service consists of interest payments plus any repayments of principal (that is, retirement of debt).

An important source of cash flow is from selling new debt. Thus, an increase in long-term debt is the net effect of new borrowing and repayment of maturing obligations plus interest expense.

Cash Flow Paid to Creditors
($ millions)

Interest	$ 147
Retirement of debt	219
Debt service	366
Proceeds from long-term debt sales	(258)
Total	$ 108

Cash flow of the firm also is paid to the stockholders. It consists of paying dividends plus repurchasing out-

standing shares of stock and issuing new shares of
stock.

Cash Flow to Stockholders
($ millions)

Dividends	$ 129
Repurchase of stock	18
Cash to stockholders	147
Proceeds from new stock issue	(129)
Total	$ 18

Several important observations can be drawn from
our discussion of cash flow:

1. Several types of cash flow are relevant to a complete
   understanding of the financial situation of the firm.
   Operating cash flow, defined as earnings before
   interest and depreciation minus taxes, measures the
   cash generated from operations, not counting capital
   spending or working capital requirements. It should
   usually be positive; a firm is in trouble if operating
   cash flow is negative for a long time, because the
   firm is not generating enough cash to pay operating
   costs. *Total cash flow of the firm* includes adjustments for capital spending and additions to net
   working capital. It will oftentimes be negative. When
   a firm is growing rapidly, expenditures on accounts
   receivable and fixed assets can be higher than cash
   flow receipts from sales.

2. Net income is not cash flow. The net income of the
   U.S. Generic Corporation in 19X2 was $258 million,
   whereas cash flow was $126 million. The two num-
   bers are not usually the same. In determining the
   economic and financial condition of a firm, cash flow
   is more relevant.

FINANCIAL ACCOUNTING: MEASUREMENT
OF ACCOUNTING INCOME VERSUS
CASH FLOW

The emphasis in accounting income statements is the
determination of the net income of the firm. The value
of a firm depends on its *cash flow.* That is, the value of
an asset (or a whole firm) is determined by the cash
flow it generates. The firm's net income is important,
but cash flow is even more important because dividends must be paid in cash and because cash is necessary to purchase the assets required to continue
operations.

Since the value of any asset, including a share of
stock, depends on the cash flow produced by the asset,
managers should act to maximize the cash flow available to its providers of capital over the long run. A
business' cash flow is equal to cash from sales, minus
cash operating costs, minus interest charges, and

minus taxes. Before we proceed further, however, we need to discuss *depreciation,* which is an operating cost, but not a cash outlay.

Recall that depreciation is an annual charge against income which reflects the estimated dollar cost of the capital equipment used up in the production process. For example, suppose a machine with a life of seven years and a zero expected salvage value was purchased in 1994 for $210,000. This $210,000 cost is not expensed in the purchase year; rather, it is charged against production over the machine's seven-year depreciable life. If the depreciation expense were not taken, profits would be overstated, and taxes would be too high. So the annual depreciation charge is deducted from sales revenues, along with such other costs as labor and raw materials, to determine taxable income. However, because the $210,000 was actually expended back in 1994, the depreciation charged against income in 1995 through 2001 is not a cash outlay, as are labor or raw materials charges. *Depreciation is a noncash charge, so it must be added back to net income to obtain the cash flow from operations.*

Because dividends are paid in cash, a company's ability to pay dividends depends on its cash flow. Cash flow is generally related to *accounting profit,* which is simply net income as reported on the income statement. Although companies with relatively high accounting profits generally have relatively high cash flows, the relationship is not always perfect. Therefore, investors are concerned about cash flow projections as well as accounting profit projections.

Firms can be thought of as having two separate but related sources of organizational value: *existing assets,* which provide current profits and cash flows, and *growth opportunities,* which represent opportunities to make new investments that will eventually increase future profits and cash flows. The ability to take advantage of growth opportunities often depends on the availability of the cash needed to buy new assets, and the cash flow from existing assets is often the primary source of the funds used to make profitable new investments. This is another reason why both investors and managers are concerned with cash flows as well as profits.

For our purposes, it is useful to divide cash flow into two classes: (1) *operating cash flows* and (2) *other cash flows.* Operating cash flows arise from normal operations, and they are, in essence, the difference between sales revenues and cash expenses, including taxes paid. Other cash flows arise from the issuance of stock, from borrowing, or from the sale of fixed assets. Our focus here is on operating cash flow.

Operating cash flow can differ from accounting profits (or net income) for three primary reasons:

1. All the taxes reported on the income statement may not have to be paid during the current year, or, under certain circumstances, the actual cash payments for taxes may exceed the tax figure deducted from sales to calculate net income.

2. Sales may be on credit and, hence, may not represent cash.

3. Some of the expenses (or costs) deducted from sales to determine profits may not be cash costs. Most important, depreciation is not a cash cost.

Thus, operating cash flow could be larger or smaller than accounting profits during any given year.

The Cash Flow Cycle

As a company operates its business, it makes sales, which lead (1) to a reduction of inventories, (2) to an increase in cash, and (3), if the sales price exceeds the cost of the item sold, to a profit. These transactions cause the balance sheet to change, and they are also reflected in the income statement. It is critical that you understand (1) that businesses deal with *physical* units such as autos, computers, or aluminum; (2) that these activities are translated into dollar terms through the accounting system; and (3) that the purpose of financial analysis is to examine the accounting numbers in order to determine how efficiently the firm is producing and selling physical goods and services.

Several mitigating factors make financial analysis of a firm's operations difficult. One is the differences that exist in accounting methods among firms. Different methods of inventory valuation and depreciation can lead to differences in reported profits for otherwise identical firms. Therefore, a good financial analyst must be able to adjust for these differences if he or she is to make valid comparisons of the operations of different companies. Another factor involves timing—actions are taken at one point in time, but their full effects cannot be accurately measured until a later date. Investments made today produce cash flow consequences over several years in the future.

To understand how timing influences the financial statements, one must understand the *cash flow cycle*. Various transactions and activities cause changes in the balance sheet accounts. For example, collecting an account receivable reduces the receivables account, but this transaction also increases the cash account.

The cash (and marketable securities) account should be the focal point of a manager. Certain activities, such as collecting accounts receivable or borrowing money from the bank, will cause the cash account to increase, while the payment of taxes, interest, dividends, and accounts payable will cause it to decline. Similar comments could be made about all the balance sheet accounts—their balances rise, fall, or remain constant depending on events that occur during the period under study.

Projected increases in sales may require the firm to raise cash by borrowing from its bank, by selling additional bonds, or by selling new stock. For example, if a firm anticipates an increase in sales, it will (1) expend cash to buy or build fixed assets through the capital budgeting process; (2) step up purchases of raw materials, thereby increasing both raw materials inventories and accounts payable; and (3) eventually build up its finished goods inventory. Cash will have been expended and, hence, removed from the cash account, and the firm will have obligated itself to expend still more cash within a few weeks to pay off its accounts payable and accrued wages. These cash-using events often will have occurred *before* any new cash has been generated from sales. Even when the anticipated sales do take place, there may still be a delay in the collection of cash. If a firm grants credit for 30 days, it will have to wait 30 days after a sale is made before cash comes in. Depending on how much cash the firm had at the beginning of the buildup, on the length of its production-sales-collection cycle, and on how long it can delay payment of its own payables and accrued wages, a firm may have to obtain substantial amounts of additional cash by selling stock or bonds or by borrowing from the bank.

If the firm is profitable, its sales revenues will exceed its costs, and its cash inflows will eventually exceed its cash outlays. However, even a profitable business can experience a cash shortage if it is growing rapidly. It may have to pay for plant, materials, and labor before cash from the expanded sales starts flowing in. For this reason, rapidly growing firms generally require large bank loans plus capital from other sources.

An unprofitable firm will have larger cash outlays than inflows. This, in turn, will drain the cash account and also cause a buildup of accrued wages and accounts payable, and lead to heavy borrowings. As a result, liabilities rise to excessive levels in unprofitable firms. Similarly, an overly ambitious expansion plan may result in excessive inventories and fixed assets, while too lenient a credit/collection policy will result in high accounts receivable, which may eventually result in bad debts and reduced profits.

STATEMENT OF CASH FLOWS

The statement of cash flows helps explain the change in accounting cash, which for U.S. Generic is $99 million in 19X2. It is very useful in understanding financial cash flow. Notice in Table 1.3 that cash increases from $321 million in 19X1 to $420 million in 19X2.

The first step in determining the change in cash is to determine cash flow from operating activities. This is the cash flow that results from the firm's normal activities of producing and selling goods and services. The second step is to make an adjustment for cash flow from investing activities. The final step is to make an adjustment for cash flow from financing activities. Financing activities are the net payments to creditors and owners (excluding interest expense) made during the year.

The three components of the statement and cash flows are determined as follows.

Cash Flow from Operating Activities

To calculate cash flow from operating activities, start with net income. Net income can be found on the income statement and is equal to 258. We now need to add back noncash expenses and adjust for changes in current assets and liabilities (other than cash). The result is cash flow from operating activities.

U.S. Generic Corporation
Cash Flow from Operating Activities
19X2

Net income	258
Depreciation	270
Deferred taxes	39
Change in assets and liabilities	
Accounts receivable	(72)
Inventories	33
Accounts payable	48
Accrued expense	57
Notes payable	(9)
Other	(24)
Cash flow from operating activities	**597**

Cash Flow from Investing Activities

Cash flow from investing activities involves changes in capital assets: acquisition of fixed assets and sales of fixed assets (i.e., net capital expenditures). The result for U.S. Generic is as follows.

U.S. Generic Corporation
Cash Flow from Investing Activities
19X2

Acquisition of fixed assets	(594)
Sales of fixed assets	75
Cash flow from investing activities	**(519)**

Cash Flow from Financing Activities

Cash flows to and from creditors and owners include changes in equity and debt.

U.S. Generic Corporation
Cash Flow from Financing Activities
19X2

Retirement of debt (includes notes)	(219)
Proceeds from long-term debt sales	258
Dividends	(129)
Repurchase of stock	(18)
Proceeds from new stock issue	129
Cash flows from financing activities	**21**

The statement of cash flows is the addition of cash flows from operations, from investing activities, and from financing activities, and is produced in Figure 1.4. There is a close relationship between the official accounting statement, called the *statement of cash flows,* and the total cash flow of the firm used in finance. The difference between cash flow from financing activities and total cash flow of the firm (see Figure 1.3) is interest expense.

FINANCIAL STATEMENT ANALYSIS

The objective of this section is to illustrate how to rearrange and interpret information from financial statements. Financial ratios provide information about five areas of financial performance:

1. *Solvency*—the ability of the firm to meet its short-run obligations
2. *Activity*—the ability of the firm to control its investment in assets
3. *Financial leverage*—the extent to which a firm relies on debt financing
4. *Profitability*—the extent to which a firm is profitable
5. *Value*—the value of the firm

Financial statements do not directly provide the preceding five measures of performance. However, management can constantly evaluate how well the firm is doing, and financial statements provide useful information regarding that. The financial statements of the U.S. Generic Corporation, which appear in Figures 1.1, 1.2, and 1.3 provide the information for the examples that follow. (Values are given in $ millions.)

Short-Term Solvency

Ratios of short-term solvency measure the ability of the firm to pay its current bills. To the extent a firm has sufficient liquid financial resources, it will be able to avoid defaulting on its financial obligations and, thus, avoid financial distress. Accounting liquidity measures short-term solvency and is often associated with the firm's net working capital position. Recall that current liabilities are debts and financial obligations that are

U.S. GENERIC CORPORATION
Statement of Cash Flows
19X2
(in $ millions)

Operations

Net income	258
Depreciation	270
Deferred taxes	39

Changes in assets and liabilities

Accounts receivable	(72)
Inventories	33
Accounts payable	48
Accrued expenses	57
Notes payable	(9)
Other	(24)
Total cash flow from operations	597

Investing activities

Acquisition of fixed assets	(594)
Sales of fixed assets	75
Total cash flow from investing activities	(519)

Financing activities

Retirement of debt (including notes)	(219)
Proceeds of long-term debt	258
Dividends	(129)
Repurchase of stock	(18)
Proceeds from new stock issues	129
Total cash flow from financing activities	21
Change in cash (on the balance sheet)	99

FIGURE 1.4 *Statement of consolidated cash flows of the U.S. Generic Corporation.*

due within one year. The primary source from which the firm will pay these debts is its current assets. The most widely used measures of accounting liquidity are the current ratio and the quick ratio.

Current Ratio

To find the current ratio, divide current assets by current liabilities. For the U.S. Generic Corporation, the figure for 19X2 is:

$$\text{Current ratio} = \frac{\text{total current assets}}{\text{total current liabilities}} = \frac{2283}{1458} = 1.57$$

If a firm is experiencing financial and liquidity problems, it may not be able to pay its bills (accounts payable) on time or it may need to negotiate an extension and/or an increase in its bank credit (notes payable). As a consequence, current liabilities may rise faster than current assets and the current ratio may fall. This may be an indication of impending financial difficulty. A firm's current ratio should be calculated over several years for a historical perspective, and it should be compared to the current ratios of other firms with similar operating activities. Generally, the similar firms are those found in the same industry.

Quick Ratio

The quick ratio is computed by subtracting inventories from current assets and dividing the difference (called *quick assets*) by current liabilities:

$$\text{Quick ratio} = \frac{\text{quick assets}}{\text{total current liabilities}} = \frac{1476}{1458} = 1.01$$

Quick assets are those current assets that can be most easily and quickly converted into cash. Inventories are generally regarded as the least liquid current assets. Many financial analysts believe it is important to determine a firm's ability to pay off current liabilities without relying on the sale of inventories. Moreover, since a firm carries its inventories on its balance sheet at cost, a fire sale may bring in less cash than the balance sheet might otherwise indicate.

Activity

Ratios of activity are constructed to measure how effectively the firm's assets are being managed. The level of a firm's investment in assets depends on many factors, such as seasonal, cyclical, and industry considerations. How can the appropriate level of investment in assets be measured? One sensible starting point is to compare assets with sales for the year to arrive at turnover. The idea is to find out how quickly assets are used to generate sales.

Total Asset Turnover

The total asset turnover ratio is determined by dividing total operating revenues for the accounting period by the average of total assets. The total assets turnover ratio for the U.S. Generic Corporation for 19X2 is:

$$\text{Total asset turnover} = \frac{\text{total operating revenues}}{\text{total assets (average)}} = \frac{6786}{5431.5} = 1.25$$

$$\text{Average total assets} = \frac{5{,}637 + 5{,}226}{2} = 5{,}431.5$$

The ratio measures how efficiently a firm is utilizing its assets. If the asset turnover ratio is high, the firm is using its assets effectively in generating sales. If the ratio is low, the firm may not be using its assets efficiently and should either increase sales or eliminate some of the existing assets. One problem in interpreting this ratio is that it is maximized by using older assets, because their depreciated accounting value is lower than that of newer assets. Also, firms with relatively small investments in fixed assets, such as retail and wholesale trade firms, tend to have high ratios of total asset turnover when compared with firms that require a large investment in fixed assets, such as manufacturing firms. Thus, industry differences must be carefully considered in assessing the asset turnover ratio.

Receivables Turnover

The ratio of receivables turnover is calculated by dividing sales by average receivables during the accounting period. If the number of days in the year (365) is divided by the receivables turnover ratio, the average collection period can be determined. Net receivables are used for these calculations. The receivables turnover ratio and average collection period for the U.S. Generic Corporation are:

$$\text{Receivables turnover} = \frac{\text{total operating revenues}}{\text{receivables (average)}} = \frac{6,786}{846} = 8.02$$

$$\text{Average receivables} = \frac{882 + 810}{2} = 846$$

$$\text{Average collection period} = \frac{\text{days in period}}{\text{receivables turnover}} = \frac{365}{8.02} = 45.5 \text{ days}$$

The receivables turnover ratio and the average collection period provide some information on the success of the firm in managing its investment in accounts receivable. The actual value of these ratios reflects the effectiveness of the firm's credit policy. If a firm has a liberal credit policy, the amount of its receivables will be higher than would otherwise be the case. However, sales would presumably be higher as well. One common rule of thumb that financial analysts use is that the average collection period of a firm should not exceed the time allowed for payment in the credit terms by more than ten days. Longer average collection periods may indicate that customers are not repaying on a timely basis.

Inventory Turnover

The ratio of inventory turnover is calculated by dividing the cost of goods sold by average inventory. Because inventory is stated in historical cost terms, it must be divided by cost of goods sold instead of sales (sales include a margin for profit and are not comparable with inventory). The number of days in the year divided by the ratio of inventory turnover yields the ratio of days in inventory. The ratio of days in inventory is the number of days it takes to get goods produced and sold; it is called *shelf life* for retail and wholesale trade firms. The inventory ratios for the U.S. Generic Corporation are:

$$\text{Inventory turnover} = \frac{\text{cost of goods sold}}{\text{inventory (average)}} = \frac{4{,}965}{823.5} = 6.03$$

$$\text{Average inventory} = \frac{807 + 840}{2} = 823.5$$

$$\text{Days in inventory} = \frac{\text{days in period}}{\text{inventory turnover}} = \frac{365}{6.03} = 60.5 \text{ days}$$

The inventory ratios measure how quickly inventory is produced from raw materials and sold to customers. They are significantly affected by, among other things, the production technology of goods being manufactured. It takes longer to produce a 747 airplane than a pint of Ben & Jerry's ice cream. The ratios also are affected by the perishability of the finished goods. A large increase in the ratio of days in inventory could suggest an excessive buildup of high inventory of unsold finished goods or a change in the firm's product mix to goods with longer production periods. Clearly, a high ratio can serve as a warning that requires further investigation.

The method of inventory valuation can also materially affect the computed inventory ratios. Thus, financial analysts should be aware of the different inventory valuation methods and how they might affect the ratios.

Financial Leverage

Financial leverage is related to the extent to which a firm relies on debt financing rather than equity. Measures of financial leverage are used in determining the probability that the firm may default on its debt contracts. The higher a firm's debt level, the more likely it is that the firm could become unable to fulfill its contractual obligations. Too much debt can lead to a higher probability of financial distress.

On the positive side, debt is an important form of financing and provides a significant tax advantage because interest payments are tax deductible. Dividends and share repurchases are not tax deductible.

Debt Ratio

The debt ratio is calculated by dividing total debt by total assets. We can also use several other ways to express the extent to which a firm uses debt, such as the debt-equity ratio and the equity multiplier (that is, total assets divided by equity). The debt ratios for the U.S. Generic Corporation for 19X2 are:

$$\text{Debt ratio} = \frac{\text{total debt}}{\text{total assets}} = \frac{3{,}222}{5{,}637} = 0.57$$

$$\text{Debt-equity ratio} = \frac{\text{total debt}}{\text{total equity}} = \frac{3,222}{2,415} = 1.33$$

$$\text{Equity multiplier} = \frac{\text{total assets}}{\text{total equity}} = \frac{5,637}{2,415} = 2.33$$

Debt ratios provide information about the relative protection for creditors from insolvency and the ability of firms to obtain additional financing for potentially attractive investment opportunities. However, debt is carried on the balance sheet simply as the unpaid balance. Consequently, no adjustment is made for the current level of interest rates (which may be higher or lower than when the debt was originally issued) or risk. Thus, the accounting value of debt may differ substantially from its market value. Some forms of debt may not appear on the balance sheet at all, such as pension liabilities, lease obligations, or guarantee for subsidiary debt.

Interest Coverage

The ratio of interest coverage is calculated by dividing earnings (before interest and taxes) by interest. This ratio emphasizes the ability of the firm to generate enough income to cover interest expense. This ratio for the U.S. Generic Corporation is:

$$\text{Interest coverage} = \frac{\text{earnings before interest and taxes}}{\text{interest expense}} = \frac{657}{147} = 4.5$$

The ratio of interest coverage is directly related to the ability of the firm to pay its ongoing interest obligations. However, it would probably make sense to add depreciation to income in computing this ratio and to include other financing expenses, such as payments of principal and lease payments. These adjustments would provide a better measure of the cash available to repay all of the firm's current financial obligations.

A large debt burden is a problem only if the firm's cash flow is insufficient to make the required debt service payments. This is related to the uncertainty of future cash flows. Firms with predictable cash flows are frequently said to have more *debt capacity* than firms with high, uncertain cash flows. Therefore, it may be useful to calculate the variability of the firm's cash flows. One possible way to do this is to calculate the standard deviation of cash flows relative to the average cash flow. Note, however, that this is done using historical information, while it is really the variability of future earnings that matters to creditors.

Profitability

Accounting profits are the difference between revenues and costs. Unfortunately, there is no completely unambiguous way to know when a firm is profitable. At best, a financial analyst can measure current or past accounting profitability. Many business opportunities, however, involve sacrificing current profits for future profits. For example, all new products require large start-up costs and, as a consequence, produce low initial profits. Thus, current accounting profits can be a poor predictor of true future accounting profitability. Another problem with accounting-based measures of profitability is that they ignore risk. It would be false to conclude that two firms with identical current profits were equally profitable if the risk of one was greater than that of the other.

An important conceptual problem with accounting measures of profitability is they do not give us a benchmark for making comparisons. Thus, profitability measures are important to understand but difficult to rely upon.

Profit Margin

Profit margins are computed by dividing profits by total operating revenue. Thus, they express profits as a percentage of total operating revenue. The most important margin is the *net profit margin*. The net profit margin for the U.S. Generic Corporation is:

$$\text{Net profit margin} = \frac{\text{net income}}{\text{total operating revenue}} = \frac{258}{6,786} = 3.8\%$$

$$\text{Gross profit margin} = \frac{\text{earnings before interest and taxes}}{\text{total operating revenues}} = \frac{657}{6,786} = 9.7\%$$

In general, profit margins reflect the firm's ability to produce a project or service at either a low cost or a high price. Profit margins are not direct measures of profitability because they are based on total operating revenue, not on the investment made in assets by the firm or the equity investors.

Return on Assets (ROA)

One common measure of managerial performance is the ratio of income to average total assets, both before tax and after tax. These ratios for the U.S. Generic Corporation for 19X2 are:

$$\text{Net return on assets} = \frac{\text{net income}}{\text{average total assets}} = \frac{258}{5,431.5} = 0.0475 \, (4.75\%)$$

$$\text{Gross return on assets} = \frac{\text{earnings before interest and tax}}{\text{average total assets}} = \frac{657}{5,431.5} =$$

$$0.121 \, (12.1\%)$$

One of the most interesting uses of the return on assets measure is to see how some financial ratios can be combined to produce ROA. The Du Pont system emphasizes the fact that ROA can be expressed in terms of the profit margin and asset turnover. The basic components of the system are as follows:

$$ROA = \text{profit margin} \times \text{asset turnover}$$

$$ROA(net) = \frac{\text{net income}}{\text{total operating revenue}} \times \frac{\text{total operating revenue}}{\text{average total assets}}$$

$$0.0475 = 0.038 \times 1.25$$

$$ROA(gross) = \frac{\text{earnings before interest and taxes}}{\text{total operating revenue}} \times \frac{\text{total operating revenue}}{\text{average total assets}}$$

$$0.121 = 0.097 \times 1.25$$

Firms can increase ROA by increasing profit margins or asset turnover. Of course, competition limits their ability to do both simultaneously. Thus, firms tend to face a trade-off between turnover and margin.

It is often useful to describe financial strategies in terms of margins and turnover. Suppose a firm selling specialized electronic equipment is considering providing its customers with more liberal credit terms. This action will probably decrease asset turnover (because receivables would increase more than sales). This suggests that the margins will have to increase to keep ROA from declining.

Return on Equity (ROE)

This ratio is defined as net income (after interest and taxes) divided by average common stockholders' equity, which for the U.S. Generic Corporation is:

$$ROE = \frac{\text{net income}}{\text{average stockholders' equity}} = \frac{86}{765} = 0.11 \ (11\%)$$

$$\text{Average stockholders' equity} = \frac{805 + 725}{2} = 765$$

The most important distinction between a firm's ROA and ROE is due to financial leverage. To see this, consider the following breakdown of ROE:

$$ROE = \text{profit margin} \times \text{asset turnover} \times \text{equity multiplier}$$

$$= \frac{\text{net income}}{\text{total operating revenue}} \times \frac{\text{total operating revenue}}{\text{average total assets}}$$

$$\times \frac{\text{average total assets}}{\text{average stockholders' equity}}$$

$$0.11 = 0.038 \times 1.25 \times 2.36$$

Based upon these calculations, it would appear that financial leverage always increases ROE. Actually, this occurs only when ROA exceeds the interest rate on a firm's debt obligations.

Payout Ratio

The payout ratio is the proportion of net income paid out in cash dividends. For the U.S. Generic Corporation,

$$\text{Payout ratio} = \frac{\text{cash dividends}}{\text{net income}} = \frac{129}{258} = 0.5$$

The *retention ratio* for the U.S. Generic Corporation is:

$$\text{Retention ratio} = \frac{\text{retained earnings}}{\text{net income}} = \frac{129}{258} = 0.5$$

Retained earnings = net income − dividends

The Sustainable Growth Rate

One ratio that is very helpful in financial analysis is called the *sustainable growth rate.* It is the maximum rate of growth a firm can maintain without increasing its financial leverage and using internal equity only. The precise value of sustainable growth can be calculated as:

$$\text{Sustainable growth rate} = \text{ROE} \times \text{retention ratio}$$

For the U.S. Generic Company, ROE is 11 percent. The retention ratio is 1/2, so we can calculate the sustainable growth rate as:

$$\text{Sustainable growth rate} = .11 \times (1/2) = 5.5\%$$

The U.S. Generic Corporation can expand at a maximum rate of 5.5 percent per year with no external equity financing or without increasing financial leverage.

Market Value Ratios

As our preceding discussion indicates, we can learn many things from an analysis of a firm's balance sheets and income statements. However, one important measure of a firm's value that cannot be found on an accounting statement is its market value.

Market Price

The market price of a share of common stock is the price that buyers and sellers establish when they trade the stock. The market value of the common equity of a firm is the market price of a share of common stock multiplied by the number of shares outstanding.

Sometimes the words "fair market value" are used to describe market prices. *Fair market value* is the amount at which common stock would change hands between a willing buyer and a willing seller, both having knowledge of the relevant facts. Thus, market prices provide an assessment of how investors value the true worth of the assets of a firm. In an efficient stock market, market prices reflect all relevant facts about firms; thus, market prices reveal the true value of the firm's underlying assets. Therefore, a stock price provides an important indication of how investors assess the operating and financial policies adopted by management.

Price-to-Earnings (P/E) Ratio

One way to calculate the P/E ratio is to divide the current market price by the earnings per share of common stock for the latest year. The P/E ratios of some of the largest firms in the United States, Japan, and Germany are as follows:

P/E Ratios 1994					
United States		**Japan**		**Germany**	
Exxon	15	Nippon Telegraph & Telephone	270	Allianz Holding	99
General Electric	19	Toyota Motor	45	Bayer	16
Coca-Cola	23	Tokyo Electric Power	70	Siemens	18

As can be seen, some firms have high P/E ratios (Nippon Telegraph & Telephone, for example) and some firms have low ones (Exxon).

Dividend Yield

The dividend yield is calculated by annualizing the last observed dividend payment of a firm and dividing by the current market price:

$$\text{Dividend yield} = \frac{\text{dividend per share}}{\text{market price per share}}$$

The dividend yields for several large firms in the United States, Japan, and Germany are:

Dividend Yield (%) 1994					
United States		**Japan**		**Germany**	
Exxon	4.7	Nippon Telegraph & Telephone	0.6	Allianz Holding	0.9
General Electric	2.9	Toyota Motor	0.9	Bayer	4.4
Coca-Cola	1.9	Tokyo Electric Power	1.5	Siemens	2.7

Dividend yields are related to the market's perception of future growth prospects for firms. Firms with high growth prospects will generally have lower dividend yields.

Market-to-Book (M/B) Value and the Q Ratio

The market-to-book-value ratio is calculated by dividing the market price per share by the book value per share.

The market-to-book ratios of several of the largest firms in the United States, Japan, and Germany are:

Market to Book 1994					
United States		**Japan**		**Germany**	
Exxon	2.2	Nippon Telegraph & Telephone	3.2	Allianz Holding	4.0
General Electric	3.3	Toyota Motor	1.6	Bayer	1.4
Coca-Cola	11.4	Tokyo Electric Power	3.1	Siemens	2.1

There is another ratio, called *Tobin's Q,* that is very much like the M/B ratio. Tobin's Q ratio divides the market value of all of the firm's debt plus equity by the replacement value of the firm's assets. The Q ratios for several firms are:

		Q ratio
High Qs	Coca-Cola	4.2
	IBM	4.2
Low Qs	National Steel	0.53
	U.S. Steel	0.61

The Q ratio differs from the M/B ratio in that the Q ratio uses market value of the debt plus equity. It also uses the replacement value of all assets and not the historical cost value.

It should be obvious that if a firm has a Q ratio greater than 1 it has an incentive to invest that is probably greater than that of a firm with a Q ratio less than 1. Firms with high Q ratios tend to be those firms with attractive investment opportunities or a significant competitive advantage.

USES AND LIMITATIONS OF RATIO ANALYSIS

As noted earlier, ratio analysis is used by three main groups: (1) *managers,* who employ ratios to help analyze, control, and thus improve their firms' operations;

(2) *credit analysts,* such as bank loan officers or bond rating analysts, who analyze ratios to help ascertain a company's ability to pay its debts; and (3) *stock analysts,* who are interested in a company's efficiency and growth prospects.

While ratio analysis can provide useful information concerning a company's operations and financial condition, it does have limitations that require caution and judgment. Some potential problems are:

1. Many large firms operate different divisions in different industries, and this makes it difficult to develop a meaningful set of industry averages for comparative purposes. Therefore, ratio analysis is more useful for small, narrowly focused firms than for large, multidivisional ones.

2. Most firms want to be better than average, so merely attaining average performance is not necessarily good. As a target for high-level performance, it is best to focus on the industry leaders' ratios.

3. Inflation may have badly distorted firms' balance sheets—recorded values are often substantially different from "true" values. Further, since inflation affects both depreciation charges and inventory costs, profits are also affected. Thus, a ratio analysis for one firm over time, or a comparative analysis of firms of different ages, must be interpreted with judgment.

4. Seasonal factors can also distort a ratio analysis. For example, the inventory turnover ratio for a toy company will be radically different if the balance sheet figure used for inventory is the one just before, versus just after, the close of the Christmas season. This problem can be reduced by using monthly averages for inventory (and receivables) when calculating ratios such as turnover.

5. Firms can employ techniques to make their financial statements look stronger. As an example, a company might borrow on a two-year basis on December 28, 1995, hold the proceeds of the loan as cash for a few days, and then pay off the loan on January 2, 1996. This economically meaningless transaction improves the firm's current and quick ratios, and made the year-end 1995 balance sheet look good. However, the improvement was strictly temporary. One week later the balance sheet was back at the old level.

6. Different accounting practices can distort comparisons. As noted earlier, inventory valuation and depreciation methods can affect financial statements and thus distort comparisons among firms. If one firm leases a substantial amount of its productive equipment, then its assets may appear low relative to sales because leased assets often do not appear

on the balance sheet. At the same time, the lease liability may not be shown as a debt. Therefore, leasing can artificially improve both the turnover and the debt ratios.

7. It is difficult to generalize about whether a particular ratio is good or bad. For example, a high current ratio may indicate a strong liquidity position, which is good, or excessive cash, which is bad (because excess cash in the bank is a nonearning asset). Similarly, a high fixed-assets turnover ratio may denote either a firm that uses its assets efficiently or one that is undercapitalized and cannot afford to buy enough assets.

8. A firm may have some ratios that look good and others that look bad, making it difficult to tell whether the company is, on balance, strong or weak. However, statistical procedures can be used to analyze the *net effects* of a set of ratios. Many banks and other lending organizations use statistical procedures to analyze firms' financial ratios, and, on the basis of their analyses, classify companies according to their probability of getting into financial trouble.

Ratio analysis is useful, but analysts should be aware of these problems and make necessary adjustments. Ratio analysis conducted in a mechanical, unthinking manner is misleading, but used intelligently and with good judgment, it can provide useful insights into a firm's operations.

THE FEDERAL INCOME TAX SYSTEM

The value of any financial asset, including stocks, bonds, and mortgages, as well as most real assets such as plants or even entire firms, depends on the stream of cash flows produced by the asset. Cash flows from an asset consist of *usable* income plus depreciation, and usable income means income *after taxes*.

Tax laws can be changed by Congress, and in recent years changes have occurred almost every year since 1913, when the federal income tax system began in the United States. Therefore, although this section will give you a good background on the basic nature of our tax system, you should be aware that any attempt to summarize current tax law will probably be outdated at some point in the future.

Currently, federal income tax rates for individuals go up to 39.6 percent, and, when social security, Medicare, and state and city income taxes are included, the marginal tax rate on an individual's income can easily exceed 50 percent. Business income is also taxed heavily. The income from partnerships and proprietorships is reported by the individual owners as personal income and, consequently, is taxed at federal-plus-state rates going up to 50 percent or more. Corporate profits are subject to federal income tax rates of up to 39 percent, in addition to state income taxes. Because of the magnitude of the tax bill, taxes play a critical role in many financial decisions.

Taxes are so complicated that university law schools offer master's degrees in taxation to practicing lawyers, many of whom are also CPAs. In a field complicated enough to warrant such detailed study, only the highlights can be covered in a chapter like this. This is enough, though, because business managers and investors should and do rely on tax specialists rather than trusting their own limited and outdated knowledge. Still, it is important to know the basic elements of the tax system as a starting point for discussions with tax experts.

Current tax law was established by the Omnibus Budget Reconciliation Act of 1993, signed into law by President Clinton on August 10, 1993. The most significant points of this act for corporate financial management include the following:

1. The top marginal rate for corporations is 39 percent. The highest marginal rate for individuals is 39.6 percent.

2. Short-term realized capital gains and ordinary income are taxed at the same rate for both corporations and individuals. However, long-term capital gains—profits from selling capital assets that are held for more than one year—are limited to 28 percent. Capital losses to offset capital gains are limited to $3,000 per year.

3. Now, 70 percent of dividends received by a corporation from the preferred stock and common stock of another corporation is exempt from corporate taxation. However, the 70 percent exclusion is reduced in proportion to the amount of borrowed funds used to purchase the stock. If a corporation is completely owned by another corporation, there is no tax on intercorporate dividend payments. The exclusion is 80 percent if a corporation owns between 20 and 80 percent of another.

Individual Tax Rates

For individuals, taxable income is defined as gross income less a set of deductions. The various brackets for 1994 are shown in Table 1.3. Income from firms that are classified as partnerships and sole proprietorships is taxed as personal income to the owners or partners. Individual tax rates apply to the profits of these firms.

Corporate Tax Rates

Corporate tax rates for 1994 are shown in Table 1.3. There are three brackets; however, an additional 5 percent tax is levied on income between $100,001 and $335,000. This creates a tax rate of 34 percent for corporations with taxable income greater than $335,000 and 39 percent on taxable income in the range from $100,001 to $335,000.

Alternative Minimum Tax (AMT)

Corporations and individuals must pay an alternative minimum tax or regular tax, whichever is higher. The alternative minimum tax requires firms and individuals to add back the benefits of accelerated depreciation and other tax-lowering devices to reported income. The alternative minimum tax rates are 26 and 28 percent of the sum of reported income plus the addbacks.

Tax Loss Carrybacks and Carryforwards

The tax law permits corporations to carry tax losses forward for up to 15 years and back for as many as 3 years.

SUMMARY

The field of accounting is a complex and challenging component of any business organization. Accountants

TABLE 1.3 TAX RATES

	Individual 1994 Income	Marginal Tax Rate (%)
Married, filing jointly	$0–36,899	15
	36,900–89,149	28
	89,150–139,999	31
	140,000–249,999	36
	250,000–up	39.6

Corporate 1994 Income	Marginal Tax Rate (%)
$0–50,000	15%
50,001–75,000	25
75,001–100,000	34
100,001–335,000	39
335,001–10,000,000	34
10,000,001–15,000,000	35
15,000,001–18,333,333	38
18,333,334–up	35

are responsible for accurately and concisely summarizing many crucial aspects of a firm's operations for a variety of internal and external constituencies. Thus, the challenge is to provide information that reflects the changing dynamics of the modern business organization. As the nature of competition and the information needs of decision makers continue to evolve, the field of accounting will continue to change in a responsible manner.

ACCOUNTING

Accounting Rate of Return (ARR)

This is a method of measuring the potential profitability of an investment. ARR is calculated by dividing net income by the amount (or average amount) of the investment during a given time period. Since this measure is based on income rather than discounted cash flows, it may not provide a good estimate value.

Activity-Based Costing

This is an accounting method that assigns identifiable costs and allocates common costs to specific product lines or business segments (also known as *product-line costing*). By using this method, a company can determine the profitability or profit contribution that each activity, segment, and product line brings to the company as a whole.

Activity Cost Drivers

This is a unit of measurement for the level (or quantity) of an activity that is performed within a business organization. Hence, an activity cost driver represents specific units of work or activities performed to satisfy customer needs but which consume costly corporate resources.

Balance Sheet

A balance sheet is a statement representing a company's financial position at a specific date, usually at the end of an accounting period; it is also called a *statement of financial position*. The balance sheet, which presents a picture at one point in time of a company's financial standing, shows a company's resources, the amount it owes creditors, and ownership value. Balance sheets categorize a company's assets, liabilities, and stockholders' equity according to the following formula:

$$\text{Assets} = \text{liabilities} + \text{shareholder's equity}$$

Benchmarking

Benchmarking is a process by which an organization reassesses its traditional business practices by comparing them with the best practices of other organizations. This process is designed to provide a manager with an understanding of how the best-performing organizations perform similar activities and processes. By studying the best practices of other organizations, the goal is to identify actions that improve in-house performance.

Capital Budgeting

Capital budgeting is the process by which management chooses investment projects. This is accomplished by considering the present value of the project's cash flows and determining how to raise the capital necessary to find the required investment. Hence, it encompasses the full image of resources and planning dedicated to the evaluation of the profitability and desirability of various long-term assets.

Capital Expenditures

Capital expenditures constitute an expenditure of corporate funds in order to acquire long-term assets. The investments are typically designed to develop or introduce new products or services, to expand existing production or service capacity, or to alter the mix of current production or service facilities.

Cash Budget

This is a schedule of expected cash receipts and disbursements. Hence, it provides a summary of all cash inflows and outflows for a corporation during the budget period.

Contribution Margin

The amount by which sales exceed the variable costs (such as materials and labor) of a product or service is the contribution margin. In other words, the amount of money that a company can use to cover fixed costs (such as rent and insurance) and generate a profit. Financial managers use contribution-margin analysis to decide, among other things, whether to maintain, drop, or add to a product line; whether to manufacture or purchase a particular part or subassembly; and whether to accept special orders. Contribution margin is calculated by subtracting variable costs from sales:

Sales − variable costs = contribution margin

Cost Center

A cost center is a unit, whether a department, piece of equipment, process, or individual, within a company, to which direct costs can be attributed. In addition to direct costs, many cost centers are also assigned a portion of the company's fixed costs, or overhead. A factory is usually considered a cost center. Managers of cost centers are usually responsible for optimizing the difference between standard costs (that is, the direct costs and overhead assigned to the cost center by management) and actual costs. Because of this, cost centers are sometimes called *responsibility centers*. The key to the effective use of cost centers is an accurate assessment and assignment of direct costs and overhead. In many cases, cost allocation is a matter of tradition rather than careful analysis. This can lead to a distorted perception of the profitability of various cost centers.

Cost of Capital

This is the rate of return available in the marketplace on investments, comparable both in terms of risk and other investment characteristics (such as marketability and other qualitative factors). A more practical definition would be: the expected rate of return an investor would require to be induced to purchase the rights to future streams of income as reflected in the business interest under consideration. Cost of capital is an integral part of the business valuation process. However, it is determined by the market and is totally out of management's control. Cost of capital represents the degree of perceived risk by potential investors: The lower the perceived risk, the lower is the cost of capital.

Cost-Volume-Profit Analysis

This involves an analysis or study of the sensitivity of corporate profits to changes in units sold or produced, assuming some variable costs in the firm's cost structure. It is a management tool that is used to examine the relationship between total volume, total costs, total revenues, and profits during the time period of interest. The relationship is often illustrated through a graph or chart.

Degree of Operating Leverage

This is a measure of the firm's operating leverage, which is calculated as the contribution margin divided by income before taxes. A firm with a high degree of operating leverage will have a large proportion of fixed costs in its total costs. This type of firm will experience a larger percentage increase in income from a given percentage increase in unit sales.

Depreciation Tax Shield

This is the reduction in corporate income taxes due to the deductibility of depreciation from the firm's taxable earnings. Although depreciation is a noncash expense, the reduction in taxes represents the cash flow effect of a firm's depreciation expense.

Discount Rate

This term relates to business valuations. It is the rate applied to a future stream of earnings or cash flow to calculate its present value. *Discount rate* and *capital-*

ization rate are used interchangeably to designate the premium charged by investors as compensation for the perceived risk, or uncertainty, in receiving forecasted future benefits. It can be thought of as the minimum rate of return required for an investment project to be considered acceptable.

Financial Accounting

This is an accounting method that records, interprets, and reports the historical cost transaction of a company. A company records these transactions in bookkeeping journals and ledgers. To interpret the transactions, it uses, among other analytic tools, a series of ratios, such as acid-test ratio, current ratio, inventory turnover, debt-to-equity ratio, and so on. Financial reports include financial statements (balance sheet, income statement, statement of cash flows), as well as special internal monetary reports that are unique to each company.

Financial Reporting

This is the process of preparing the corporation's financial statements in accordance with generally accepted accounting principles. The statements prepared include an income statement, a balance sheet, and the statement of cash flows.

First-in First-out Method (FIFO)

FIFO is a method of inventory valuation based on the concept that merchandise is sold in the order of its receipt. In other words, if an electronics store buys 100 stereos in January and 50 in February, FIFO assumes that the units purchased in January will be sold before the units purchased in February. When inventory is valued with FIFO, cost of goods sold is based on the cost of older inventory.

Fixed Costs

Charges that stay constant regardless of increases or decreases in sales activity are fixed costs. Rent on a factory building, for example, is a fixed cost, since it remains the same no matter how many units the factory produces. Although fixed costs do not change, fixed cost per unit changes as volume changes.

Full Costs

Full costs include all variable and fixed costs and costs at all activity levels in a corporation. It is the total cost of producing and selling goods.

Future Value

This is the value of an investment, based on the rate of interest paid at set time periods, at some point in the future. Future values incorporate both the earned rate of interest and the amount of interest compounded on interest already earned. Interest may be compounded annually, monthly, weekly, or even daily. The more frequently interest is compounded, the higher the future value of the investment.

Income Statement

This is a formal statement of the elements used in determining a company's net income; also called *profit and loss statement.* The categories reported in an income statement are as follows: sales, gross margin, income from operations, income before tax, income from continuing operations, income before extraordinary items or cumulative effect, and net income.

Internal Rate of Return

This is the discount rate at which the net present value (that is, the value of all future cash flows, in excess of the original investment, expressed in today's dollars) of an investment equals zero. Internal rate of return is frequently used by financial managers to decide whether to commit to an investment. In most cases, an investment opportunity is accepted when the internal rate of return is greater than the opportunity cost (that is, the projected return on an investment of similar risk) of the capital required for the investment.

Inventory Turnover

In accounting, inventory turnover is a measure of the number of times that the average amount of inventory on hand is sold within a given period of time. In other words, the inventory turnover ratio shows how many times a company emptied its warehouse over a particular period of time. This ratio is calculated by dividing the cost of goods sold for a specified period of time by the average amount of inventory on hand for that same time period (average inventory is calculated by adding beginning inventory and ending inventory for a given time period and dividing the sum by 2), or

$$\text{Inventory turnover ratio} = \frac{\text{cost of goods sold}}{\text{average inventory on hand}}$$

Investment Tax Credit

This is a reduction in corporate income taxes equal to a percentage of the cost of a new asset in the year the new asset is placed into service. The credit is periodically allowed by the federal tax authorities but is not always available. The actual rules and rates change over the years. Currently, there is no investment credit available to firms that purchase new equipment.

Just-in-Time Inventory Management

This is an approach to dealing with materials inventories that emphasizes the elimination of all waste and the continual improvement of the production process. The process focuses on policies, procedures, and attitudes by managers and other employees, designed to result in the efficient production of high-quality goods while simultaneously allowing the firm to maintain the minimum level of inventories.

Management Accounting

This is an accounting discipline concerned with the use of financial information and the use of other relevant information by managers and other decision makers inside a specific organization. The information is designed to facilitate strategic, organizational, and operational decisions. The objective is to enhance the ability of management to perform its job of decision making, planning, and control.

Marginal Cost

The increase or decrease in the total costs of a company that results from the output of one unit more or one unit less is the marginal cost, also called the *incremental cost.* In manufacturing firms, marginal cost typically decreases as the volume of output increases. This is a result of fixed costs being spread over a greater number of output units, thereby reducing the amount attributable to each unit. Conversely, fixed costs spread over a lesser number of output units result in a higher cost per unit. The analysis of marginal costs can be a handy tool for deciding whether to increase or decrease production.

Marginal Revenue

This is the additional revenue a company receives resulting from the sale of one more item of output. Marginal revenue is calculated by taking the difference between the total revenue both before and after the production of the extra unit. As long as the price of a product or service remains constant, marginal revenue equals price.

Mutually Exclusive Investments

These are investment alternatives that are substitutes, so that the acceptance of one of the projects eliminates the possibility of undertaking the remaining projects.

Net Present Value (NPV)

In corporate finance, NPV is the present value (that is, the value of cash to be received in the future expressed in today's dollars) of an investment in excess of the initial amount invested. When an investment or project has a positive NPV, it should be pursued. When an investment has a negative NPV, it should not be accepted.

Operating Budget

This includes a collection or set of formal financial documents that details expected revenues and expenses, as well as all other expected operating and financial transactions over some particular period of time. Thus, it outlines the firm's operating plans over that time period. The operating cycle usually covers one year.

Opportunity Cost

The amount that is sacrificed when choosing one activity over the next best alternative is the opportunity cost. In industry, an example of opportunity cost is seen in the concept of the *hurdle rate* used by financial analysts in deciding whether to pursue a particular investment project. In financial analysis, the hurdle rate is the minimum acceptable rate of return needed to justify the investment in a capital project. If a company's managers can demonstrate that a particular project would have a rate of return that is higher than this, they are, in effect, saying that the benefits of this project exceed the opportunity cost of using the company's funds in this project.

Organizational Cost Drivers

These are the cost consequences that result from managerial choices concerning the organization of activities as well as the involvement of persons inside and outside the organization in the decision-making process.

Outsourcing

This is the purchase of parts from outside suppliers. It is the external acquisition of services or components used in the production of goods or services in an organization.

Payback Period

This is the amount of time, usually measured in years, it takes before the undiscounted cash inflows from a project equal the cash outflow. It indicates the length of time necessary for the firm to recover its initial investment in a project.

Present Value

This is the current value of a future payment or stream of payments. Present value is calculated by applying a discount (capitalization) rate to the future payment(s). If $100 were invested today at 10 percent interest, compounded annually, for a period of ten years, its present value would be approximately $38.55. The present-value method forms the cornerstone of business or equity interest valuations and is also referred to as the *discounted cash flow method* or the *discounted earnings method*. It is widely used by companies and investors to determine the fair market value of a potential investment. Although it is extremely time-consuming to calculate present value manually, annuity tables, programmable calculators, and computer programs make the calculations easy and fast.

Product Margin

This is calculated as product sales minus the direct costs of selling the product.

Profit Center

A profit center is a separate unit or department within a company that is responsible for its own costs, revenues, and, thus, profit. Profit center managers are generally free to make their own decisions regarding key issues such as price, marketing, and product positioning.

Pro Forma Financial Statements

In accounting, these are financial statements in which the amounts stated are fully or partially estimates (from the Latin for "as a matter of form"). For example, a company making a change in accounting principle must prepare pro forma financial statements estimating what the previous year's earnings would have been if the new principle had been in use. Usually, companies also disclose the underlying assumptions of any pro forma statement.

Relevant Costs

These constitute the increase in costs that a firm incurs if it undertakes an incremental activity or if the firm decides to produce or sell a new product.

Residual Income

For external reporting purposes, *residual income* refers to the net income available for distribution to the firm's common stockholders. In managerial accounting, it refers to the excess divisional or segment income over the product of the cost of capital for the company multiplied by the average amount of capital invested in the division during the period over which the income was earned.

Return on Investment (ROI)

In accounting, ROI is a measure of the earning power of a company's assets. A high return on investments is desirable. ROI is broadly defined as net income divided by investments. However, the term *investments* has three distinct interpretations in financial analysis, each of which leads to a different calculation of return on investment: return on assets, return on owners' equity, and return on invested capital.

Revenue

Revenue is the gross income received before any deductions for expenses, discounts, returns, and so on. Revenue is also called *sales* in most companies. A much less common usage refers to interest income, dividends, royalties, refunds, and claim settlements as revenue. Generally, however, each type of income carries its own designation—sales, income, fees, claims, and so on.

Sales Budget

This is a forecast of unit sales volume and sales dollars. Oftentimes, the budget will also contain a forecast of sales collections if the firm sells a significant portion of its products on credit terms.

Segment Margin

This is the amount that a business segment in an organization contributes toward the common or indirect cost of the organization. Hence, it represents that segment's contribution to the overall profitability of the organization. It is usually measured as segment sales minus direct segment costs.

Standard Cost

This is a predetermined cost representing the ideal or norm achievable by a company. Standard costs form the basis of a standard cost system used extensively in manufacturing companies. At the beginning of each year, companies normally review standards for material price and usage, labor efficiency and wage rate, and overhead rates based on budgets.

Statement of Cash Flows

This is a formal statement of the cash received and disbursed by a company. The statement of cash flows is divided into three sections: operating activities (usually a source of cash), investing activities (usually both a source and a use of cash), and financing activities (usually a source and use of cash). When cash is received or paid for more than one activity, it is allocated to that activity that is the prime motivation for the cash flow. For example, many companies consider cash spent on new equipment to be an investment activity rather than an operating activity.

Strategic Cost Management

This is a management philosophy in which decisions concerning specific cost drives are made within the context of an organization's business strategy, its internal value chain, and its position in a larger value chain encompassing the initiation of a project and the delivery of the final product to its customers.

Sunk Costs

In accounting, a cost that has already been incurred and cannot be affected by any present or future decisions is a sunk cost.

Transfer Price

This is the price charged when one segment of a company provides goods or services to another segment of the company.

Value Chain

This is the collection of activities within a company that allow it to compete within an industry. The activities in a value chain can be grouped into two categories. The first is primary activities, which include inbound logistics such as materials handling; operations; outbound logistics, such as distribution; marketing and sales; and after-sales service. The second is support activities, which include human resources management, company infrastructure, procurement, and technology development. Note that each of the primary activities involves its own support activities. By considering each activity within a company in terms of the value chain, it is possible to isolate a potential source of competitive advantage.

Variable Costs

These are expenses that vary directly with changes in business activities. For example, the cost of raw materials increases and decreases as the volume of production units changes. Total variable cost rises with the number of units produced. Per-unit variable costs remain constant.

MORE READINGS
Critical References

Atkinson, Anthony A., et al. *Management Accounting.*
Englewood Cliffs, N.J.: Prentice-Hall, 1995.
    This is an inviting, colorful textbook that intro-
duces students to the new role for management
accounting and control information in organizations. The text focuses on organizational activities
and there is an emphasis on real-world examples.
Contents covered are: management accounting
(information that creates value), managing activities, cost concepts, cost behavior, budgeting for
operations, basic product costing systems, two-
stage allocations and activity-based costing systems, pricing and product-mix decisions, process
and activity decisions, capital budgeting, planning
and control, financial control, compensation and
behavioral and organizational issues in management accounting and control system design.

Choi, Frederick D. S. *Handbook of International
Accounting.* New York: Wiley, 1991.
    This book is helpful for anyone interested in the
international aspects of accounting, reporting, and
control. The text consists of 30 different articles,
which are divided into 8 different sections. Each
article is written by different leading academics
and practicing businesspeople. All of the Big-Six
accounting firms contributed articles to the book
and all of the contributing academics have had
experience as consultants in their given fields.

Davidson, Sidney. *Intermediate Accounting: Concepts,
Methods, and Uses.* Chicago: Dryden, 1982.
    This is a textbook to help students further
understand economic events, accounting concepts, and accounting methods and uses. The
comprehensive and lengthy text is broken down
into five major parts: (1) "Review of Basic Financial Accounting Concepts and Principles," (2)
"Asset Valuation and Income Measurement," (3)
"Liability Recognition and Related Expenses," (4)
"Shareholders' Equity," (5) "Financial Statement
Preparation and Analysis."

Demski, Joel S. *Managerial Uses of Accounting Information.* Boston, Mass.: Kluwer Academic, 1994.
    This book studies how managers can make use
of accounting information. Three themes are
present in this book. The first theme states that
managers must be willing to thoroughly search
financial statistics in order to find important
information. The second is that managers must
learn how to use, and mix, this information,

together with nonaccounting information. The third theme is a general focus on the skills that are necessary for a quality, professional manager. The book assumes that its readers are familiar with financial accounting, economics, statistics, the economics of uncertainty, strategic or equilibrium modeling, abstract notation, linear programming, and how to take a simple derivative.

Gates, Sheldon. *101 Business Ratios: A Manager's Handbook of Definitions, Equations, and Computer Algorithms: How to Select, Compute, Present, and Understand Measures of Sales, Profit, Debt, Capital, Efficiency, Marketing, and Investment.* Scottsdale, Ariz.: McLane, 1993.

This book is directed mostly toward managers of small and medium-sized businesses. The book is divided into two major parts. The first part introduces the reader to ratio analysis and then describes 101 specific measures, as well as formulas for their computation. The second section focuses on the use of these ratios (how to find the input numbers, how to calculate the ratios, and how to present them). The book also contains a glossary of technical terms, a list of ratios, a list of input statistics, a usage table, suggestions for acronymic naming of variables, and stock market ratios.

Horngren, Charles T. *Introduction to Financial Accounting.* Englewood Cliffs, N.J.: Prentice-Hall, 1988.

This textbook is meant to provide students with the essentials of financial and managerial accounting. It is for introductory courses and assumes the reader has no prior knowledge of accounting. The text consists of three major sections: (1) "The Fundamentals of Accounting," (2) "Some Major Elements of Financial Accounting," (3) "Some Financial Reporting Perspectives." Problems and cases can be found throughout the text.

Huefner, Ronald J. *Advanced Financial Accounting.* Chicago: Dryden, 1986.

This textbook is intended to teach students some of the more advanced accounting topics. Topics covered in this text are: entity concept and personal financial statements, partnership accounting, fiduciary accounting, home office and branch accounting, business combinations and consolidated financial statements, segment and interim reporting, the Securities and Exchange Commission (SEC) and its role in financial accounting and reporting, accounting for international operations and government and nonprofit organizations. Exercises and problems are found throughout the text.

Kieso, Donald E. *Intermediate Accounting.* New York: Wiley, 1989.

This lengthy textbook is intended to give students an in-depth study of traditional financial accounting topics and accounting valuation and reporting practices. Examples from actual businesses are used to help students further understand the theories and practices. The text is divided into six main parts: (1) "Financial Accounting Functions and Basic Theory," (2) "Assets—Recognition and Measurement," (3) "Liabilities—Recognition and Measurement," (4) "Stockholders' Equity, Dilutive Securities, and Investments," (5) "Issues Related to Income Measurement," (6) "Preparation and Analysis of Financial Statements."

Shank, John K., and Vijay Govindarajan. *Strategic Cost Management: The New Tool for Competitive Advantage.* New York: Free Press, 1993.

This award-winning book, published in seven languages, presents a point of view in which issues of cost and profit are seen in their strategic context, rather than as topics in accounting methodology. Concepts such as value chain, activity costing, cost of quality, competitor costing, and balanced scorecard are described, illustrated, and evaluated.

Stickney, Clyde P. *Financial Accounting: An Introduction to Concepts, Methods, and Uses.* Fort Worth: Dryden, 1994.

This textbook was created to help students understand the basic concepts of financial statements and to train them in accounting terminology and methods. The text has 16 chapters consisting of 4 major sections: (1) "Overview of Financial Statements," (2) "Accounting Concepts and Methods," (3) "Measuring and Reporting Assets and Equities," (4) "Synthesis." Problems and cases based on financial statement data are at the end of most chapters.

Stickney, Clyde P. *Financial Reporting and Statement Analysis: A Strategic Perspective.* Fort Worth: Dryden, 1996.

This textbook teaches students to analyze financial statements by performing the analysis on actual companies. The text explains the important concepts and analytical tools, and then applies them to the financial statements of Coca-Cola and Pepsi. Each chapter also contains problem sets that are based on the financial data of actual companies.

Communication

Defined in its broadest sense as "the exchange of thoughts, messages, or information, as by speech, signals, writing, or behavior," communication, more than any other subject in business, has implications for everyone in the organization—from the newest mailroom clerk to the CEO. We all have to communicate no matter what our role and, as a result, the subject is often taken for granted.

Given the broad nature of the topic, we will have to narrow our focus on communication to two areas: (1) the management communication discipline and (2) the corporate communication function. What makes both of these aspects of communication in business different from other kinds of communication is their focus on audience or constituencies.

MANAGEMENT COMMUNICATION

The field of management communication is one of the more recent additions to the business school curriculum. Most graduate business schools added such courses to their rosters about 20 years ago in response to requests from the business and academic communities for better written and oral skills from graduates.

Although all college and even high school graduates in the United States receive some formal instruction in writing, it tends to focus on basic skills (grammar, spelling, usage, etc.) rather than on communication strategy or issues of organization, which are critical in business writing. And few graduates receive any training prior to graduate school in the art of oral presentation.

Thus, the first management communication courses developed in the early part of this century (Harvard Business School and Dartmouth's Tuck School were pioneers in this effort) tended to focus on developing writing and speaking skills that would help students prepare themselves for managerial careers. Today, virtually all graduate schools teach a combination of management communication, which includes: communication strategy, managerial writing, oral presentation, cross-cultural communication, as well as corporate communication.

Communication Strategy

Most managers have learned to think strategically about their business overall, but few think strategically about what they spend most of their time doing—communicating. In fact, several studies have shown that CEOs spend as much as 85 percent of their time communicating. Management communication expert Mary Munter writes in her *Guide to Managerial Communication* that managerial communication is successful only if you get the desired response from your audience. To get that response, you have to think strategically about your communication before you start to write or speak.

In addition, a more strategic focus on communication allows managers to determine their communicator strategies, to analyze their audiences, to determine whether their messages should be direct or indirect, and to choose the appropriate communication channels.

Communicator Strategy

Managers who set objectives before communicating will be more efficient and more effective. Setting objectives in this context means putting yourself in the shoes of your audience and determining their response ("As a result of this communication, my audience will . . .").

For example, instead of saying that you want to write a memo requesting funding for a business trip to meet with the sales force, you would set your communication objective as follows: "As a result of reading this memo, my boss will agree that I need to travel to meet with the sales force." This subtle shift makes all the difference in how you organize your message, what tone you use, and what information to include.

In addition, the communicator must think about what communication style to use. Tannenbaum and Schmidt wrote about communication style in a landmark *Harvard Business Review* article. Their approach (as translated for management communication by Munter) breaks down style into four categories: tell, sell, consult, and join. If you want simply to instruct or explain something (e.g. "use this exit in an emergency"), use a "tell" style. If, instead, you want to persuade your audience to do something (as in the preceding request for funding), use a "sell" style. If you need to confer with your audience and need more information from them (as in a question and answer session after a presentation), use a "consult" style. If you need collaboration (as in preparation for a meeting), use a "join" style of communication.

Finally, the communicator must also think about what kind of credibility he or she has with the audience. This can be based on rank, goodwill, expertise, image, or even shared values. Communicating strategically means thinking about what kind of credibility you have going into the communication and what you might do to acquire such credibility over time.

To get back to our earlier example, if the communicator has asked for travel funding several times over the past year and accomplished little as a result, chances are that the boss will not grant the request because the communicator has lost goodwill credibility.

Audience Analysis

In addition to thinking about the objectives for a given communication, you need to determine who the audience should be, what the audience members know about you and the topic, how they feel about it, and what sorts of appeals might work best.

When you communicate with someone, you are, in essence, also communicating with all of the people that person communicates with as well. Many managers do not think about this beforehand. Thus, the secondary or hidden audience is as important to think about when communicating in business as the primary audience. If, for example, you are sending a message about employee benefits to the person who works for you, you must also think about the needs of that person's family, who will be a part of the audience for that communication.

One of the great difficulties in management communication is that the same message may appeal to some members of your audience but not others. This may require that you tailor your message for different audience members, depending upon their needs. For example, what is in the company's best interest may not be so good for its employees and families.

As important as analyzing the audience is analyzing its knowledge base. How much do the audience members know about the topic you are discussing? If they know very little, you have to include more background information; if they know a lot, you need to come up with a new approach to the topic.

Similarly, what do they know about you? If they do not know you very well, chances are your credibility will be lower, making it harder for you to reach your objective. This may mean that you need to build up your credibility at the same time you are covering the main topic.

Their feelings about the topic are also an important part of the analysis. If the audience is positively disposed toward your topic, it will be more inclined to agree with you; if the audience is negative, you have more work to do to reach your objective.

Message Strategy

Once you have determined your objectives as a communicator and analyzed your audience, you must also think about how you want to organize your message for the communication. As writing expert Barbara Minto has pointed out, the two most important ways to structure a message are the direct approach and the indirect approach.

The direct approach follows the old dictum, "tell them what you are going to tell them, tell them, and then tell them what you told them again." Most communications experts agree that the direct approach is preferable in business because of the emphasis on efficiency and the bottom-line orientation of managers. But, in addition, the audience prefers a more direct approach in business.

Despite the agreement among experts, however, most people in business still tend to communicate in an indirect manner. This is the result of years of training by English teachers who tend to focus on narrative derived from literature, from a reluctance to state one's opinion emphatically for fear that it might actually be understood, and from a lack of strategic thinking.

The indirect approach, which means to build your argument or get to the main point last, however, may be appropriate when communicating bad news, when dealing with analytical or academic types, or when trying to create interest in your audience. Remember that this approach is harder to understand and takes longer for the audience to process. Several studies have shown that millions of dollars a year are wasted in trying to decipher indirect messages in business. Thus, you should use the direct approach whenever possible.

Channel Choice

Managers today have a much greater range of choices when it comes to distribution channels than ever before. Aside from the obvious choice of whether to write or speak, for example, we must also consider new technologies that have dramatically changed the way we write and speak.

Speaking is still the dominant form of communication in business because it allows for two-way interaction. Even in a speech to a large group, the speaker can determine the audience's reaction by looking at its nonverbal responses. The choices for managers include speaking to groups, meetings, conversations with one person, telephone calls, voice mail, and videoconferences.

Writing has in the past been a one-way communication activity because of the time involved in waiting for a response. Electronic mail and chat rooms have changed that somewhat, but the nonverbal portion is still missing from the picture. The choices for managers include traditional memos, letters, and reports, as well as e-mail. Writing offers one distinct advantage in that it provides a permanent record for the communication, which can be extremely valuable for legal, historical, and reference purposes.

Often the key strategic choice is deciding whether to communicate at all. Thinking about this can prevent you from communicating something you may later regret. This is particularly true in writing.

Managerial Writing

Managerial writing differs from other types of writing in terms of its focus on brevity, its emphasis on the direct approach, and the severe time pressure associated with its production. While style is part of managerial writing, it is much less important than in other kinds of writing such as fiction or journalism. Given the emphasis on efficiency in business, managerial writers need to produce the material quickly for an audience that is interested in getting to the core idea as soon as possible. Perhaps the easiest way to understand managerial writing is to think of it in terms of the process as well as the final product.

The Managerial Writing Process

Most people have experienced what is known as writer's block when trying to produce important documents for classes in school or for work in business. Most of the time this results from writers trying to do too many things at once. Many students, for example, under pressure to produce reports in college, will try to develop ideas, organize material, draft, and edit all at the same time. Each part of the process is equally important and takes a different set of skills to succeed. An attempt to do all of these things at the same time is likely to produce frustration.

Step 1: Developing ideas, for example, takes research skills. You might need to go to the library, search for information on the World Wide Web, brainstorm, or interview people to come up with ideas that will help you reach your objective. Most of us would not consider this *writing,* but it is an important part of the process nonetheless.

Step 2: Once you have the ideas, you then need to organize them in a coherent form. As mentioned earlier, the best approach in business is to use the direct approach, but organization involves more than just the choice between using the direct or indirect approach in managerial writing.

Managerial writers also need to decide how to categorize or "bunch" the information developed earlier. This is simple for ideas that are easy to put into categories. Usually, however, this is one of the most difficult steps for writers. Impressed by all of the research he or she has done, the writer will fight valiantly to fit all of the material into some category.

Once the information has been placed in the appropriate categories, you then need to decide which order is best for the categories themselves. For example, you might decide to organize the material chronologically or by some logical method. Chronological organization is easy because one idea flows obviously into the next, but logic is much more difficult to achieve and demands that writers think of ways to link material through transitions.

Step 3: This part of the process is sometimes referred to as *drafting* by writing experts. It means actually putting the words physically onto the page or computer screen.

Drafting is the most creative part of the writing process as you struggle to put your stamp on the material. As a result, it should not be mixed with editing, which is a much more logical process that can easily stifle creativity. You should feel free to write sections in any order without thinking about whether words are spelled correctly or if the punctuation is just right.

Step 4: Once you have produced a draft, you are ready to go back and edit the material in several different ways. First, you should see if it fits in with your overall communication strategy and whether you should be writing at all. Next, you should be sure that the material is organized logically, with transitions that help bridge ideas. Third, you should edit to see if the document is easy for busy readers to skim. And, finally, you should edit for microissues such as spelling and grammar. Most writers spend an inordinate amount of time on the last step at the expense of the more important issues of strategy and organization.

Although the process might proceed easily from step 1 to step 4 as outlined here, it is more likely to involve movement from one step to the next and back. For example, you might find when editing (step 4) your draft (step 3) that you need more material (step 1). This leads you back to the drafting and organizing (step 2) steps before editing all over again. Writing is recursive and thus involves going over the material again and again in the quest for the best way to reach your communication objective.

The Written Product

The product is the end result of the writing process. Managerial communication expert, Mary Munter, has broken the product into two separate categories: macrowriting and microwriting.

Macrowriting refers to the document as a whole— including its organization, logic, flow, and design. The biggest difference between managerial writing and other kinds of writing (such as fiction or academic writing) is the importance of design, or visual appearance.

Good document design allows the reader to see your organization more readily through devices such as headings, subheadings, use of white space, paragraphs, typography, lists, indentations, bullet points, and enumeration.

In addition to design, macrowriting also refers to the use of effective introductions and conclusions in your documents. An effective introduction tells the reader why you wrote the document and how it is organized; the introduction should also give the reader a context for the information. For example, you might refer the reader back to a conversation that led to the creation of the document to put it into perspective.

The conclusion should either summarize what you wrote in a longer document or refer the reader to the next step in the communication process. Both of these devices used to end the document, as well as the logical flow of information within the body of the document, go into the development of effective macrowriting.

Microwriting refers to issues at the sentence and word level. Most writers have had extensive training in dealing with microlevel issues through composition courses in school and thus feel more comfortable with their microwriting.

As taught at the top business schools in the United States, however, microwriting strives to make business writers easier to understand and more conversational by stressing use of the active rather than the passive voice, by stressing the importance of writing short sentences with varied structure, by stressing the importance of brevity in style, and by teaching the importance of avoiding jargon in managerial settings.

Managerial writing comes in many different forms, from memos and reports to letters and e-mail messages. These different forms are often called *genres* by writing experts. While they certainly differ in terms of the way they look or the style you might use to produce one versus another, all share the need for good macro- and microwriting as well as a clear communication strategy.

Oral Presentation

Oral presentations in business are both prevalent and varied. Included in this area are speeches to large audiences, group presentations, meetings, and brainstorming sessions. Each of these activities, while different in form, relies upon three basic components to be successful: structure, visual aids, and nonverbal delivery.

Structure

Presentation structure should also include four parts: the opening (or grabber), the preview (or agenda), the main points (or body), and the conclusion (or next steps).

Part 1: The grabber. A speaker needs to connect with the audience at the beginning of the presentation. Traditionally, this has led many to make the mistake of telling inappropriate jokes. Instead, a speaker should establish rapport by arousing the audience's interest in the topic. Often, using statistics that present the topic in a new light can help grab the audience's attention.

For example, if you were making a presentation about an investment opportunity to a group of potential customers, you might begin by citing relevant numbers: "While even the most optimistic investors count on a return of only 10 percent a year from their investments, our mutual fund has produced returns over 25 percent for each of the last three years. . . ."

Part 2: The agenda. Since an audience cannot skim your presentation in the same way one can skim a document, the speaker must provide an introduction or "table of contents" that will help guide the listener through the main points of the presentation. This preview should be explicit and presented both visually and orally for the greatest impact.

For example, to continue with the presentation on the mutual fund previously described, the speaker might continue as follows: "Today, I would like to share with you how this fund has been able to achieve such success by first looking at our investment philosophy, by looking at how we determine which stocks to include in our portfolio, and by describing how we have been able to build the portfolio to its current size through investors like you. . . ."

Part 3: The main points. As in writing, the body of a presentation should be organized coherently, based on some principal such as chronology, importance, or just the logic of the material itself.

Speakers often make the mistake of including too much information in an attempt to make sure they have enough to say. In general, instructors in management communication courses suggest limiting the number of main points to five to seven ideas. In addition to limiting the number of main points, speakers need to make sure to provide clear transitions between sections to connect ideas for listeners. Transitions can be as simple as enumeration (e.g., citing the second reason) and as complex as repeating ideas in a couple of sentences for longer sections in a complicated presentation.

Part 4: The conclusion. Speakers often fail to take advantage of one of the most critical parts of any presentation: the ending. Most communications experts agree that audiences are most likely to pay close attention and remember what you say at the beginning and end of your presentation. This means you have an obligation to provide closure.

You can achieve such closure by referring to the grabber ("So, if you are interested in taking part in this investment opportunity with greater than average returns . . ."), by referring to next steps ("Now that we have seen how this company is able to provide such staggering returns, let's set up a meeting for you to meet with our investment advisors. . . ."), or by summarizing the main ideas ("So let me repeat the ideas that we have covered today. . . .").

Visual Aids

Speakers have a variety of options available today to present ideas visually. In addition to traditional possibilities such as overhead transparencies and 35mm slides, for instance, you now have access to technologically based visuals through computer projection. The medium you use should be based on the audience's needs and the level of formality you are looking for in the presentation. Whatever medium you choose, however, the visuals themselves will fall into one of two categories: text and graphics.

Text visuals are used to show the structure of the presentation. Many speakers tend to use text visuals ("Follow the bouncing ball!") for every idea they present rather than for just the most important ideas. In general, the best way to use text visuals is for the agenda, which tells the reader what the presentation is all about, and for major sections within a longer presentation.

These text visuals should be well designed and easy to read. They should also include message titles that indicate the main idea of the visual to the viewer. Good design means lettering that is large enough for the situation and a font that is pleasing to the eye.

Graphic visuals include pictures (such as photographs, drawings, or videos), as well as charts and graphs (including pie charts, bar charts, flowcharts, and other diagrams).

Visual communication expert Edward Tufte suggests that speakers should avoid graphics that are too complicated and include what he refers to as "chartjunk" (e.g., shading, 3-D effects, legends, and hash marks). Researchers have shown repeatedly that simpler charts and graphs with message titles that act as topic sentences are best to use in almost all situations. Unfortunately, technology has made it easier for us to create overly complex visual aids.

Nonverbal Delivery

While communication strategy, presentation structure, visual aids, and the content itself are all critical to the success of a presentation, what really keeps many speakers awake at night in a cold sweat are the nonverbal components of a presentation. Most communication studies have shown that speaking in front of a group is one of the greatest fears that people have. Practice can help speakers lose their fear over time, so repeated rehearsals are the best antidote for anyone preparing a presentation.

But speakers also need to be aware of the specific physical and vocal characteristics that determine successful nonverbal delivery. These include posture, body movement, eye contact, hand gestures, facial expressions, inflection, rate, filler words, and enunciation.

Most oral communication experts suggest that the best way to improve nonverbal delivery and avoid nervousness is to relax both the body and the mind. Exercising specific parts of the body and warming up the voice before a presentation help the speaker to gain confidence during the performance. Likewise, trying to build your self-confidence by avoiding self-criticism and looking at yourself in a practice session on videotape can do wonders for timid speakers. You might also try to use some of Dale Carnegie's proven methods of positive thinking to relax yourself mentally before a presentation.

Cross-Cultural Communication

In addition to providing training in skills such as written and oral presentation, management communication courses also cover the cultural context for managers who wish to succeed in an increasingly diverse and global environment.

Managers can obviously become more sensitive to cultural differences by studying about or experiencing different cultures firsthand. But this is not always possible, given the pressures of contemporary business life. Instead, managers should try to apply frameworks like those in the following three examples culled from a variety of disciplines that are used to teach business students how to succeed in diverse cultures.

Cultural Values Systems

Anthropologists Kluckhohn and Strodtbeck's Cultural Values Systems framework looks at how attitudes differ about nature, time, social relations, activity, and humanity across cultures. For example, in the United States, we tend to believe that we can control and challenge nature, while in Middle Eastern cultures, such as Saudi Arabia, they tend to believe that life is determined by God or fate. This can have many implications for you in terms of the success or failure of your communication objective if you are trying to communicate with someone in Saudi Arabia.

Other cultures have beliefs about humanity that differ widely, from a feeling that people are basically evil and hard to change to a feeling that people are basically good and should be trusted. This can make a huge difference in terms of motivating your audience to do what you want them to do.

Work-Related Values

Hofstede's Differences in Work-Related Values shows how to analyze a culture's attitude toward authority. Hofstede studied managers in 40 countries to look at how they accept unequal distribution of power, their attitudes toward individualism versus a group orientation, their tolerance for ambiguity, and their materialism versus concern for others.

Hofstede refers to power distribution in a culture in terms of *power distance*, the extent to which power is autocratic. Cultures such as Sweden and Israel tend to be more democratic, which would imply that communication is more participative. France, on the other hand, exemplifies a high power distance, which means the people tend to have less concern for participative management and greater concern with who has the power.

In terms of the individual versus the group, the United States was one of the most individualistic of the 40 countries that Hofstede studied, while Venezuela and Peru tended to be much more collectivist in orientation. This has implications for what communication style might work best in a particular culture.

High- and Low-Context Cultures

Another framework that is useful to study in terms of management communication across cultures is Hall's analysis of high- and low-context cultures. Hall finds that cultures range from *high-context*, which implies the need for a prior relationship or *context*, to *low-context* cultures that like to get right to the business at hand.

Several Asian countries, such as China, Japan, and Vietnam, were high-context in their orientation in Hall's study. This means that they tend to establish social trust first, value personal relationships and goodwill, agree by general trust, and negotiate slowly and ritualistically.

Low-context cultures, on the other hand, such as Germany, Switzerland, and most North Americans, tend to get down to business first; value expertise and performance; agree by specific, legalistic contracts; and negotiate as efficiently as possible.

This framework has implications for communicators in terms of how you establish credibility in different cultures, how you socialize with people in those cultures, and how you approach business situations, such as a simple negotiation. For example, if a stereotypical American were to begin negotiating a contract with a Chinese bureaucrat without trying to understand the high-context nature of that individual, he or she might try to do business before socializing (for example, sharing a meal), which could easily prevent the American from reaching the ultimate communication objective (to get the bureaucrat to sign the contract).

Thus, cross-cultural communication in business relies on the sensitivity of the communicator in dealing with diverse cultures, the specific knowledge about that culture, and the ability of the communicator to use analytical frameworks such as those just described in dealing with a more complex and diverse environment.

CORPORATE COMMUNICATION

In the first part of this chapter, we looked at the field of management communication, which tends to focus on specific skills and frameworks that managers can use individually to succeed in any organization. The term *corporate communication,* however, refers to how the organization itself communicates.

In most companies today, corporate communication is a distinct functional area similar to the marketing, finance, production, accounting, and human resource functions. In this section, we will look at the changing environment for business and its influence on the development of a corporate communication function, the rise of public relations firms, as well as the specific subfunctions that make up the core of a modern communication department in a corporation.

The Changing Environment for Business

Although earlier this century corporations had no specific strategy for dealing with communication as a functional area, they often had to respond to external and internal constituencies, whether they wanted to or not. As the environment for business became more hostile, laws also began to change, forcing companies to communicate in new and much more public ways.

According to three different polls, while close to three-quarters of the population agreed in the late 1960s that business balanced profit and the public interest, only 15 percent would agree with the same statement by the mid-70s. This radical shift in attitudes created a dramatic need for corporate communication to develop as a functional area in business.

Because of the changing environment, the responses to constituencies became frequent enough that someone who was not responsible for another function, such as marketing or administration, had to take control of certain aspects of communication.

The Development of the Function

This function was almost always called either *public relations* (also known as PR) or *public affairs.* Typically, it included a component that would attempt to allow the organization to interact with the press. More often than not, however, the function in its emerging days really existed to keep the press away from the inner workings of the corporation. Thus, the pejorative term *flak* came into existence as a way to describe what PR people were actually doing: shielding top managers from "bullets" thrown at them from outside the boundaries of the organization.

Since the press was used to this sort of relationship, and the general public was less interested in the inner workings of business than they are today, the flak era of public relations lasted for many years. As companies needed to add other communications activities to the list, public relations personnel were the obvious choice. For example, in the 1960s it was not unusual to find public relations officials handling speech writing, annual reports, and the ubiquitous "house organ" (or company newspaper).

Given that the majority of work in this area involved dealing with the press (television was not a factor until the early 1970s), former journalists were typically hired to handle this job. They could, after all, write quickly and coherently, which were the most important skills necessary for a discipline revolving around the writing of press releases and speeches.

These journalists-turned-flaks brought the first real expertise in the area of communication to the corporation. Most other managers in large companies, until recently, came from very traditional business-oriented backgrounds such as engineering, accounting, finance, production, or at best (in terms of sensitivity to communication issues) sales or marketing. Their understanding of how to communicate depended on abilities that they might have gained by chance or through excellent undergraduate or secondary school training rather than years of experience. Given their more quantitative orientations, these old-style managers welcomed a professional communicator who could take the heat for them and offer guidance based on something other than seat-of-the-pants reasoning.

The Rise of Public Relations Firms

At the same time these developments were taking place within corporations, another group of communication professionals was working independently to handle the growing need for communication advice. The legends of the public relations field, like Edward Bernays, David Finn, Harold Burson, and (more recently) Robert Dillenschneider, helped the profession develop away from its journalism roots into a more refined and respected field. They were the founders and leaders of the PR firms that were often hired by corporations to deal with inadequacies in their own public relations or public affairs departments.

As a result, schools of communication sprang up to train the consultants who would work in these firms. Hill and Knowlton, Burson Marsteller, Ruder and Finn, just to name a few, still exist today to service the needs of organizations in the area of public relations. And schools of communication still provide the natural resources for entrants into these firms.

For many years, those PR firms dominated the communication field. They essentially operated as outsourced communication departments for many organizations that could not afford their own or that needed extra help for special situations, such as crises or promotional activities. Even today, these firms provide some of the best advice available on a number of issues related to corporate communication. But, for the most part, they are unable to handle the day-to-day activities required for the smooth flow of communication from organizations to constituents.

Thus, as problems in the 1970s developed outside of companies, requiring more than the simple internal PR function supplemented by the outside consultant from a PR firm, the roots of the new corporate communication function started to take hold. At the same time, this new functional area started to look more like other functional areas within the corporation.

These changes created the need for business-school-trained professionals who could understand and converse with other managers in their own language. It also created a much more complex functional area with many different subfunctions besides just media relations.

Functions within the Discipline of Corporate Communication

Perhaps the best way to discuss the different subfunctions of the corporate communication discipline is to look at the different parts of a modern corporate communication function. The areas under consideration are image and identity, corporate advertising, media relations, financial communication, employee relations, community relations and corporate philanthropy, government relations, and crisis communication. Although this is not an all-encompassing list of activities, it represents the most important subfunctions within a large corporation.

Image and Identity

Image is a reflection of the organization's reality. It is the corporation as seen through the eyes of constituents. Thus, an organization can have different images with different constituencies. For example, forest products companies may have a very negative image among environmental activists, but a very positive image among employees in firms engaged in this endeavor. Corporate communication departments conduct research (similar to marketing research for products and services) to understand different constituents' needs and attitudes. They then try to work on better communication with those constituents to enhance their image.

Identity, on the other hand, is the visual manifestation of the company's image as seen in the corporate logo, its stationery, its uniforms, its buildings, its brochures, and its advertising. Identity consulting firms work with organizations to create logos and other manifestations of identity. These firms increasingly rely on business schools to provide personnel for this growing field.

Corporate Advertising and Advocacy

Image and identity are often reflected in a company's *corporate advertising.* Corporate advertising differs from product advertising or marketing communication. Instead of trying to sell a company's product or service, corporate advertising tries to sell the company itself—usually to a completely different constituency than customers. For example, companies with a diverse product range might try to run umbrella ads that show potential shareholders what the company is all about, oil companies might try to influence public opinion about their environmental friendliness, and chemical companies might try to show themselves as good places to work for young people entering the job market.

Advocacy programs are a subset of corporate advertising and represent the organization's attempt to influence public opinion on an important issue related to the firm's business. The most famous examples are Mobil Oil's ads, which run on op-ed pages and cover a broad range of topics important to the corporation, and Philip Morris's advertising to defend itself against those who would attack the tobacco industry.

The professionals in a corporate communication department typically develop the strategy and shape the messages for these advertisements. They also act as a liaison with advertising agencies.

Media Relations

Unlike the paid advertising just described, the *media relations* subfunction allows an organization to shape its image through third parties. This is the last vestige of the old PR department and a mainstay of any corporate communication function. Most of the personnel for corporate communication will typically be found within this subfunction, and the person in charge of the department as a whole must also be capable of dealing with the media as a spokesperson (in addition to other top managers) for the firm.

Media relations specialists today go far beyond their predecessors in managing this subfunction. They must be more adept at developing background material on writers and producers, at training managers for interviews based on their best guess at what the story is all about, and at handling the actual relationships with reporters and editors themselves. Given the typically adversarial relationship between business and the media, this subfunction is often one of the most critical to senior managers hoping to present a positive image to shareholders and other critical constituents.

Financial Communications

Also called *investor* or *shareholder relations,* this subfunction has emerged as one of the fastest-growing subsets of the corporate communication function and an area of intense interest at all companies. Traditionally, this subfunction has been handled by the finance or treasury department, but the focus today has moved away from just the numbers to the way the numbers are actually communicated to various constituencies.

This subfunction deals with securities analysts on both the buy and sell sides who are often also direct sources for the financial media, which this subfunction cultivates in conjunction with experts from the media relations area. Financial communication also involves direct contact with investors, both large and small. In addition, every public firm must produce financial statements and annual reports, which are produced by financial communication professionals. Financial communicators especially must have a broad understanding of business in general and finance and accounting in particular. Training in these subjects is most easily found today within business schools.

Employee Relations

As companies become more focused on retaining happy workforces with changing values and different demographics, they have necessarily had to think more seriously about how they communicate with employees through what is also often referred to as *internal communication.* Companies today must explain complicated health and benefit packages, changes in laws that affect employees, and changes in the marketplace that might affect the company in the future. And increasingly, they must boost the morale of employees after downsizing and reengineering.

While many of these activities can be handled through personnel departments, the communication itself and the strategy for communicating these ideas should come from communication experts in the corporate communication function. Most of the Fortune 500 corporations now use corporate communication departments (rather than human resource departments) to deal with these issues. Like financial communication, this area is growing at a rapid rate in most organizations and requires a deeper understanding of the business as a whole than it did in the past.

Community Relations and Corporate Philanthropy

Many companies have a separate subfunction outside of the corporate communication function to deal with each of these areas. Community relations is often housed in the human resource department for historical reasons, while corporate philanthropy is often set up as a separate foundation from the organization itself in larger companies. But the need for a more strategic focus and the difficulties in dealing with growing concerns in communities about the role of the corporation create the need for corporate communication departments to handle both of these subfunctions.

In addition, given the limited resources available today in communities and not-for-profit organizations, most companies are much more strategic in their focus on philanthropy. Many try to balance the need to help less fortunate people within the communities in which they do business with the demands of shareholders.

Government Relations

This subfunction, often called by the more global name of *public affairs,* is more important in some industries than in others, but virtually every company can benefit by having ties to legislators on both a local and national level. Many companies have established offices in Washington, D.C., to find out what is going on in government that might affect the company and influence the discussion.

Because of its importance in heavily regulated industries, such as utilities, government relations are often dealt with at an industry level (as in the electric utilities and tobacco industries) in addition to the individual company effort. In these industries, companies and lobbying groups spend far more time trying to influence legislation that might have an effect on the industry or firm than one would find in less heavily regulated industries.

Crisis Communication

While not specifically a separate function, responses to potential crises need to be planned for and coordinated by the corporate communication function. Usually, a broad group of managers from throughout the organization is included in all planning for crises, but the actual execution of a crisis communication plan is the purview of the corporate communication department.

Responsibilities for planning would include assessing risks, setting communication objectives for potential crises, assigning teams to each crisis, planning for centralization, and deciding what to include in a formal plan. In terms of actual execution of a crisis communication plan, communicators are responsible for taking control, gathering information, creating a centralized crisis management center, doing the actual communication, and making plans to avoid other crises.

SUMMARY

The field of communication in business—which includes both management communication and corporate communication—is one of the most critical to managers in a rapidly changing and increasingly hostile environment. The references included at the end of this chapter offer readers an opportunity to learn more about specific topics of interest.

In addition, the key concepts offer readers an opportunity to learn more about specific terms to which you may want to refer later on.

CONCEPT **COMMUNICATION**

Audience Analysis

To enhance communication with your audience, you must analyze it carefully to formulate a message in a way that the audience members will understand and find meaningful. Audience analysis can be accomplished in a variety of ways. Sometimes market research or demographic data is available, but frequently audience analysis is based on thinking about your impressions, empathizing and imagining that you are a member of your audience, or by asking the advice of someone you trust. The audience can be analyzed individually or trends can be considered collectively for a group.

Business Communication

A term used to describe both a field of study (at the undergraduate level) as well as the process of communicating in business, business communication focuses primarily on skills, with a strong emphasis on writing. It also focuses on the micro instead of the macro level of communication. Business communication as an academic discipline derives its content, by necessity, from other fields, as a result of its focus on skills. Where corporate communication is narrow in its focus on function, business communication is broader, though at the same time more fragmented and practical.

Communication Channels

These are distribution vehicles for any kind of communication (e.g., memos, telephones, speeches, one-on-one meetings, etc.). Choosing the proper communication channel is frequently a challenge for organizations, because there are more ways to communicate as well as a wider range of constituents today than ever before. With the development of a corporate communication strategy, it is important for the organization to select the best channel for the message, and it is also critical to select the proper structure and include the right information in the message itself. Together, these components enable the appropriate delivery of the desired message. With modern technology, the possibilities for channel-choice strategy have widened to include choices among direct contact, telephone conversations, and computer-mediated communications.

Communication Strategy[1]

Communication strategy serves as the basis for all management communication. Figure 2.1 shows a circu-

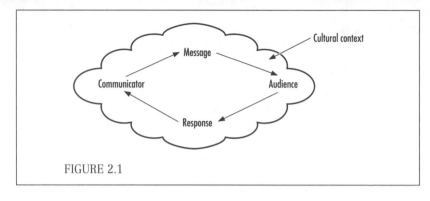

FIGURE 2.1

lar model of communication that includes five components: (1) communicator strategy, (2) audience strategy,
(3) message strategy, (4) channel-choice strategy, (5)
culture strategy. Variables that influence communicator
strategy include setting objectives, selecting a communication style, and establishing credibility. Audience
strategy recognizes the importance of knowing who will
be included in your audience and then analyzing how
best to direct a message to them based on their level of
knowledge and their probable biases. Message strategy
entails the incorporation of either a direct or indirect
communication approach and a designed organizational structure. Channel choice is a consideration of
the means of communication in terms of either writing
or speaking. Culture strategy recognizes that business
operates in multicultural settings and, hence, needs to
be sensitive and flexible to be most effective.

Communication Style

The act of communicating a message can be divided
into four separate styles, as adapted from the organizational theorists Tannenbaum and Schmidt (see Figure
2.2). The two dimensions consider how much you want
to maintain control over your content and how much
you want to involve your audience. The more you control, the less you involve and the more you involve, the
less you control. The four styles are tell, sell, consult,
and join. The *tell* style provides information with the
objective of teaching the audience. For the *sell* style,
you are persuading with the goal of convincing the
audience to perform an action. In the *consult* style you
are interacting with your audience with some control
(as in a question and answer session). For the *join*
style, you and your audience are in collaboration to
derive the content (as in a brainstorming session).

Community Relations

This is a subfunction of corporate communication that
focuses on the relationship between an organization

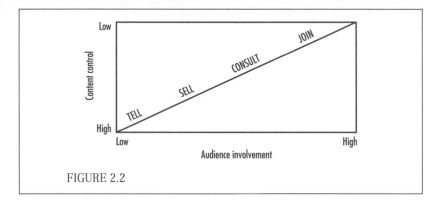

FIGURE 2.2

and its community. Community relations were traditionally handled by human resources departments, but the need for a greater strategic focus and unified message with the corporate image and identity for the constituent community indicates the growing need for community relations to assume the status of a corporate communication subfunction. The greater strategic focus stems from growing concerns about the perception of corporations in the larger community and, in particular, their relationship with the environment.

Constituency Analysis

This involves identification of specific groups and subgroups within the community at large that contain certain qualities as a group that will influence how they receive and interpret an external communication message about a company. The objective with constituency analysis is to first identify who the constituency really is, then determine what its attitude is toward the organization, and then determine what the constituents already know about the communication in question. It is not always obvious who the main constituency is, and subgroups with different qualities will also likely exist. Thus, the analysis of relevant constituents is an important issue that ultimately determines the nature of the message for organizations.

Corporate Advertising

This is a subfunction of corporate communication that differs from product advertising or marketing communication. Instead of trying to sell a company's products or services, corporate advertising tries to sell the company itself—usually to a completely different constituency than customers. Image and identity are reflected in corporate advertising. For example, companies with a diverse product range might try to run umbrella advertisements that show potential shareholders what the company is all about.

Corporate Communication

An emerging field that has been increasingly recognized as a critical functional area within business organizations, corporate communication focuses on an entire function of management. The field of study has been evolving throughout the twentieth century in schools of communication and journalism under the areas of public relations or public affairs, and the concept has infiltrated into the business realm, as most large corporations in the United States today have departments called "corporate communication."

Corporate Image

Image is a reflection of the organization's reality—the corporation seen through the eyes of its constituents. Hence, an organization will likely have different images with different constituencies. For example, forest product companies may have a very negative image among environmental activists, but a very positive image among employees. Corporate communications departments conduct research to understand different constituents' needs and attitudes and then they try to develop better communications with those constituents to enhance their image.

Corporate Identity

This comprises the visual manifestation of the company's image as seen in the corporate logo, stationery, uniforms, buildings, brochures, and advertising. Identity consulting firms and graphic designers work with organizations to create logos and other manifestations of identity. These firms increasingly rely on business schools to provide personnel for this growing field.

Corporate Philanthropy

This term refers to corporate donations to communities and other nonprofit organizations. Philanthropy was originally established as a separate foundation from the organization itself in larger companies. As a result of the need for a more strategic focus to address the growing concerns of constituents in communities about the role of the company and to foster a unified corporate image and identity, corporate communication departments will increasingly have a role in this sub-function. Additionally, since resources available today for not-for-profit organizations are often limited, companies are increasingly strategic in their philanthropic focus. For example, many try to balance the need to help people within the communities in which they do business with demands of the shareholders.

Crisis Communication

Most managers and all communications experts agree that crises need to be planned for and coordinated by the corporate communication function (or its equivalent). Typically, a broad group of managers from various parts of the organization are included in this process, but the actual execution of a crisis communication plan is the purview of the corporate communication department. Responsibilities for planning include risk assessment, setting communication objectives for potential crises, assigning teams to each crisis, planning for centralization, and deciding what to include in a formal plan. For the actual execution of a crisis communication plan, communicators are responsible for taking control, gathering information, creating a centralized crisis management center, doing the actual communication, and making plans to avoid other crises.

Cross-Cultural Communication

This term refers to the communication of the same message to different geographical regions that do not share the same cultural background, ideas, and practices. The impetus behind cross-cultural communication is the recognition that, in the modern global economy, business success frequently necessitates the ability to function or communicate with multicultural suppliers, employees, and clients. Before attempting to communicate cross-culturally, it is important to develop first a basic understanding of another culture. The better your understanding of another culture, the more successful you will be in developing an effective communication strategy.

Document Design

This refers to the overall look and design, rather than the content of a document. Specific elements enhance the readability of a document's design, such as white space, limited paragraph length, lists, indentations, and effective margins. Additionally, using headings and subheadings for organizational factors and having an easily readable type create a more powerful form of written communication.

Employee Communication

More broadly called *internal communication,* employee communication is an important component in retaining a happy and productive workforce. Companies must explain complicated health and benefit packages, changes in laws that affect employees, and changes in the marketplace that might affect the company in the future. Additionally, they must boost the morale of employees after downsizing and reengineering. Although many of these activities can be handled through personnel departments, the communication itself and the strategy for communicating these ideas must come from communication experts in the corporate communication function. Most Fortune 500 companies now use corporate communication departments, instead of human resources departments, to address these issues. This subfunction of corporate communication is growing rapidly in most organizations and requires a deeper understanding of business as a whole than it did in the past.

Financial Communication

This subfunction of corporate communication has also emerged as a fast-growing subset of the function and an area of intense interest to companies. Also called *investor* or *shareholder relations,* this subfunction moves away from the traditional handling of the finance or treasury department presentation of numbers toward greater care in how the numbers are actually communicated to various constituencies. Financial communication involves direct communications with both large and small investors. Public firms have financial communication professionals that produce financial statements and annual reports. This subfunction also deals with securities analysts on both the buy and sell sides. These analysts are often also a direct information source for the financial media, which this subfunction cultivates in conjunction with experts from the media relations area. Financial communicators must have a broad understanding of business and particular knowledge of finance and accounting, and they are typically educated in graduate business schools.

Government Relations

This is a subfunction of corporate communication more frequently called *public affairs.* The importance to companies varies by industry, but virtually every company can benefit by having connections to legislators on both local and national levels. Many companies have established offices in Washington, D.C., to be at the forefront of knowledge about government action that might affect the corporations. Government relations professionals try to influence the discussion and the debate. Government relations are particularly important in heavily regulated industries, such as utilities. Government regulations are frequently dealt with at an industry level in addition to the individual company effort. Companies and lobbying groups spend much more time trying to influence legislation that might have an effect on the industry than one would find in less heavily regulated industries.

Investor Relations

See Financial Communication.

Listening Skills

Communication is not a one-way street. Therefore, effective communication is not one individual dominating a conversation. Hence, a masterful communicator will not only know how to express his or her ideas, but should also be a good listener. By listening well to others, you will increase your understanding, receive more detailed information, and increase cooperation. One component of listening skills is nonverbal and includes maintaining good eye contact and looking and acting interested in what other people are saying. Show your interest by nodding your head and using brief encouragers such as "I see" or "yes." Avoid obvious signs of impatience such as looking at your watch, reading, or looking out the window. Listening skills involve improving the ability to be objective and empathetic.

Macrowriting

This term refers to issues in written documents that have to do with the document as a whole. These components include the overall organization, logic, flow, and layout. These issues apply to all types of written communication. The goals of macrowriting are to increase readability, emphasis, and appeal by using white space, headings, and typography to produce a document with clear and coherent organizational structure and design. Another objective is to place ideas together in a way that promotes a logical flow by means of linking transitions and clear openings and closings to produce a coherent document with organized paragraphs. Strategies for editing at a macrowriting level include making the writing comprehensible if a reader were to skim the document and using introductions and conclusions in paragraphs as coherent links to convey the intended message.

Management Communication

Both the academic discipline (typically at the graduate level) and the process of communicating in management itself, management communication appears in professional settings where a given message is designed for a particular audience with the objective of eliciting a specific response. Effective managerial communication, either written or spoken, is based on a cohesive strategy combining communicator strategy, audience strategy, message strategy, channel-choice strategy, and culture strategy.

Managerial Writing

This refers to a channel for management communication. Writing as a means of communication has specific advantages and disadvantages. Advantages include saving your audience time, since reading is three to four times faster than listening. Writing also offers you the ability to convey larger volumes of detailed information and provides a permanent and legal record. Writing is a good channel when you do not need a response immediately or at all, as it enables you to clearly clarify, confirm, announce, or report. Writing is also more consistent than speaking, as exact wording will remain consistent and people can assimilate a greater volume of written details than through audio messages.

The disadvantages to writing include the inability to control whether, when, and how thoroughly your message will be read. Additionally, writing can be misinterpreted in tone or meaning because of the lack of nonverbal interaction. With the advent of modern technology, electronic and computer-mediated writing are additional possibilities for written communication. E-mail and faxes provide written forms of communication that are spontaneous and interactive, but they have the potential disadvantage of limited privacy.

Microwriting

Microissues in writing entail choices about sentences and words. A goal inherent in microwriting is making written communication concise. Editing for brevity can be achieved by avoiding wordiness and overlong sentences. Another goal is to make the tone of the writing appropriate by choosing the proper writing style.

Nonverbal Communication

In addition to words and visual aids, communication also consists of nonverbal messages. Nonverbal messages include the way you look, appear, and sound to other people. Experts estimate that nonverbal delivery elements account for 65 to 90 percent of what gets communicated, so nonverbal delivery is an extremely important element of speaking skills. Elements to consider when analyzing nonverbal skills include body language, vocal qualities, and use of space. Practice and relaxation are two tools that can help nonverbal communication.

Oral Presentation

This refers to spoken, rather than written, communication, where information is presented to a group. This is a frequent forum of information exchange in a corporate setting as a means of revealing research and analysis results. Oral presentations can also be used to foster internal and external promotions of image and identity. The spoken word is frequently augmented by visual aids such as graphs, charts, graphics, and multimedia presentations. Before giving an oral presentation, you should be certain to prepare a communication strategy to accommodate the specifications of the situation.

Organizational Communication

This is the study of communication within organizations, which fits well as a subset of corporate communication because it enables organizations to approach employees as one of numerous constituencies as opposed to the narrower perspective of human resource management. Hence, corporate communication's ability to unify internal and external communications under one business unit enables greater consistency in the corporate image and identity. Therefore, corporate communication can be used as a tool to facilitate more effective organizational communication.

Persuasion

When communicating, your objective often is to persuade the audience to accept the message that you are conveying to it. Persuasion is connected to the feasibility of the message that you are promoting, but there are other factors that can also enhance the persuasiveness of your argument. Establishing credibility, based both on initial impressions of the audience as well as the credibility acquired while speaking, are integral elements that enhance persuasiveness. The implementation of an appropriate audience strategy to promote the audience's evaluation of your message in a way that appeals to it is also a factor in creating a persuasive forum for audience acceptance of your message.

Reputation

This is a critical component in establishing credibility and an underlying component in successful corporate communication. Reputation is intricately related to shaping corporate image. A company with a good reputation strives to perpetuate that image successfully through its corporate identity. Reputation is the factor that precedes a company's product or services, and a good reputation can be a factor that causes clients to select one company over another. Just as reputation can enhance business, it is also the component that can be harmed through poor crisis management or that can sustain a company in a time of corporate disaster.

Visual Aids

These are tools for gaining and sustaining audience attention when presenting oral presentations. Visual aids provide support for your ideas and keep the audience's concentration on your presentation. Visual aids increase audience comprehension and retention by making the audience members actively analyze the visual information presented. Visual aids enhance the presentation by adding interest, variety, and impact and may create a visual memory that stays with the audience longer than words do.

MORE READINGS

Critical References—Articles

Argenti, Paul A. "Corporate Communication as a Discipline: Toward a Definition," *Management Communication Quarterly* (August 1996). This article traces the academic development of corporate communication as a discipline.

Munter, Mary M. "Cross-Cultural Communication for Managers," *Business Horizons* (May-June 1993).
This article synthesizes multiple insights about cross-cultural communications—from fields as diverse as anthropology, psychology, communication, linguistics, and organizational behavior—and applies them specifically to managerial communication.

Tannenbaum, R., and W. Schmidt. "How to Choose a Leadership Pattern," *Harvard Business Review* (March-April 1958): 95–101.
This article describes how managers need to use different communication styles to reach various communication objectives.

Critical References—Books

Argenti, Paul A. *Corporate Communication.* Burr Ridge, Ill.: Irwin, 1994.
This book presents the new concept of corporate communication as a functional area of business management. The goal, in theory, is to facilitate unified internal and external communication strategies to create a totally integrated communication function. Evolution of corporate communication is explained in an historical context with specific emphasis on current business demands for a more strategic approach to communication. Case studies on General Electric, Exxon, and Adolph Coors, among others, are included to demonstrate application of theory to companies as well as the importance of communication as a tool for resolving corporate crises.

Aristotle. *The "Art" of Rhetoric.* Vol. 22. Translated by John Henry Freese. Cambridge: Harvard University Press, 1982.
Aristotle was head of the Lyceum of Athens in 336 B.C. and this collection of his works encompasses his teachings on the art of communication. Aristotle defines the tripartite system in terms of speech that includes a speaker, the subject of discussion, and the person to whom it is addressed. This concept forms the basis for communication

strategy at both the individual and organizational level.

Barton, Laurence. *Crisis in Organizations: Managing and Communicating in the Heat of Chaos.* Cincinnati: South-Western, 1993.

This book explains strategic challenges facing hundreds of organizations such as Chrysler, Coca-Cola, Dow Corning, Walt Disney, and Tylenol. The book examines potential crises such as strikes, hostile takeovers, product recalls, and accidents through case studies supplemented with interviews of CEOs, managers, and attorneys. The gamut of potential business problems is covered as well as the development and implementation of crisis management plans to resolve these actual corporate disasters.

Brothers, Theresa, and Holly Gallo, eds. *Corporate Strategies for Effective Communications.* New York: The Conference Board, 1992.

This offers an application of effective communication strategies to business, with a specific focus on developing corporate strategies for a range of business needs including internal and external communications.

The Chicago Manual of Style. 14th ed. Chicago: University of Chicago Press, 1993.

Comprehensive reference tool for authors, editors, copywriters, and proofreaders with guidelines on written communication.

Culture-grams for the Nineties. Provo, Utah: Brigham Young University, David M. Kennedy Center for International Studies, published yearly.

Culture-grams provide information relevant to business travelers for specific countries.

Cutlip, Scott M. *Public Relations History: From the 17th to the 20th Century.* Hillsdale, N.J.: Lawrence Erlbaum Associates, 1995.

This book traces the dynamics of public relations in its practices and manifestations of events from the seventeenth through the twentieth century. It analyzes public relations in the foundation of America and throughout its history and demonstrates that public relations continues to play an important role in a modern context for businesses, colleges, and nonprofit agencies.

Filson, Brent. *Executive Speeches: Tips on How to Write and Deliver Speeches from 51 CEOs.* New York: Wiley, 1994.

The art of oral presentations is presented based on the insights of top CEOs, using an informative format for honing speech-writing and presentation skills based on practical advice from executives who recognize that communication is an integral component of leadership and business success.

Fombrun, Charles J. *Reputation: Realizing Value from the Corporate Image.* Boston: Harvard Business School Press, 1996.

This book develops an explanation of why reputation can play an integral role in business success. Reputation is intricately interwoven with the development and the retention of corporate image.

Fowler, H. W. *A Dictionary of Modern English Usage.* 2d ed. Edited by Sir Ernest Gowers. Oxford: Oxford University Press, 1985.

This is a reference for the orderly use of precise words for effective communication.

Heffernan, James A. W., and John E. Lincoln. *Writing: A College Handbook.* 4th ed. New York: W. W. Norton, 1994.

This reference offers guidelines for English grammar usage.

Hildebrandt, Herbert W., ed. *International Business Communication: Theory, Practice, Teaching Throughout the World.* Ann Arbor: Division of Research, Graduate School of Business Administration, University of Michigan, 1981.

This is number 17 of the Michigan International Business Studies Series, and presents an extensive consideration of the components of international business communication in theory and also applied throughout the world. It includes comparisons of business communication education in different geographical regions of the world.

Lanham, Richard A. *Revising Business Prose.* New York: Scribner's, 1981.

This book promotes the more effective use of language, postulating that modern communication has assumed a bureaucratic writing format in the business world. Lanham proposes the Paramedic Method as a means of solving the "plague" of bureaucratic writing by offering a quick, self-teaching method for translation of verbose language into comprehensible English.

Munter, Mary. "Management Communication" in *Business Administration Reading Lists and Course Outlines.* Vol. 16. Series edited by Richard Schwindt. Chapel Hill: Eno River, 1995.

This is a compilation of course syllabi from professors teaching management communication to MBAs at Cornell University (Johnson), Dartmouth College (Tuck), Duke University (Fuqua), Emory University (Goizueta), Massachusetts Institute of Technology (Sloan), University of Michigan, University of New York (Stern), Notre Dame, University of North Carolina (Kenan-Flagler), and the University of Virginia (Darden). The book is a means of exploring the ideas being taught in top MBA programs and demonstrates a range of teaching styles.

Munter, Mary. *Business Communication: Strategy and Skill.* Englewood Cliffs, N.J.: Prentice-Hall, 1987.
This comprehensive text is designed for undergraduate business communication classes. The text has three components: communication strategy, writing skill, and speaking skill.

Munter, Mary. *Guide to Managerial Communication.* 4th ed. Upper Saddle River, N.J.: Prentice-Hall, 1997.
This book offers practical communication strategies and skills for speaking and writing. Its organized and easy-to-read format provides general guidelines for managerial communication as well as answers to specific questions.

Richards, Ian. *How to Give a Successful Presentation: A Concise Guide for Every Manager.* London; Boston: Graham & Trotman, 1988.
This book is part of the Better Business Series and is a reference designed specifically for managers but also applicable to all whose jobs entail oral presentations. It offers concise guidelines for effective and successful presentation in a corporate setting.

Tannen, Deborah. *Talking from 9 to 5: How Women's and Men's Styles Affect Who Gets Heard, Who Gets Credit, and What Gets Done at Work.* New York: Morrow, 1994.
This book considers gender factors in communication dynamics. It also focuses on the differences in men's and women's conversational styles and the results in a business forum. It explores the means of bridging the communication styles of women and men to create more successful business results.

Thill, John V., and Courtland L. Bovee. *Excellence in Business Communication.* 2d ed. New York: McGraw-Hill, 1994.
This is a presentation of the factors in business communication and the development of strategies that promote excellence in corporate communication.

Zelazny, Gene. *Say It with Charts: The Executive's Guide to Visual Communication.* 3d ed. Homewood, Ill.: Irwin, 1996.

This book explores the selection and use of charts in the 1990s, with advice on how to take advantage of new technology to create impressive graphics and visual aids for business presentations.

Critical References—Journals

Business Communication Quarterly: A Publication of the Association for Business Communication (previously *The Bulletin of the Association for Business Communication*).

This organization is made up of academicians who study communication in business and the publication covers an array of business communication themes as well as book reviews in its quarterly issues (commonly known previously as the *abca Bulletin*).

Communication Quarterly (previously *Today's Speech*).

This journal focuses on oral communication. It is published by the Speech Association of Eastern States and contains current research and book reviews.

Communication Research.

This quarterly journal, published by Sage Publications, has current communication research and book reviews.

Communication World (previously *International Association of Business Communicators [IABC] News Journal of Communication Management*).

This monthly periodical, published by the International Association of Business Communicators (a group made up of corporate communicators), includes current communication research with a global reach, as well as book reviews.

Journal of Business Communication.

Published by the Association for Business Communication, the topical focus of this journal is communication in management with a specific emphasis on writing and speaking skills. This journal has a more theoretical focus, given its academic orientation.

Journal of Business and Technical Communication: JBTC (previously *Iowa State Journal of Business and Technical Communication: JBTC*).

Published quarterly by Iowa State University, the focus of this journal is on research that considers the communication of technical information, technology, and management communication systems. It includes recent research and book reviews.

The Journal of Communication.
　　Published quarterly by the National Society for the Study of Communication, this publication includes recent communication research and book reviews.

Journal of Communication Management (previously *Journal of Organizational Communication;* commonly called I.A.B.C. Journal).
　　Published quarterly by the International Association of Business Communicators, this journal has a global reach in studies with a focus on research in management communication. It includes recent research and book reviews.

Management Communication Quarterly: MCQ.
　　This quarterly journal, published by Sage Publications, focuses on issues of communication in effective management. It contains essays on current research as well as book reviews. This journal represents the most cutting-edge ideas from the academic community.

Public Relations Review: A Journal of Research and Comment.
　　Published quarterly by Communication Research Associates, each volume has a specific theme for which it presents research essays and book reviews.

Economics

Traditionally, the study of economics has been broken down into two major disciplines. *Macroeconomics* is the study of business forces in the aggregate, or on a national or global level. *Microeconomics* is the study of the business dynamics that affect economic behavior within firms. The first part of this chapter will present a discussion of key concepts in macroeconomics and describe how managers can use this information to make better business decisions. The second part of this chapter will present and explain key concepts in micro-economic theory and conclude with a discussion of microeconomic business analyses.

MACROECONOMICS

Gross Domestic Product

The study of macroeconomics is made in an attempt to measure and understand relationships governing over-all economic activity. *Gross domestic product,* or GDP, is the most comprehensive measure of this activity. GDP measures economic activity from the perspective of the total income generated by different entities within an economy, as well as by measuring the total expenditures of those entities. Thus, GDP sets up a fun-damental macroeconomic equation in which the sum of income generated from domestic sources equals the sum of the expenditures generated by the same domes-tic sources, such that:

$$GDP = C + I + (X - M) + G$$

In this equation, *C* represents consumer goods, *I* represents investment goods, (*X* – *M*) represents exports less imports (or net exports), and *G* represents government spending.

This equation can be read as the sum of all expenditures from these sources, or the sum of all income from these sources. In the case of the income application, GDP can be presented as a market value, or it can be adjusted for inflation. A GDP value adjusted for inflation is also called *real GDP*.

Business managers use GDP values to get a feel for overall economic conditions and for trends prevailing in the business environment. An increase in GDP has many economic and business-related implications. A consistently increasing GDP, for example, indicates that an economy is healthy and expanding. Managers may perceive a GDP increase as an indication that there may be an accompanying increase in the demand for goods and services within an economy. This might have the positive effects of increasing business revenue and creating more jobs. Managers could also perceive a potential economic expansion in terms of having potentially negative effects if demand exceeds the current supply or if capacity within a market has already been fully utilized and cannot expand to meet the new production levels.

Leading Economic Indicators

Another tool set managers use to get a feel for trends within an economy, or to predict economic activity related to a particular industry, are the *leading economic indicators*. Although there are eleven recognized leading economic indicators, this chapter will focus on the four most commonly used in business. GDP is the first of these four.

Employment statistics, the second indicator, measure how much of the available labor capacity of a country is being used. In the United States, the Bureau of Labor Statistics compiles data and publishes *The Employment Situation* report monthly. This report focuses on changes in payroll employment, broken down by industry. While the report captures data on the number of payroll jobs available and occupied, there is an implicit assumption that there is one person per job. The report does not make any provision for measuring the number of persons who hold more than one of these jobs.

Employment data can be used by managers in several ways across many industries. In the simplest terms, managers can use employment data to project levels of disposable income, which affect a consumer's willingness and ability to make purchases. Managers may also use *The Employment Situation* to get information on average wages paid by industry.

An even more sophisticated managerial application of employment data involves predicting the response of the Federal Reserve Bank (the "Fed") to changes in employment. As the bank that sets interest rates, the Fed pays close attention to employment data as an indicator of upcoming economic trends. If there is a steep drop-off in employment from one month to another, for example, the Fed might interpret this information in such a way that it responds by lowering interest rates. Clearly, any change in interest rates has an immediate and profound effect on the financial services industry. A manager in the financial services industry would be better able to take advantage of an interest rate change if he or she had anticipated it.

The third indicator, *personal income,* tracks both how people earn income as well as how they spend it. As a result, the personal income report, while far less timely than the employment report, is thought to be a better indicator of spending power within an economy and is used widely by managers in consumer products industries.

The *Personal Income and Consumption* reports are generated by the Bureau of Economic Analysis. This agency has identified the primary sources for income as wages and salaries, income from other labor, proprietors' income, rental income, personal dividend income, interest income, and net transfer payments. The primary uses of income break down to personal tax payments, consumption spending, interest payments, and personal savings.

The fourth indicator is *industrial production.* The Federal Reserve Board tracks the production of all intermediate and finished goods, including utilities, produced in the United States. The Fed responds to changes in the economy's output of goods as an indication of a strengthening or weakening of the economy overall, and it changes interest rates accordingly. The industrial production data, however, reflects production of goods only and does not include any measure of production of services.

Other economic indicators include the *consumer confidence index,* the *consumer price index,* the *producer price index, unemployment, housing starts and permits,* and the *National Association of Purchasing Management Diffusion (NAPM) index.* Depending on a manager's industry or particular concern, different economic indicators can be used to predict upcoming trends in the overall economy or in a specific industry.

The Federal Reserve Bank System

The Federal Reserve system, or the central bank of the United States, consists of 12 Federal Reserve banks, 7 members of the Board of Governors of the Federal

Reserve system, and 12 members of the Federal Open Market Committee (FOMC). The members of the FOMC include the 7 members of the Board of Governors, the president of the Federal Reserve Bank of New York, and the presidents of 4 other Federal Reserve banks; these last 4 persons change periodically. Within the Federal Reserve system, there is also the Federal Reserve Council and approximately 5,000 member commercial banks. This number of commercial banks represents approximately 40 percent of all commercial banks in the United States. While it is not a requirement for a commercial bank to be a member of the Federal Reserve system, all commercial banks are subject to the rules and regulations handed down by the Fed.

The Federal Reserve's aim is to regulate the growth of monetary aggregates to ensure sufficient credit expansion to foster economic growth, without inflation, while maintaining orderly financial markets. The Fed controls U.S. monetary policy, primarily through the use of three policymaking instruments. These tools include controlling open-market operations, interest rates, and reserve requirements.

The FOMC is the branch of the Fed largely responsible for influencing open-market operations. This is done through the direct influence the FOMC has on the Federal Reserve Bank of New York, which houses the domestic market operations trading desk. Effectively, the FOMC decides what trades get done with respect to government and agency securities.

All members of the Board of Governors and presidents of Federal Reserve banks contribute to decisions regarding issues such as the setting of interest rates and reserve requirements. As a more in-depth discussion of interest rates will follow, we will address the issue of reserve requirements first.

The term *reserve requirements* refers to the amount of funds that a member bank must have on hand as some percentage of the total deposits of the bank. It is the province of the Fed to decide what this percentage is. The Fed also controls the *federal funds rate,* or the interest rate that American banks that have funds in excess of the requirements dictated by the Federal Reserve can use to make overnight loans to banks whose funds do not meet the levels dictated by the Fed.

Finally, the last responsibility of the Fed is to set the *prime lending rate.* While commercial banks and other lending agencies can offer lending rates higher than that offered by the Fed, these rates are generally expressed as *prime plus* rates. To appreciate the significance of the power to set interest rates and the influence that this power brings to bear on the overall economy, one must understand how interest rates affect the overall money supply and economy.

The Money Supply—Monetary Aggregates

The Fed identifies three different components of the overall money supply:

1. *M1*—This is the narrowest category, consisting of only currency, checks, demand deposits, and traveler's checks. Of all the categories, M1 has the highest liquidity.

2. *M2*—This category includes all M1 money, but also includes savings, deposits under $10,000, money market deposit accounts, money market mutual account balances, overnight repurchase agreements, and overnight Eurodollar deposits.

3. *M3*—This category contains all M2 but also includes term deposits for repurchase agreements, and Eurodollar deposits, as well as dealer-only money market funds.

The supply of these aggregates available to the public is monitored through the joint activities of the Federal Reserve and the commercial banks. Commercial banks make the decision either to extend or to not extend credit to a particular individual or company based on the amount of capital it has to lend. The Fed determines the reserve rates the banks must maintain on outstanding deposits, thereby reducing the amount of capital available to lend to credit customers.

Money Supply and Demand

Interest rates also play a key role in determining the available money supply. If interest rates are high, customers may prefer to save money rather than spend it, increasing the available reserves the commercial banks have to work with. Yet the banks, which must pay the interest on these outstanding deposits, must find customers who want to borrow funds so that the bank can earn enough interest revenue to cover depositor interest payments and, hopefully, have funds left over in the form of profits.

Interest rates also affect the demand for money. Economic activity can be viewed as a series of transactions, where money is the vehicle on which these transactions are based. If there is a great deal of economic activity, or a high number of transactions, the demand for money increases.

The IS/LM Curves

The complicated relationship between money supply, demand, and output in an economy is summarized through the use of IS/LM analyses. The IS curve represents the different possible combinations of aggregate output and interest rates such that the total quantity of goods produced equals the total number of goods demanded, or those combinations of output and interest that achieve market equilibrium.

The LM curve represents the combinations of aggregate output and interest rates such that the total amount of money demanded equals the quantity of money supplied, or those combinations of output and interest that achieve money market equilibrium.

Taken together, the IS/LM curves intersect at a point that indicates the equilibrium levels for aggregate output as well as for interest rates such that both goods market equilibrium and money market equilibrium are achieved and maintained. Moreover, the IS/LM analysis illustrates the inextricable relationship between interest rates, the money supply, and GDP. (See Figure 3.1.)

MICROECONOMICS

As mentioned previously, the study of macroeconomic relationships can assist a business manager in making more informed and better business decisions in relation to the overall economy. The study of microeconomics, however, can assist managers with making better decisions on a firm-specific level.

Microeconomics deals with how the relationship between supply and demand affects business decisions at the level of a firm. More specifically, microeconomic analyses can help a manager make the most efficient

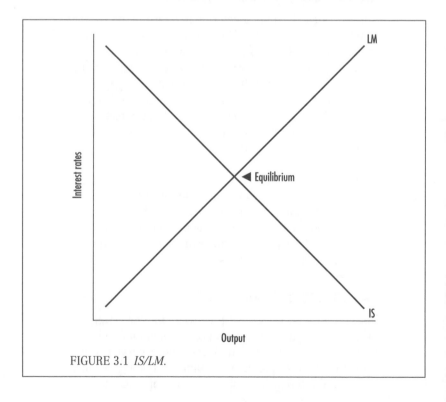

FIGURE 3.1 *IS/LM.*

use of the limited resources under his or her jurisdiction to manage. Further, microeconomic principles can be used to set production limits to maximize revenue, minimize costs, and determine appropriate prices for products and services.

Supply and Demand Curves

In microeconomics, the term *supply* refers quite literally to the amount or quantity of a product available for consumption in a given market. The term *demand,* however, is a measure of how much a consumer wants a product, expressed as a function of how much that consumer is willing to pay for the product.

Supply and demand curves are graphic representations of how each functions in relation to the other. More simply put, a supply curve expresses the behavior of the supply function, where quantity serves as the independent or X axis, and price serves as the dependent or Y axis. Across these axes, the supply curve is an increasing function. This represents the desire of firms to sell more and, thereby, make greater quantities of product available when prices are high than when prices are low.

The demand curve also expresses the behavior of the demand function across the same axes. This behavior, however, is opposite in nature, as the demand function is represented by a decreasing function. This means that when there is a lesser quantity of a product available, people are willing to pay more for it. When a product is available in abundant supply, people are willing to pay less for it.

The point of intersection of these two curves represents the price and quantity amounts when a given market is in *equilibrium,* or when supply equals demand. From this point, a manager can evaluate the outcomes of changes in supply and the corresponding effects on price, and vice versa. (See Figure 3.2.)

Revenue, Cost, and Profit Equations

Managers can also use microeconomic tools to assess the maximum and minimum values for revenue, cost, and profit equations. To understand these relationships, however, one must understand what components make up these three equations.

Revenue, simply put, is all the money a firm makes before any expenses are taken out. In other words, revenue is equal to the number of units of product sold times the price each unit is sold for. In its simplest form:

$$\text{Revenue} = \text{price} \times \text{quantity sold}$$

Clearly, this equation becomes slightly more complex for firms that produce more than one product, but the general principle remains the same.

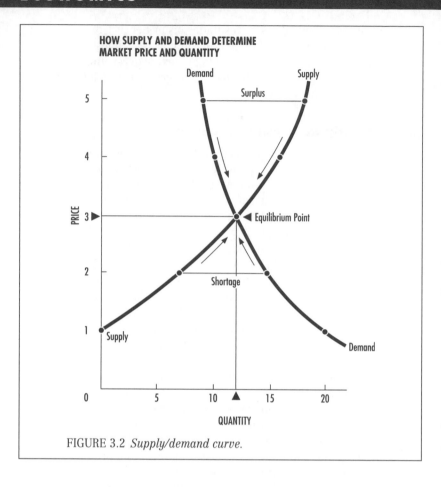

HOW SUPPLY AND DEMAND DETERMINE MARKET PRICE AND QUANTITY

FIGURE 3.2 *Supply/demand curve.*

Cost equations can be slightly more complex than their revenue counterparts. *Total cost* equations consist of a part that represents *variable costs,* or costs that change depending on how many units a firm produces, and *fixed costs,* which do not change with production. An example of a variable cost would be material expenses, whereas an example of a fixed cost would be a company's rent. Thus, in its simplest form:

Total cost = variable cost × quantity sold + fixed costs

Profit equations measure what a firm makes after it covers its costs of production. This translates to a firm's revenue less its costs, or:

Profit = (price × quantity sold)
— [(variable costs × quantity sold) + fixed costs]

Elasticity of Demand

Elasticity of demand refers to the change in behavior of buyers when there is a change in the price of a product. More specifically, elasticity of demand is calculated as:

$$\text{Elasticity of demand} = \frac{\%\text{ change in quantity of product demanded}}{\%\text{ change in price}}$$

Under the most basic conditions, the supply and demand curves presented earlier indicate that buyers are directly sensitive to price, such that the lower the price of an item, the greater the quantity of the item the buyers are willing to purchase, and the reverse. There are conditions, however, when the relationship of price to quantity is not so direct, nor is selling fewer units of a product necessarily a negative outcome. Consider the revenue equation:

$$\text{Revenue} = \text{price} \times \text{quantity}$$

It is the objective of the manager to maximize revenue. The concept of demand elasticity allows for the possibility that an incremental increase in price will not necessarily result in an identical decrease in the quantity sold, where the net change in revenue is zero. It is possible that an incremental increase in price, while it might prompt a decrease in demand, will prompt a lesser decrease incrementally, resulting in an overall increase in revenue.

While the concept of elasticity is a useful one, few if any managers have the luxury of randomly choosing prices for products until revenue is maximized. Fortunately, there is a more scientific method.

Optimization

The concept of *optimization,* or the practice of maximizing revenue and profits and minimizing costs, rests on the idea of marginal analysis. Reconsider the plight of the manager who wants to maximize revenue for a specific product. Ideally, the manager wants to find the right combination of price and quantity so that when they are multiplied, they yield the highest revenue amount possible. Since trial and error is not an option, how can this be done?

Suppose trial and error were an option. The manager's strategy might be to increase the price of a product by one dollar each week and note the corresponding effect on quantity sold and overall revenue. Effectively, the manager would be evaluating the corresponding change in revenue for every one unit change in price. If the current price of the product is lower than the market will bear, then increasing the price will yield a positive change in revenue. If the manager overdoes it and sets the price of the product too high, the change in revenue will be negative. From this, it stands to reason that the manager will know when he or she has hit the right price when the change in revenue is neither positive or negative. This is the heart of marginal analysis.

Performing marginal analyses enables managers to find the right combination of price and quantity that maximizes revenue without trial and error. To derive a marginal function given a total function, one must take the first derivative of the dependent function with respect to its independent variable. In this case, one would find marginal revenue by taking the first derivative of the total revenue function and solving for the quantity that made marginal revenue equal to zero. For example, if *total revenue* (TR) $= 120Q - 3Q^2$, where Q is quantity sold, and TR $= P \times Q$, then *marginal revenue* (MR) $= 120 - 6Q$ and marginal revenue would be optimized where $120 - 6Q = 0$, or $Q = 20$.

Managers also use techniques of optimization to find levels of production that minimize total costs. Recall that:

$$\text{Total cost} = \text{variable costs} + \text{fixed costs}$$

or

$$TC = AQ + C$$

where Q is quantity and A and C are constants. In marginal analysis, only terms that contain variables get differentiated on. Thus, the marginal cost function (MC) represents the transition of variable costs to marginal costs, where the marginal cost associated with a given unit represents the additional cost of producing the next unit. Total costs can be minimized by setting the marginal cost equation to zero and solving for a Q value.

The last critical value that managers want to maximize is *profit.* Recall that:

$$\text{Profit } (\pi) = TR - TC$$

or

$$P \times Q - (AQ + C)$$

Profit is optimized by finding the values for which the marginal profit function equals zero. Taking the first derivative of the profit function requires taking the first derivatives of the revenue and total cost functions, respectively, such that:

$$M\pi = MR - MC$$

or

$$MR = MC$$

This final equation is one of the founding rules and neatest applications of microeconomics for real-world managers. It states that profit is maximized when a company produces a level of output such that the incremental revenue earned on producing the next unit is equal to the incremental cost incurred of producing the next unit. Since producing one unit more would result in the company incurring an incremental cost greater than the incremental revenue benefit from selling that unit, the company should limit production to the number of units that make its marginal profit equation equal to zero.

SUMMARY

Macroeconomics, or the study of how the economy behaves in the aggregate, can be used by business managers to understand and predict how changes in the overall economy may affect the success of the businesses they run. Managers can draw inferences about the economy in terms of the general business climate, or they can assess how specific changes in fiscal or monetary policy will drive trends in a particular industry.

Microeconomics, or the study of the dynamics of the firm, can also be used to aid managers in making critical business decisions on a daily basis. More specifically, managers can use their understanding of the dynamics of supply and demand to predict business changes. In addition, managers can use marginal analysis to target optimum levels of production to maximize revenues and profits while minimizing costs.

When used in conjunction, macro- and microeconomic concepts can enable a manager to understand, predict, and manage market forces to a company's benefit. Otherwise, a company is left to manage in the aftermath of what it could not capitalize on in the forefront.

CONCEPT ECONOMICS*

Aggregate Demand

When referred to in the context of GNP or GDP, aggregate demand measures the sum of what is spent by different parties in the United States for goods and services. These parties include:

1. *Households.* This value measures what households spend on personal consumption items, as well as what investments they make in residential housing.

2. *Businesses.* This value measures what businesses spend on nonresidential property, plant, and equipment, as well as inventory.

3. *Foreign entities.* This spending measures the value of all goods exported by the United States, less the value of all goods imported by the United States, or net exports.

4. *Government.* This value measures what American government entities spend on goods and services.

Aggregate Supply

When referred to in the context of GNP or GDP, aggregate supply refers to the labor and capital required to produce the level of goods and services required to meet aggregate demand.

Allocation Function

This involves the shifting or reallocation of production resources into or out of markets, based on shifts in prices for the goods or services produced in that market. If price moves in such a way that indicates an increase in demand, more firms may try to enter that market and provide a supply to meet that demand. Conversely, if price shifts in such a way that demand seems to be diminishing, some firms may choose to leave the market and direct their resources elsewhere.

Allocative Efficiency

This is the production of goods and services such that levels of production are closely tied to levels of consumer demand.

*Many terms here are adapted from Philip Y. K. Young and John J. McAuley, *The Portable MBA in Economics* (New York: Wiley, 1994); Paul A. Argenti, *The Portable MBA Desk Reference* (New York: Wiley, 1994); and Frederic S. Mishkin, *The Economics of Money, Banking, and Financial Markets* (Boston: Little, Brown, 1986). Please see these texts for an even more comprehensive list of terms.

Balance of Trade

This is the net difference between the dollar value of a country's imports and exports over a specific period of time.

Break-even Point

This is the quantity of goods or services a company must sell in order for its revenue from sales to equal its cost of production for the same number of units. Thus, setting a firm's revenue equation equal to its total cost equation and solving will yield the production quantity at which revenue equals cost.

Budget Deficit and Debt

A budget deficit occurs when the costs of running a country exceed the revenues that country generates. This applies specifically to federal revenue and federal spending. The outcome of a budget deficit is usually the incurment of debt.

The federal budget deficit represents a shortfall in savings in the federal government sector. When the federal government runs a deficit, households, businesses, state and local governments, and foreign entities must make up the difference. Economic forces, like recession or recovery, dictate which of these supplemental sources will have the actual resources to make up a federal shortfall.

Business Cycle

A business cycle comprises the graphic representation of the recurring pattern of macroeconomic activity and industry trends that affect the expansion or contraction of markets, a company's sales, inflation, employment, interest rates, and financial market share prices. One business cycle can be measured from peak to peak or expansion to expansion, or from trough to trough or recession to recession.

Capital Stock

This comprises the physical, nonhuman, reusable inputs used to make a product. Capital stock is measured by investment in things like property, plant, and equipment, less the replacement investment for items that have worn out or become obsolete.

Cartel

A cartel is a group of sellers in a particular market that has banded together in order to influence the price of a good or service by controlling the market supply. Although illegal in the United States as a violation of the Sherman Antitrust Act, cartels are not illegal in other parts of the world and enjoy the economic benefits of exerting such power. One very famous example of a cartel is the Organization of Petroleum Exporting Countries (OPEC).

Command Process

This is the use of central authority, usually in the form of government, to decide policy regarding central issues faced by every economy. Usually, these questions stem from basics such as: What will we produce? How much of it will we produce? To whom will we sell it?, and they involve government intervention in the allocation of resources to meet these ends.

Central Bank

This is the national bank at the apex of a national banking system. In the United States, it is the Federal Reserve Bank, in Great Britain it is the Bank of England, and in Japan it is the Bank of Japan. In the United States, the Fed acts independently of federal fiscal policy. Like many other central banks, however, the Fed determines the nation's monetary policy by setting interest rates and determining the money supply for the country.

Consumer Price Index (CPI)

This is a measure of the prices consumers pay for a representative "basket of goods and services." This measure is compiled monthly by the Bureau of Economic Analysis and expressed on an index basis.

Consumption Function

This is a function capturing the dependent relationship between consumer spending and income, where changes in consumer spending are directly proportional to changes in income, but these changes do not occur in a one-to-one fashion. This means that if someone were to get a raise, the person would not spend the entire increase on goods and services available in the economy, but he or she would spend some of it.

Contribution Margin

This is a measure of a firm's profitability and performance and of how much a firm's revenue exceeds its variable costs of production, thereby contributing to covering the fixed costs associated with all levels of production.

Cost-Benefit Analysis

This is a method of determining whether the results or outcome of a business undertaking outweigh the costs associated with pursuing the undertaking. Generally, cost-benefit analyses start with the extrinsic considerations of the cost of a product versus the revenue it will generate. Intrinsic considerations, which are harder to quantify, are then evaluated and the overall go or no-go decision is made.

Cost-Plus Pricing

This is a technique for pricing goods and services where managers evaluate the cost of producing a good or service and then determine their corresponding prices by multiplying by a desired profit factor. Cost-plus pricing requires that a manager have a good sense of what the market demand is for a particular good or service, such that the manager can negotiate between a desired profit factor and what a consumer will actually pay for a good or service.

Cost Structure

This involves the relationship of a firm's fixed costs to its variable costs. Firms with high fixed costs and low variable costs have a cost structure in which a high volume of production is more desirable, whereas firms with low fixed costs and high variable costs benefit from lower levels of production.

Cross-Price Elasticity

This is the numerical value that represents the relationship between the quantity demanded for a good or service and the price of a substitute or complementary product. Generally, firms try to minimize cross-price elasticity through efforts to eliminate substitute products as viable options in the minds of consumers. Firms may also choose to minimize cross-price elasticity by packaging complementary products together.

Current Account

This is the main measure of the international exchange of goods and services in the United States, measured by the net purchase of all goods, services, and investments made by foreign parties of U.S. products, less those purchases of goods, services, and investments made by the United States in other countries.

Demand Function

This is the function capturing the dependent relationship between the price people are willing to pay for a good or service and other factors related to that good or service. These other factors include the cost associated with making the product, the technology employed in making the product, the number of vendors operating in a market, the price at which competing vendors are offering similar products, and the supply of the product available to consumers.

Diseconomies of Scale

This refers to an increase in a firm's cost of producing an additional unit as all other factors of production increase. Diseconomies of scale can be caused by poor and inefficient management or disproportionate increases in indirect costs of production.

Disposable Personal Income

This is the amount of money remaining after taxes are removed that an individual has the opportunity to spend.

Economic Efficiency

This refers to the effort to produce goods and services in the least costly way without sacrificing quality.

Economic Profit

A firm's total revenue less its average total costs of production is its economic profit.

Economies of Scale

This refers to the decrease in the cost of each additional unit produced as all factors of production increase. Factors contributing to economies of scale include discounts on bulk purchases of raw materials, the ability to use fixed assets to full capacity, the ability to use specialized labor to its fullest capacity, and the ability to use management to govern the greatest number of people as effectively as possible.

Economies of Scope

This refers to the ability of a company to reduce its unit costs by producing two or more goods or services that involve complementary skills, experience, and production facilities.

Employment

Employment is the measure of human input to the production process. In the United States, there are two major measures of employment, as determined by the Bureau of Labor Statistics. The first is the Household Survey of Employment, which measures the employment status of the population by counting the number of employed persons, regardless of how many jobs one person may hold. The second is the Establishment Survey of Employment, which measures the number of payroll jobs in the nonfarm economy, and not the number of persons who hold them.

Federal Funds Rate

This is the interest rate used by American banks that have funds in excess of the requirements dictated by the Federal Reserve to make overnight loans to banks whose funds do not meet the levels dictated by the Federal Reserve.

Federal Open Market Committee

The principle policymaking body of the Federal Reserve, the FOMC consists of 7 governors of the Federal Reserve system and 12 Federal Reserve District Bank presidents, where only 5 of the 12 members are voting members and the right to vote is rotated.

Federal Reserve System

This is the central banking institution in the United States responsible for determining U.S. monetary policy, including the setting of interest rates. The Federal Reserve system consists of a Board of Governors in Washington and 12 regional district banks.

Fiscal Policy

This refers to the government's use of spending and taxation to affect the level of macroeconomic activity. In theory, weak economic activity requires stimulative fiscal policy, which is delivered in the form of tax cuts, spending increases, or both. Restrictive fiscal policy, used to suppress robust economic activity, can come in the form of tax increases, spending cuts, or both.

Fiscal Year

A period of 12 consecutive months used by a company to account for and report the results of its operations is a fiscal year.

Fixed Costs

These are the costs a firm incurs in doing business that do not change in relation to production. Rent, for example, is a fixed cost because it remains constant whether goods and services are sold or not.

Foreign Exchange Rate

This is the proportional value of one currency to another, used to change currency from one denomination to another. For example, one British pound is worth approximately 1.6 American dollars or $1.60.

Gross Domestic Product

A measure of national economic activity, GDP is measured from two different approaches. GDP can be viewed as the total value of all goods and services produced in the United States, or as the total value of all payments made to produce all American goods and services. Other measures of GDP exist that take into account inflation factors, so that the adjusted GDP is a more accurate representation of economic activity in the United States in real dollars.

Hard Currency

This is currency in which there is wide confidence in the world markets, as opposed to *soft currency,* which is not widely accepted as legal tender outside the country of origin. Hard currencies can be exchanged for other hard currencies at a designated exchange rate.

Housing Start

This refers to the start of the construction of a new housing unit. Housing starts are used as an indicator of economic development, as if there is increased demand for new homes, which means that families are prospering and are able to make long-term investments.

Income Elasticity

This refers to the functional relationship between the change in the quantity demanded for a good or service and the change in income of those persons demanding the good or service. If the demand for a good increases as a person's income increases, that good is said to be "normal." If the demand for a good decreases as a person's income rises, that good is said to be "inferior."

Incremental Cost

This is the measured change in a firm's cost of production due to an additional activity pursued by the firm. Incremental costs can be measured as the cost difference between two business alternatives or as the added cost a firm must incur to expand its operations. In the first case, the incremental costs would equal the difference between the production costs of two like products that differ on the basis of features only. In the second case, the incremental cost would be a measure of the cost of buying a new piece of equipment relative to the revenue that new piece of equipment enabled the firm to generate.

Industrial Goods

This refers to all goods and services that are used in the production of other goods and services subsequently supplied to consumers. Industrial goods fall into one of three categories: raw materials and components, capital goods and services, and suppliers.

Industrial Market

This refers to all individuals or companies that produce or acquire goods or services that are incorporated into the production of other finished goods or services subsequently sold to customers. The industrial market is also referred to as the *business* or *producer market*.

Industrial Policy

This is the course of action set by the government to influence the development of domestic industrial sectors in particular and the direction of the national industrial growth in general. A government's industrial policy may comprise such instruments as subsidies, tax incentives, regional development programs, training programs for workers, and R&D assistance.

Industrial Production Index

This is the measure of the combined output of all mining, manufacturing, and electric and natural gas utilities companies in the United States, as compiled by the Federal Reserve. The industrial production index, when divided by an index of productive capacity, yields the capacity utilization rate, which is a measure of capital use identical to the way the unemployment rate measures labor use.

Inflation

This refers to an overall and general increase in price level for goods and services in a particular economy. Inflation can be viewed as either an increase in the general cost of living or an erosion of purchasing power. Inflation is a state of macroeconomic disequilibrium, usually associated with strong demand pressures on the economy.

Interest Rates

These are the payments borrowers make for the used of borrowed funds and the payments that lenders demand for the use of the funds they lend, expressed as a percentage of the principal amount borrowed. Interest rates are expressed as percentages and basis points, where 1 percentage point equals 100 basis points.

Market interest rates are determined based on four major factors:

1. *Risk premium*—a measure of the likelihood that the loan will not be repaid
2. *Liquidity premium*—a measure directly related to the duration of the loan
3. *Inflation premium*—a measure directly related to the expected inflation over the life of the loan
4. *Tax treatment premium*—a measure directly related to any tax benefits or liabilities associated with the loan.

Leading Economic Indicators

These constitute a complete index of 11 key economic indicators that have been found to lead business-cycle turning points.

Marginal Cost

This refers to the change in a firm's cost of production relative to a unit change in its output or the added cost of producing the next unit. The marginal cost function can be found by taking the first derivative of the total cost function, and the marginal cost for a unit of production can be found by substituting that quantity into the marginal cost function.

Monetary Aggregates

These are the Federal Reserve's three main classifications of what is regarded as money in the United States. These categories include:

1. *M1*—This is the narrowest category, consisting of only currency, checks, demand deposits, and traveler's checks. Of all the categories, M1 has the highest liquidity.
2. *M2*—This category includes all M1 money, but also includes savings, deposits under $10,000, money market deposit accounts, money market mutual account balances, overnight repurchase agreements, and overnight Eurodollar deposits.
3. *M3*—This category contains all M2, but also includes term deposits for repurchase agreements and Eurodollar deposits, as well as dealer-only money market funds.

Monetary Policy

This refers to the Federal Reserve's aim to regulate the growth of the monetary aggregates in order to ensure sufficient credit expansion to foster economic growth, without inflation, while maintaining orderly financial markets.

Opportunity Cost

This is the cost that is incurred when a person or company chooses one course of action over the next best alternative.

Perfect Competition

This refers to a market in which conditions prevail such that buyers and suppliers are without the ability to manipulate price in any significant way; the market dynamics are determined almost completely by the forces of supply and demand.

Price Discrimination

A practice whereby one firm sells the same product at different prices in different markets constitutes price discrimination.

Price Elasticity

This measures the change in demand for a product relative to unit changes in the price of the product. If the percentage change in quantity demanded is greater than the percentage change in price, the response to a change in price is said to be "elastic."

Producer Price Index (PPI)

This is a measure of the prices of all goods produced in the United States. Unlike the CPI, the PPI is comprehensive and includes all goods produced, excluding imports. The PPI is organized into three subgroups, including crude goods, intermediate goods, and finished goods.

Productivity

A measure of a firm's efficiency, productivity is calculated by dividing a firm's output by the number of hours people worked to produce the output. Productivity can be increased by either increasing outputs, decreasing worker hours, or both.

Profit Margin

A measure of company performance, profit margins calculate the percentage return a company is earning over the cost of production of the items sold.

Savings

The part of after-tax personal income that is not spent is savings.

Shortage

A shortage is a condition under which the quantity demanded for a good or service exceeds the available supply for that good or service. Shortages usually cause an increase in price to restore market equilibrium in the short term.

Sunk Cost

This is a cost that has already been incurred and cannot be affected by present or future decisions.

Surplus

A surplus is a condition under which the supply for a good or service is in excess of the demand for that good or service. When this happens, there is usually a reduction in price to restore market equilibrium in the short term.

Trade Deficit

This is an inbalance of merchandise trade within a country that results in an excess of imports over exports.

Unemployment Rate

A measure of labor-force utilization, the unemployment rate is equal to the number of people unemployed as a percentage of the total labor force.

Variable Cost

This is the component of a total cost function that increases as levels of production increase.

MORE READINGS
Critical References

Dornbusch, Rudiger, and Stanley Fischer. *Macroeconomics.* 3d Ed. New York: McGraw-Hill, 1984.

This comprehensive macroeconomics text is utilized by various top business schools. It presents development of a theory supported by case studies and diagrams and is a good source for a broad overview of macroeconomics or a reference for greater detail on a specific subcomponent of macroeconomics.

The Economic Report of the President.

One of the three most important sources of officially compiled data, this is published annually by the Council of Economic Advisors and consists of approximately 300 pages of analysis and discussion on the U.S. macroeconomy. There are an additional 100 pages of tables presenting annual data on a range of U.S. economic data for the post–World War II period. The tables are organized into 10 areas: (1) national income or expenditure; (2) population, employment, wages, and productivity; (3) production and business activity; (4) prices; (5) money stock, credit, and finance; (6) government finance; (7) corporate profits and finance; (8) agriculture; (9) international statistics; (10) national wealth.

The Federal Reserve Bulletin.

This is one of the three most important sources of officially compiled data. Published by the Board of Governors of the Federal Reserve System, it is the main source of data on money, banking, credit conditions, and additional U.S. financial sector indicators. *The Federal Reserve Bulletin* consists of three main sections: (1) articles on aspects of financial economy or monetary policy, (2) legal notices of changes in banking regulations, (3) monetary and financial indicator statistics that appear monthly in tabular form at the back of the bulletin.

Friedman, David. *Hidden Order: The Economics of Everyday Life.* New York: Harper Business, 1996.

An application of economic principles to daily life. Friedman masterfully utilizes economics to understand people's behavior on a daily basis and what action they will likely follow in the future. *Hidden Order* is an unfolding of witty examples to demonstrate strategies for various economic decisions of daily life. Some examples are: driving in rush hour traffic, negotiating the best job offer, choosing the right career, buying the best car at the lowest price. Friedman gives new meaning to the concept of applied economics as he integrates economics into the decision-making processes of people's daily lives.

Galbraith, John Kenneth. *A Journey Through Economic Time*. New York: Houghton Mifflin, 1994.

Galbraith traces the course of the history of capitalism in an international context from the late eighteenth century through the 1990s. The book effectively conveys the central core of economic life in the progression of the decades. The book is structured so that each chapter addresses a specific point in the history of economics, with titles such as "The Crash," "The Great Depression," "The New Deal," "Revolution" by John Maynard Keynes, "The Second War," "The Good Years." The book is a valuable source for demonstrating the progression of economics throughout the last century and offers a distinct historical perspective of the dynamics of economics.

Keynes, John Maynard. *The General Theory of Employment, Interest and Money*. New York: Harcourt Brace, 1964.

This critical book has changed the previous conceptions held by economists as to the working of the capitalist system and, as a result, established Keynesian economics. The effects of this work have been called the Keynesian Revolution, as they reshaped economic theory by modernizing business-cycle theory and establishing the framework for modern macroeconomic analysis. Keynes' work has a profound historical influence and the importance of his thinking serves as the basis for classic economic theory today.

Pindyck and Rubinfield. *Microeconomics*. New York: Macmillan, 1992.

This text is used by various top business schools and presents a comprehensive approach to microeconomics. The book incorporates microeconomic theory and applies these principles to specific examples. It is a good text for learning or honing details of microeconomics.

The Survey of Current Business.

One of the three most important sources of officially compiled data, this is the primary publication through which the Commerce Department presents economic and business data. The monthly publication consists of three parts. (1) The white pages in the front contain articles and supporting tables on various aspects of aggregate economic activity. (2) The yellow pages present tables of data and charts that show the business-cycle behavior of 250 key economic indicators that have cyclical characteristics. (3) The blue pages consist of tables of roughly 1,900 series, covering most aspects of general business activities and specific industry measures.

Young, Philip K. Y., and John J. McAuley. *The Portable MBA in Economics.* New York: Wiley, 1994.

This book is designed for managers and entrepreneurs to hone their working knowledge of economics and apply it effectively to their respective businesses. It covers both macro- and microeconomics and demonstrates their interrelationship and how both are applied to the daily interworkings of business. The book incorporates insights from experts at top business schools and demonstrates concepts with real-world examples and case studies. An invaluable source for expanding and solidifying economic knowledge and then applying that information to improve business performance.

Entrepreneurship

The concept of entrepreneurship is one of the founding principles on which American culture, if not American industry itself, is based. As the Land of Opportunity, from its inception as a country the United States has always offered determined would-be business owners the opportunity to succeed—and fail—at starting and managing a new venture. Several hundred years later, the United States remains the Land of Opportunity for many entrepreneurial ventures.

This chapter will begin with a discussion of the entrepreneurial character profile. It will continue to discuss the process for identifying opportunities, business areas charged with entrepreneurial potential, as well as defining a few forms new businesses can take. This chapter will then provide an overview for writing a business plan for a new venture and conclude with a discussion of sources of financing for new ventures.

THE ENTREPRENEURIAL PROFILE

Let us begin with one critical assertion: *Entrepreneurial* is not a synonym for *unemployable.* It is a mistake to confuse the drive it takes to be an entrepreneur with a personal reluctance, no matter how profound, to work for someone else. There is also an enormous difference between being an entrepreneur and being self-employed. Before a person begins any steps down the entrepreneurial path, he or she is well advised to give issues of motivation serious consideration, as this will prevent a person from making precipitous decisions and, possibly, grave mistakes.

What, exactly, is an entrepreneur? According to Joseph Schumpeter, a prominent economic theorist writing in the early 1900s, an entrepreneur is "a person who destroys the existing economic order by introducing new products and services, creating new forms of organization, or by exploiting new raw materials. This destruction can be done through forming a new business, or by working within an existing business."[1] For the purposes of this chapter, an alternative, simpler definition of the entrepreneur is "someone who perceives an opportunity and creates an organization to pursue it."[2]

Given this definition, are there personal characteristics that make one person more apt to be successful at entrepreneurship than another? While there is no cookbook set of personal attributes that constitute the perfect entrepreneurial personality, research has shown that successful entrepreneurs do have certain character traits and skills largely in common. These include:

- *Vision:*   The successful entrepreneur has a clear and communicable vision of the opportunity his or her business will create or exploit and is completely dedicated to making this vision a reality, even when it means taking risks.

- *Determination:*   The successful entrepreneur must be completely determined to succeed, even in the face of doubts of close friends and associates. This determination must empower the entrepreneur to be decisive and to follow through once decisions are made. This determination must also fuel the entrepreneur's energy level to complete tasks, even when this means working tirelessly or incessantly.

- *Motivation:*   For the entrepreneur, making the vision a reality takes on a self-actualizing importance. As a result, very little takes priority over moving toward the goal of realization. "Very little" can include personal relationships, outside interests, or other projects that may be more financially rewarding in the short term.

- *Focus:*   As the bearer of the vision, the entrepreneur must make sure that all central plans are executed while all critical details are addressed. The entrepreneur must keep his or her eye on the ball at all times, never allowing precious time, energy, and other resources to be usurped from the project at hand.

- *Devotion:*   Entrepreneurs, in order to maintain the level of the characteristics mentioned above, must be completely devoted to the project, enjoy working on the project, and be deeply committed to the ideas and beliefs on which the project is founded. Many entrepreneurs are motivated by the power of having full responsibility for the success or failure of a venture. Entrepreneurs are rarely motivated by financial gain, as money alone is not enough of a motivator to do all the work involved in starting a new venture. Further, if the venture is successful in all other aspects, the money will follow.

As previously stated, there is no magic formula that yields the ideal entrepreneur. However, anyone even considering launching an entrepreneurial venture should realize that being an entrepreneur means always having the final word. This means always having ultimate responsibility for making decisions, solving problems, resolving conflicts, and keeping morale high when things get tough.

ENTREPRENEURIAL OPPORTUNITIES

An entrepreneurial venture is usually the product of the culmination of several factors. First, there must be a person who discovers or conceptualizes an innovation that is marketable. This person must then have the expertise and desire to bring this innovation to the market. He or she must also have access to the resources needed to produce this innovation and must operate within an environment conducive to perpetuating the project's success. Even with all these factors in play, there is still no guarantee that the innovation will come to fruition or that the venture will be a success, but the odds for success do increase dramatically. Let us discuss these steps in order.

1. *The idea.*   One major pitfall to avoid when conceptualizing an idea for a new product or service is that the idea must be unique. It is neither likely nor required for a business idea to be new; odds are that someone, somewhere, has had the idea before. Truthfully, what is far more relevant than an entrepreneur's idea-generation skills are his or her implementation skills. The reason that an idea may appear new to a would-be entrepreneur is that the last person to have the idea was not able to make it a reality and, as a result, was not able to bring a product or service to the market for anyone to be aware of its existence. While an entrepreneur must pay some attention to protecting his or her ideas, it is a waste of time and energy to get obsessed over it. An idea is no more than a pleasant thought, however, without the ability to implement it, and most people are without the interest and resources to really steal an idea.

2. *The product concept and market need.*   An entrepreneur must be able to describe a product or ser-

vice in terms of its features and benefits, as well as be able to describe the target markets for this product or service. An idea, no matter how ingenious, is simply not enough. For a venture to be successful, the entrepreneur must have a clear and specific idea about what a product or service does and how it does it.

Moreover, the entrepreneur must also know who is going to be interested in having this product or service when it exists. As well as possible, an entrepreneur must be able to identify the target population in terms of number, demographics, and potential sales. A venture based on a product for which there is no demand will be an unsuccessful venture and a waste of valuable time and resources.

3. *Expertise, resources, and environment.* Once an entrepreneur has a product concept, he or she must also have access to the expertise to translate the concept into a reality. This is either done through the entrepreneur's own education or training, or through knowing others who have the knowledge base that the entrepreneur does not and who are willing to work on the project.

The entrepreneur must also have the physical resources to bring an idea to life. Physical resources can include everything from access to the materials, production facilities, and technology needed to make a product, to the office space needed to present the product. And, of course, the entrepreneur must have access to the capital required to pursue the project. (A discussion of potential capital sources will follow at the end of this chapter.)

Lastly, the entrepreneur must be in an environment that supports his or her business efforts. This could mean everything from working for a company that supports innovation and new product development among its employees, to living in a situation where the entrepreneur is motivated by issues of basic survival to make a project work. Of course, there is a broad spectrum between these two extremes. Fundamentally, however, entrepreneurs fare better in an environment that, in some way, supports the entrepreneurial effort.

PROMISING BUSINESS AREAS

While an entrepreneurial idea can emerge within any industry, there are several industries that by nature encourage entrepreneurial innovation. These include the following:

1. *Personal computing services.* Advances in personal computing, dynamic data exchange, and the proliferation of the Internet have created widespread opportunities in the personal computing industry. This is an industry where the demand for technology applications grows as the available technology increases.

For example, the development of user-friendly Web-site technology has created a significant demand for content development to be used on Web sites, as well as enabled many young entrepreneurs to develop new content that uses the Web-site medium. Further, the demand for related products, such as instructional guides and manuals, has also increased.

2. *Telecommunication services.* The growth of the personal communication services market has created enormous opportunity, both domestically as well as internationally, for new products and services. The emergence of wireless communication, for example, created market opportunity for such services as paging, wireless messaging, and instantaneous results reporting. Changes in government regulations continue to open this market to innovation and create more opportunities for entrepreneurial ventures.

3. *International goods distribution.* Changes in the global political climate have opened new markets for entrepreneurs to provide needed services. The relaxation, and in some cases elimination, of trade barriers in many Eastern European and Asian countries creates significant opportunities for the export and distribution of products desired but previously unavailable in these markets.

BUSINESS FORMS

Whatever the nature of the venture pursued, the entrepreneur must at some point direct his or her attention to creating a formal, legally recognized business entity. There are many business forms to choose from. The choice of which form to take usually rests on considerations dealing with the nature of the good or service a business provides, as well as personal preferences of the parties that compose the business.

The most common business forms are as follows:

1. *Sole proprietorship:* This business form is the legal default form for any person who does business in the United States and who make no efforts to organize the business otherwise. This is a business owned and operated by one person who assumes total control and liability for the business. No legal entity is formed. While the sole proprietor may have employees, he or she does not have co-owners.

2. *Partnership:* This form is when two or more parties go into business together to make a profit and share profits, losses, and liability for the business.

3. *Corporation:* This is a business form created by state government upon the filing of an application and payment of a fee. It creates a legal entity, sepa-

rate from its owners (the shareholders). It also eliminates any personal liability the owners have for the business.

4. *Subchapter S corporation:* This is a subclassification of corporation that can be requested and granted after the organization applying passes a number of tests. The primary difference between an S-corp and a regular corporation is the ability of the owners to pay the corporation's taxes directly.

5. *Limited partnership:* This business form is a combination of a partnership and a corporation. It affords general partnership status to some parties, and all benefits and liabilities that go along with it. It also affords limited-partnership status to some parties, where limited partners are entitled to rights and liabilities similar to those of shareholders.

6. *Not-for-profit entity:* This business form is similar to that of a corporation. The primary differences include the absence of a profit-making initiative and the exemption from government tax liabilities.

Usually, issues of control over the business, willingness to accept personal liability for the business, and the nature of the service the business is providing dictate what form a business should take.

BUSINESS PLANS

A business plan is a document summarizing the key objectives and strategies on which a venture idea is based. Business plans serve many purposes and can be used for everything from helping an entrepreneur to evaluate an idea to see if it is worth pursuing, to helping an entrepreneur obtain bank financing or investment funds.

Business plans can vary in length, depending on the specific purpose for writing the plan or the specific audience to whom the plan is directed. In general, a summary business plan, of about ten pages, is a good place to start. A summary business plan should include the following sections:

1. *Cover page:* This is simply a page including the company's name, address, and phone and fax numbers. The cover page may also include the name of the person to contact with questions and his or her direct phone number. The cover page is also a good place to include a message regarding the confidential nature of the document and to establish any rules for sharing or reproduction of the information contained therein.

2. *Table of contents:* This page should be as detailed as possible, providing section titles and their accompanying page numbers.

3. *Executive summary:* This page should include a concise summary of information on the company, the product, the target market, the strategy for pursuing the market, a timetable, and the action step you want whoever is reading the business plan to take. Executive summary pages should be broken down into subsections whenever possible and should never exceed two pages in length.

4. *The company:* This section should provide information on the company's management team, including biographical information as well as business experience and role within the new company. It should also provide a detailed, easy-to-follow account of the company's overall business strategy and philosophy. This can be accomplished by providing a history of the company, giving a report on its current status, and describing the company's future goals and the process by which these goals will be reached. This is also the place to include a company mission statement.

5. *The product:* This should include a discussion of what the product or service does, its main features and benefits, and how it will appeal to the target audience. Discussions of pricing can be included in this section, as well as any pictures, diagrams, or other helpful visual aids.

6. *The market:* This section should define the target audience as specifically as possible. This section can also include a detailed discussion of the existing market need that the product or service satisfies, other products or services that can be viewed as competitors or substitutes, and how the new product is superior to these potential competitors or substitutes.

7. *Marketing plan:* This section should describe how the entrepreneur plans to introduce, promote, and sell the given product or service. This section should also be as specific as possible, providing a detailed description of all elements in the marketing mix and their expected degrees of efficacy.

8. *Key issues:* This section should identify and address any key problems or difficulties the business may encounter. It should also present proposed solutions or strategies for dealing with these problems. Any potential problem an investor may recognize should be mentioned and explained in this section to the greatest degree possible.

9. *Financial statements:* The financial statement section should include a balance sheet, income statement, and cash flow statement for any historical period of operation as well as for the period of projected operation. If the business plan is being

directed at a specific investor, the entrepreneur should include any supplemental analyses that the investing party requests or traditionally wants to see.

Typically, an entrepreneur will discover weak spots in a business structure or feel the need to revise parts of his or her business strategy, after completing a business plan. In fact, this is one of direct benefits to the entrepreneur of completing this document. Better to fix problems before presenting an idea to an important third party than have the third party point them out to you. Further, in customizing a business plan to fit the needs of a particular third party, the entrepreneur can get a sense of precisely what criteria the third party will use to evaluate the venture, and the entrepreneur can structure the accompanying presentation accordingly.

SOURCES OF FINANCING

An amazing number of sources of capital are available to the entrepreneur. While some may be more favorable than others, a determined entrepreneur can find the funds to get his or her business off the ground. The following is a brief list of some of the potential sources available to entrepreneurs.

Grants and Loans

Both private and government entities make millions of dollars per year available to invest in entrepreneurial ventures. Some grants are reserved to encourage entrepreneurship among certain population groups, such as persons of color or women. Some grants are awarded to businesses that open within certain geographic areas, sometimes called *empowerment zones.* Some grants are awarded based on the nature of the venture being pursued. Some government agencies, like The Small Business Association, provide low-interest loans to entrepreneurs who apply and meet certain professional requirements.

Bank Loans

Many private banking institutions will grant low- or competitive-interest, noncollateralized loans to entrepreneurs for the purposes of starting a business. Applications and conditions vary from institution to institution, which means that loan rejection at one bank may not mean that every bank will respond the same way.

Private Investors

There are many people, called *angels,* who choose to make private capital investments in entrepreneurial ventures. These arrangements are usually done on the basis of a privately negotiated agreement in which the investor earns a high return on invested capital if the business succeeds, to compensate for the risk associated with an unproven business.

Venture Capital

Venture capital firms are financial institutions that specialize in providing new or start-up firms with capital in exchange for a high return on the capital invested and an equity stake in the new company.

Depending on the person, some forms of capital are more attractive than others. For the die-hard entrepreneur, however, any form of capital is better than no capital at all. Many start-up ventures have been financed on personal savings and credit cards. This option is not optimal. The general rule of financing that many entrepreneurs follow is never to invest their own money in a venture. If the venture is really worth doing and the entrepreneur has done a good job of presenting the idea, there should be enough external capital available to meet the venture requirements.

SUMMARY

The United States fosters an entrepreneurial spirit, both through its national culture as well as through public and private support. Entrepreneurial opportunity is everywhere. If someone can recognize an opportunity, has the right skills and resources available to capitalize on that opportunity, and is completely committed to turning a concept into a reality, then starting a new venture is a risk worth taking.

CONCEPT ENTREPRENEURSHIP*

Angel

This term is used for a wealthy individual who invests in private companies.

Antidilution of Ownership

This is the right of an investor to maintain the same percentage ownership of a company's common stock in the event that the company issues more stock.

Asking Price

The price level at which sellers offer securities to borrowers is the asking price.

Asset Acquisition

This is an alternate means of conducting a buyout by purchasing certain assets a company may have instead of purchasing that company's stock.

Balance Sheet

This is a summary statement of the accounting value of a company's assets; liabilities; preferred, common, and treasury stock; and retained earnings over a specific period of time.

Bear Market

A bear market is one in which stock prices are expected to fall.

Best Efforts Offering

Unlike a firm commitment offering where a price is set and a fixed monetary amount is expected, the underwriter in a best efforts offering makes its best efforts to sell as many shares as possible at the initial offering price, and then adjusts the price as necessary to sell the rest.

Bid

The price a buyer offers to acquire a security from a seller is a bid.

*Adapted from Paul A. Argenti, *The Portable MBA Desk Reference* (New York: Wiley, 1994), and William Bygrave, *The Portable MBA in Entrepreneurship* (New York: Wiley, 1994). For an even more comprehensive list of terms, please see these two volumes.

Blue Sky

This refers to laws that safeguard investors from being misled by investment people who misrepresent the value of investments to get the money of the financially naive.

Bridge Financing

This refers to short-term financing used to cover a short-term need that is expected to be repaid relatively quickly.

Bull Market

A bull market is one in which stock prices are expected to rise.

Burn Rate

The negative real-time cash flow from a company's operations, usually computed monthly, is the burn rate.

Business Plan

This is a document that details a business concept, its present and future strategy for development, and its financial position.

Capital Gain

The amount by which the selling price of an asset exceeds the seller's initial purchase price is the capital gain.

Capitalization Rate

This is the internal interest rate a company uses to discount future income streams to arrive at their present value.

Carried Interest

A venture capital firm's share of the profit earned by a fund is the carried interest. In the United States, the venture capital firm usually earns 20 percent of the profit after all investors have been repaid any principal investments.

Cash Flow Statement

This is a financial statement that summarizes a company's sources and uses of cash over a specific period of time. Cash flow statements are generally broken down to include detail on the operations, financing activity, and investment activity of a firm. Free cash flow is also calculated from these statements.

Collateral

This is an asset identified as forfeitable to secure a loan.

Common Stock

This includes shares of a company's equity that represent ownership in that company.

Confidentiality Agreement

This is a legal contract protecting the rights of a business in cases where company or trade secrets or other confidential information must be revealed in the course of doing business. Entrepreneurs who are presenting ideas to potential investors use confidentiality agreements to prevent potential investors from replicating the proposed business concept on their own after a detailed investment presentation.

Conversion Ratio

This indicates the number of shares of a company's common stock associated with one share of that company's convertible security.

Convertible Security

This is preferred stock for a company that is convertible into common stock for that company at a previously specified ratio. It is the security holder's choice or option to make this conversion.

Corporation

This is a type of business that the law recognizes as a separate entity from those persons who run it. A corporation's important features include limited liability, easy transfer of ownership, and unlimited life.

Copyright

A copyright is a legal proviso indicating ownership of written material such that the material cannot be reproduced without the expressed consent of the author.

Cost of Capital

This is the weighted average of all types of capital a firm uses and their associated return rates. Generally, the cost of capital is determined by multiplying the amount of debt a company has by the rate paid on the debt and adding that to the amount of equity a company has multiplied by the rate paid on the equity.

Cost of Debt

The interest rate or rates charged to a company by its lenders for use of the capital is the cost of debt.

Cost of Equity

The rate of return required by a company's shareholders as compensation for the investment of capital is the cost of equity.

Covenant

A covenant is a set of restrictions imposed by a lender on a borrower regarding how the borrower must operate the business for which the capital is being borrowed. Violation of debt covenants is grounds for recalling a loan.

Debenture

This is a document containing an acknowledgment of indebtedness on the part of a company, usually secured by a charge on the company's assets.

Double Jeopardy

This refers to a situation in which an entrepreneur's main source of income and net worth depend on the entrepreneur's business.

Due Diligence

This refers to the investigative process an investor should conduct into the operations and business plan assumptions of a company soliciting investors.

Employee Stock Ownership Plan (ESOP)

This is a trust established to acquire shares in a company for subsequent allocation to employees over a period of time.

Employment Agreement

This is a contract between senior managers of a company and the company guaranteeing that the managers will live out a specific tenure with the company before even considering moving on to another company.

Exit Strategy

This refers to the means by which investors in a company realize all or part of their investment.

Expansion Financing

Expansion financing is the securing of the working capital required for the support of an increase in accounts receivable and inventory associated with a company's initial expansion period.

Factoring

This refers to a means of enhancing a business's cash flow whereby an outside company pays a firm a certain portion of its trade debts and then receives the full amount of cash from the debtor companies directly.

Firm Commitment Offering

An underwriter guarantees to raise a fixed amount of capital through an IPO.

First-Round Financing

This refers to the first investment made by internal investors.

First-Stage Financing

This refers to the process of securing the capital required to initiate full manufacturing and sales efforts.

Five Cs of Obtaining Credit

The five crucial elements lenders examine before issuing credit include:

1. *Character*—This is a measure of the borrower's integrity as related to seeing the loan as an obligation that must be repaid.
2. *Capacity*—This is a measure of a business's ability to generate the cash flows required to service the debt on hand.
3. *Capital*—This is a measure of the borrowing firm's net worth.
4. *Collateral*—This is a measure of the firm's assets available to secure the debt requested.
5. *Conditions*—This is a measure of the conditions of the loan, as well as prevailing industry and general economic conditions that might affect the loan repayment.

Franchising

This is a form of organization in which a firm sells the rights to produce its product or service to other service providers, who must then operate under the selling firm's name and pay fees to the original firm.

Golden Handcuffs

This refers to the combination of rewards and penalties given to managers to dissuade them from leaving a company.

High-Potential Venture

A company started with the intent of growing quickly to annual sales of at least $30 million to $50 million in five years is a high-potential venture. It also has the potential to have a firm-commitment IPO.

Income Statement

This is a summary statement of a company's revenues, expenses, and profits over a specific period of time.

Initial Public Offering (IPO)

This refers to the process by which a company raises money by issuing equity and gets listed on a stock exchange.

Internal Rate of Return

This is the profit percentage a company will earn on a proposed investment once all costs are considered.

Investment Bank

This is a lending entity engaged in all phases of security offerings, including managing, underwriting, trading, and distributing new security issues.

Invisible Venture Capital

This refers to venture capital supplied by wealthy individuals, or angels.

Leveraged Buyout (LBO)

This refers to acquisition of a company through the accumulation of 70 percent or more of the company's total capitalized debt.

Lien

A lien is a legal claim on specific assets that were used to secure a loan.

Liquidity

Liquidity is the ability of an asset to be converted into cash as quickly as possible and without any discount to its value.

Listing

This refers to acceptance of a security for trading on an organized stock exchange.

Management Buyout (MBO)

This refers to the transfer of ownership of an entity to new owners in which the old management and employee base are significant elements.

Mezzanine Financing

This includes any form of financing that falls between senior debt and common shares in terms of priority of repayment.

Net Income

What remains of a company's revenue after all expenses and taxes have been paid is net income.

Out of Cash

This point is calculated by taking a company's cash on hand divided by its burn rate, yielding the time period that the company will have enough cash to cover its needs.

Over the Counter (OTC)

This refers to financial securities whose sale and purchase is not conducted over a stock exchange.

Partnership

A partnership is a legally recognized business form in which two or more partners are co-owners, sharing profits, losses, and liabilities associated with the business they own.

Patent

A patent is a legal document ensuring exclusive rights to a process or product using a unique technological or structural innovation.

Private Placement

This refers to the direct sale of securities to a small number of investors.

Prospectus

A prospectus is a document containing all relevant investor information regarding the operations of a company issuing securities.

Put

An agreement allowing a holder of securities to sell them back to the issuer at a specified amount during a specified time interval is a put.

Red Herring

A preliminary prospectus circulated by underwriters to gauge investor interest in a planned offering, which has yet to gain final approval from the SEC, is a red herring.

Second-Round Financing

This refers to the introduction of further funding by original investors or new investors to enable a new company to deal with unexpected problems or finance growth.

Securities and Exchange Commission (SEC)

This is the regulatory body for investor protection in the United States, created by the Securities Exchange Act of 1934.

Seed Financing

This refers to a small amount of money used for initial market research or product development for a new venture.

Sensitivity Analysis

This is a test of a company's performance projections based on varying the key assumptions used for forecast performance.

Sole Proprietorship

This refers to a form of business where the owner is personally responsible for all liabilities associated with the business.

Start-up Financing

This consists of capital provided to companies that have been in operation for less than one year to facilitate all phases of bringing their products to market.

Subchapter S Corporation

This is a small business corporation form in which the owners pay the corporation's income taxes personally.

Syndicate

A syndicate is group of investors who act together when forming a company.

Trademark

This is the right of a seller to exclusive use of an identifying symbol or brand.

Underwriting

This refers to an arrangement under which investors each agree to buy a certain amount of securities of a new issue at a given date for a given price, thereby insuring that the issuer gets the full proceeds of the issue.

Venture Capitalist

This refers to a company in the practice of providing capital to fledgling companies with high growth potential in exchange for high-percentage returns on the capital once the business has grown.

Visible Venture Capital

This includes the organized, established firms that constitute the venture capital industry.

Vulture Capital

This is a derogatory term for venture capital.

Warrant

This is a long-term call option to purchase common stock at a specified price.

White Knight

This refers to a friendly potential acquirer sought by a target company threatened by a less welcome suitor.

MORE READINGS
Critical References

Bygrave, William. *The Portable MBA in Entrepreneurship.* New York: Wiley, 1994.

This book provides a comprehensive overview of relevant topics for those interested in the study or practice of entrepreneurship. Topics include start-up strategies, guidance on how to spot market opportunities, how to prepare a business plan, how to secure financing and manage debt, and central legal and tax information. The reader does not need any formal business education or any other prerequisite, aside from interest, to enjoy and get value from this book.

Gladstone, David. *Venture Capital Investing.* Englewood Cliffs, N.J.: Prentice-Hall, 1988.

This book provides a detailed account of the process associated with investigating private business opportunities, complete with a checklist of questions to ask before investing in a small or private business. It also provides an in-depth analysis of the venture capital process, including locating and structuring suitable investments, legal closings, monitoring the investor, and realizing a gain on the investment. The book was written by the president of Allied Capital Corporation, the largest venture capital company in the United States.

Higgins, Robert C. *Analysis for Financial Management.* Homewood, Ill.: Irwin, 1992.

This comprehensive, straightforward book serves both as a text for explanation as well as a manual for generating the key financial statements every business plan must have, including balance sheets, income statements, and cash flow statements. Set forth in very easy to understand language, this book provides theory, numerical examples, a glossary of key terms, and sample problems with accompanying solutions. This is a must-have for those without a formal finance education.

Keen, Peter. *Every Manager's Guide to Information Technology.* Cambridge, Mass.: Harvard Business School Press, 1991.

Since many new ventures stem either from a technological innovation or a product concept to fill a technological need, entrepreneurs and investors alike must be well versed in the technology terms and concepts. This guide provides information on both key terms as well as key concepts that dominate in the information technology industry. The book can be used either as a glossary for looking up key information or as an instructional volume that presents information in a clear, logical format that is easy for even the novice reader to understand.

Timmons, Jeffrey. *Venture Capital Creation.* Homewood, Ill.: Irwin, 1994.

This book provides insight into the traditional profile of the entrepreneur in an effort to expand this conception to fit the entrepreneur of today. Further, it works to assist the entrepreneur in understanding him- or herself in an effort to facilitate the readers' better self-management as well as their managerial skills in relation to others. It focuses specifically on the topics of entrepreneurship defined, the entrepreneurial environment, the entrepreneurial task, the entrepreneurial personality, and the entrepreneurial career.

Finance

The field of finance consists of three interrelated areas: (1) money and capital markets, (2) investments, and (3) financial management. *Money markets* are the markets for debt securities that must be repaid within one year. *Capital markets* are the markets for debt securities that repay beyond one year and for equity shares. *Equity shares* can be one of two types: *preferred stock* or *common stock*. Common stock is a financial study that represents an ownership of a corporation. Common stockholders are entitled to receive distributions of corporate earnings or assets only after all other capital claimants have been paid. Preferred stock is a type of stock whose holders receive priority over common stockholders in the payment of dividends. Usually, however, dividend payments to preferred stockholders are fixed. Investments focus on the decisions of individual and institutional investors as they choose securities for their portfolios. Successful investing requires an understanding of how to analyze the potential risks and rewards of individual securities and the ability to profitably combine securities in a portfolio.

Financial management describes the actual management of a firm. Financial managers are important because their decisions influence the value of their firms. In order to increase value, financial managers make decisions in three important areas. First, financial managers must somehow choose which long-term investment projects the firm should undertake. This is referred to as the *capital budgeting decision*. Second, the financial manager must raise the money needed to finance the investment projects. This is referred to as the *financing decision.* Third, the financial manager must determine how the firm's cash position and other short-term financial affairs (e.g., inventory policy or credit extension decisions) should be managed. This is the *net working capital and cash management decision.*

Finance has become one of the most fascinating and complex fields in business today. Therefore, we must focus our attention on a broad discussion of finance in this book. Our focus in this chapter, therefore, is on financial management within the modern business corporation. Our discussion emphasizes the critical role of the finance function in managing corporate resources in a profitable manner. The distinctive contribution of finance to the management of the modern corporation is the measurement of value. Finance values the operating policies and business strategies of the firm, thereby providing an objective assessment of acceptable and poor decisions.

GOALS OF THE MODERN CORPORATION

Sound business decisions are not made in isolation. Decision makers must have specific goals and objectives in mind. In this chapter we assume that a financial manager's primary goal is maximizing stockholder wealth, which is equivalent to maximizing the price of the firm's common stock. Managers do, of course, sometimes establish and pursue other objectives as well. For example, managers who make the actual decisions regarding the use of corporate resources are interested in their own personal welfare, in their employees' welfare, as well as their perceived standing in their communities. Still, for the reasons we describe throughout this chapter, share-price maximization should be the most important goal of most corporations. Moreover, share price maximization also creates the most value for managers and shareholders seeking to also pursue other objectives. Thus, shareholders' and stakeholders' interests can be balanced by managers so that all constituencies prosper.

Some Factors That Encourage Managers

Stockholders own the firm and elect the board of directors, who then appoint the corporation's management. Management, in turn, is supposed to make decisions that are in the best interests of all the stockholders. Later in this chapter, we discuss the most important decisions that managers make to achieve this objective. We know, however, that because the stock of most large corporations is widely held, managers of large corporations have a great deal of autonomy. Because most corporations have a large number of owners (stockholders), each with a relatively small ownership of the corporation, managers might be tempted to pursue goals other than stock price maximization. For example, managers of a large, well-established corporation might decide to work just hard enough to keep stockholder returns at a "reasonable" level and then devote the remainder of their efforts and resources to higher executive salaries or to other activities or expenditures that don't necessarily increase the firm's stock price. An extreme example of this type of management behavior is RJR Nabisco, as described in the book by Bryan Burrough and John Helyar *Barbarians at the Gate* (New York: Harper & Row, 1990). There, the authors describe many examples where management spent corporate resources on activities that rewarded management but not necessarily the firm's shareholders.

Unfortunately, it is difficult to determine whether a particular management team is continually striving to maximize shareholder wealth or is merely attempting to keep stockholders satisfied while pursuing their own personal goals. For example, how can we tell whether employee or community benefit programs are in the long-run best interests of the stockholders? Similarly, was it really necessary for Walt Disney to pay its chairman more than $200 million in the mid-1990s to obtain and reward his services, or was this just another example of a manager taking advantage of stockholders?

It is almost impossible to give definitive answers to these critical questions. However, managers of firms operating in markets subject to intense competition from other corporations will be forced to undertake actions that are reasonably consistent with shareholder wealth maximization. If they depart too far from this objective, they risk being removed from their jobs by their own boards of directors or through a hostile takeover or a proxy fight.

A *hostile takeover* is the acquisition of one company by another despite the opposition of management, while a *proxy fight* involves one group trying to gain management control of a corporation by getting stockholders to vote a new management group into place. Both actions are more likely to occur and succeed if a firm's stock price is low, so to retain their jobs, managers try to keep stock prices as high as possible. Successful hostile takeovers and proxy fights often result in the dismissal of top management from their jobs. Therefore, while some managers may be more interested in their own personal welfare than in maximizing shareholder wealth, the threat of losing their jobs still motivates them to try to maximize stock prices. Many of the most spectacular takeover contests during the past two decades were precipitated by the conflict of interest between managers and shareholders. A crucial task for any modern-day manager is to manage corporate resources efficiently to achieve all of his or her objectives.

Stock-Price Maximization and Social Welfare

From a societal perspective, is it desirable or undesirable for corporate managers to pursue an objective of maximizing their firm's share price? Aside from such illegal actions such as attempting to monopolize markets, violating safety codes, and failing to meet pollution control restrictions, *the same actions that maximize stock prices also benefit society.* Therefore, society as a whole benefits from the actions of managers designed to maximize share prices. Consider, for example, the following societal benefits that accrue from such managerial actions. First, stock-price maximization requires the development, manufacturing, and distribution of products that consumers want, need, and are willing to pay for. Therefore, managers seeking to maximize share price also create new technology, new products, and new jobs. Second, stock-price maximization requires efficient, low-cost plants that produce high-quality goods and services at the lowest possible cost. Finally, stock-price maximization requires efficient customer service and satisfaction, adequate supplies of merchandise, and geographical convenience to facilitate mutually beneficial transactions. These factors are all necessary to make profitable sales. Therefore, actions that help a firm increase the price of its stock are also beneficial to society at large. This line of reasoning also suggests why capitalist, free-enterprise economies have been so much more successful than socialist and communist economic systems. Since financial management plays a crucial role in the operation of successful firms, and since successful firms are absolutely necessary for a healthy, productive, and growing economy, it seems clear why finance is also important from a social standpoint. Throughout the remainder of this chapter, we describe and develop a basic understanding of how a successful manager can make sound financial decisions.

WHAT IS FINANCIAL MANAGEMENT?

Financial Objectives in Complex Organizations

Thus far, we have suggested that the financial manager should act to increase the value of the shareholders' investment in the firm. But thousands of people are employed in a large company. Each individual considers his or her own personal interests as well as that of the shareholders. Modern corporate finance deals not only with the financial objectives of the firm, but also with the selection of appropriate reward and penalty systems to ensure that each member of the organization works toward the same objective.

Think of the company's net revenue as a pie divided among a number of claimants. These include the management and the employees as well as the lenders and shareholders who have put up the money to establish and finance the continuing operations of the business. The government is a claimant, too, since it gets to tax the profits of the enterprise.

All these claimants are bound together in a complex web of contractual relationships, alliances, and understandings. For example, when banks lend money to the firm, they insist on a formal legal contract which specifically lists the interest rate and repayment dates, plus some additional restrictions (called *covenants*) on dividends or further borrowing in the future. Such a contract serves as a binding legal restriction on the future actions of the firm. Realistically, however, it is impossible to devise reasonable restrictions to cover every possible future event. So the explicit legal contracts are often supplemented by implicit or explicit understandings. For example, managers understand that in return for a high salary they are expected to work hard on behalf of shareholders and not to divert corporate resources for their own personal benefit.

What enforces this type of understanding? Is it realistic to expect financial managers always to act on behalf of the shareholders? Most shareholders can't afford to spend their time monitoring every action of the manager to ensure that sound decision-making practices are being followed.

Various institutional arrangements have developed through time in an effort to help align managers' and shareholders' interests. Consider the following two examples.

1. Managers are subject to the scrutiny of specialists. Their actions are monitored by the board of directors; managers are also reviewed by banks, which keep an eagle eye on the progress of firms receiving their loans. Also, institutional investors have become very active in recent years in an effort to ensure that firms are indeed being operated in the interest of shareholders.

2. Managers are motivated by incentives schemes, such as stock options, which pay off big if stock prices increase but are worthless if they do not.

These observations are not meant to suggest that all corporate life is a sequence of conflicts. It isn't, because practical corporate finance has gradually developed a variety of solutions to reconcile personal and corporate interests—to keep everyone working together to increase the value of the whole pie, not merely the size of each person's slice.

Nevertheless, the financial manager must stay alert to potential problems caused by conflicts of interest. We, too, have to think about potential conflicts to understand fully why takeovers occur, why lending contracts restrict dividend payouts, or why companies sometimes prefer to issue bonds that investors can convert to shares. We discuss some of these arrangements in more detail in the following section.

The Balance-Sheet Model of the Firm

Suppose we take a financial snapshot of the firm at a single point in time. The snapshot should contain a summary of all of the investment and financing decisions made by a firm throughout its relevant history. This type of information is contained in a firm's balance sheet, which shows where and how the company raised its money and how it has spent it. Figure 5.1 shows a graphic conceptualization of the balance sheet that will help introduce you to corporate finance.

The assets of the firms are on the left-hand side of the balance sheet. Assets represent how a firm has spent its time and money, and are usually categorized as either current or fixed. *Fixed assets* are those that will last a long time, such as a building. Some fixed assets are tangible, such as machinery and equipment. Other fixed assets are intangible, such as patents, trademarks, and the quality of management. The other category of assets, *current assets,* comprises those that

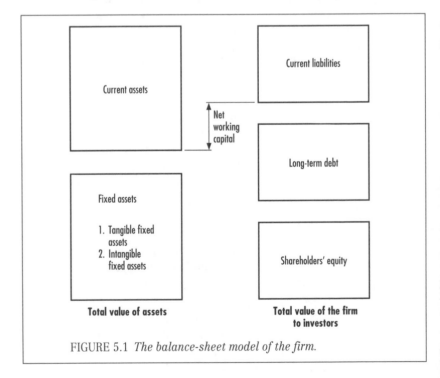

FIGURE 5.1 *The balance-sheet model of the firm.*

have short lives, such as inventory or accounts receivable. The products that your firm has made but has not yet sold are part of its inventory. Unless you have over-produced, the products will eventually be sold. At that time, one asset (inventory) will be converted into another (cash).

Before a corporation can invest in an asset, it must obtain funding, which means that it must raise the money to pay for the investment. Many firms obtain funding from a variety of different sources. The right-hand side of a firm's balance sheet sometimes summarizes the outstanding different types of financing the firm has used, hence, we often observe a number of sources rather than just a single provider. A firm will issue (sell) pieces of paper called *debt* (loan agreements) or *equity shares* (stock certificates). Debt obligations are owed to creditors, and the stockholders are the debtors. Typically, however, shareholders have the right of limited liability, which means they are not personally responsible for repaying the firm's credit obligations. Therefore, lenders base their loan decisions on their assessment of the corporation's ability (and willingness) to repay their credit obligations. Similar to our classification of assets as long-lived or short-lived, so too are liabilities. A short-term loan or debt obligation is called a *current liability.* Short-term debt represents loans and other obligations that must be repaid within one year. Long-term debt is debt that does not have to be repaid within one year. Shareholders' equity represents the difference between the value of the assets and the debt of the firm. These are the claims held by the owners of the corporation. In this sense, it is considered a residual claim on the firm's assets. That is, shareholders get paid only after all other financial obligations of the firm have been satisfied.

From the balance-sheet model of the firm, it is easy to see why finance can be thought of as the study of the following three questions:

1. In what long-lived fixed assets should the firm invest its financial resources? This question concerns the left-hand side of the balance sheet. Of course, the nature of the business the firm has chosen to operate in typically determines the type and proportions of assets the firm needs. We use the terms *capital budgeting* and *capital expenditure* to describe the process of committing investment capital and managing expenditures on long-lived assets. An example would be whether Ben & Jerry's should build a new manufacturing plant to meet the expected increase in demand for its ice cream products.

2. How should the firm raise the cash necessary to finance its capital expenditures? This question concerns the right-hand side of the balance sheet. These

decisions establish the firm's *capital structure,* which represents the proportions of the firm's financing from current and long-term debt and equity. Continuing with our Ben & Jerry's plant expansion decision, if the management decides to proceed with its planned capital expenditure, should it issue debt or equity to finance the project?

3. How should short-term operating cash flows be managed? This question concerns the upper portion of the balance sheet. Depending on the business(es) a firm operates, there may be a mismatch between the timing of cash inflows and cash outflows during its operating cycle. Furthermore, both the amount and the timing of operating cash inflows and out-flows are not known with certainty. Financial managers must establish policies and procedures to manage the temporary shortfalls (or excess inflows) in cash flow. Short-term management of cash flow is described by a firm's *net working capital* position. Net working capital is defined as current assets minus current liabilities. From a financial perspective, the short-term cash flow problem comes from the mismatching of cash inflows and outflows. It is the subject of short-term finance. Decisions such as how much inventory to carry and how much customer credit should be extended are typical problems addressed here.

Capital Structure

Sometimes it is useful to think of the firm as a pie. The size of the pie will depend on how well the firm has made its investment decisions. After a firm has made its investment decisions, the value of its assets (e.g., its buildings, land, and inventories) is determined.

Financing arrangements determine how a firm's value is divided among the various entities that have provided funding for the corporation. The persons or institutions that buy debt from the firm are called *creditors.* The holders of equity shares are called *shareholders.* In terms of our firm-as-a-pie analogy, financing arrangements determine how the pie is sliced. Creditors and shareholders are entitled to slices, and the size of those slices depends on how well the firm makes its investment decisions as well as how much money each initially contributed to the firm.

The firm then determines its capital structure. The firm might initially have raised the cash to invest in its assets by issuing more debt than equity. Subsequently, it might consider changing that mix by issuing more equity and using the proceeds to invest in new projects or to buy back some of its debt. Financing decisions like the latter can often be made independently of the original investment decisions. The decisions to issue debt and equity should be thought of as affecting primarily how the pie is sliced. They can, however, also affect the size of the pie itself. Thus, a creative financial manager can impact value through both investing and financing activities.

Figure 5.2 provides a pictorial representation of this discussion. The size of the pie is the value of the firm in the financial markets, and it reflects the investors' understanding of the investing and financing activities of the firm. We can describe the value of the firm, V, as consisting of two parts:

$$V = B + S$$

where B is the value of the debt and S is the value of the equity. The pie diagram illustrates two different ways of slicing the pie (i.e., financing the firm): 50 percent debt and 50 percent equity, and 25 percent debt and 75 percent equity. The way the pie is sliced could affect its value. If so, the goal of the financial manager will be to choose the optimal financing arrangement that makes the value of the pie—that is, the value of the firm, V—as large as possible.

THE ROLE OF THE MODERN FINANCIAL MANAGER

In large firms, the finance activity is usually associated with a top officer of the corporation, generally a vice president and chief financial officer, and some lesser officers and employees. The treasurer and the controller each report to the chief financial officer, and both have well-defined areas of responsibility within the firm. The treasurer is responsible for handling short-term (daily) cash flows, making capital-expenditures decisions and recommending financial plans to raise funds from external sources. Typically, these decisions are projected over a three- to five-year time horizon. The controller handles the accounting responsibilities, which include tax management and planning, cost and financial statement accounting, and information systems.

The most important job of a financial manager is to create value from the firm's capital budgeting, financ-

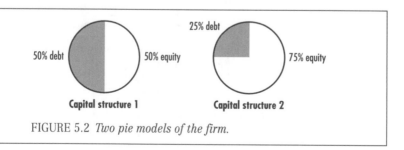

FIGURE 5.2 *Two pie models of the firm.*

ing, and working capital management decisions. Financial managers create value in two general ways:

1. The firm acquires assets that generate more cash for the firm than they cost.

2. The firm sells bonds and stocks and other financial instruments that raise more cash than they cost in terms of expected future payments.

Thus, in both cases, the firm must create more cash flow than it uses to increase value. The cash flow paid to bondholders and stockholders of the firm should be higher than the cash flows put into the firm by the bondholders and stockholders. To see how this is done, we can trace the cash flows from the firm to the financial markets and back again.

The interaction of the firm's financial decisions with the financial markets is illustrated in Figure 5.3. The arrows in Figure 5.3 trace cash flow from investors in the financial markets to the firm and back again. Consider first the firm's financing activities. To raise money, the firm sells debt and common stock to investors in the financial markets. This results in cash flows from the financial markets to the firm (A). This cash is invested in the investment activities of the firm (B) by the firm's management. The cash generated by the firm (C) is paid to shareholders and bondholders (F). The shareholders receive cash in the form of dividends or share repurchases; the bondholders who loaned funds to the firm receive interest payments and, when the initial loan is repaid, principal. Not all of the firm's cash is paid out. Some is retained to repay the firm's future financial obligations or reinvested in new assets (E), and some is paid to the government as taxes (D). Over time, if the cash paid to shareholders and bondholders (F) is greater than the

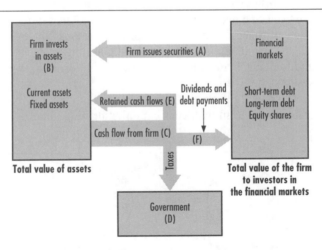

FIGURE 5.3 *Cash flows between the firm and the financial markets.*

cash raised in the financial markets (A), value will be created.

While this process may seem quite straightforward, the best financial managers must actively coordinate a wide variety of activities within the firm to ensure consistency of objectives. Here are some specific activities that the financial manager participates in to maximize the value of the firm:

1. *Forecasting and planning.* The financial staff must interact with officers and employees from other departments, such as marketing, engineering, and production, as they project the firm's future plans and assess the impact of those plans on the firm's financial health.

2. *Major investment and financing decisions.* A successful firm usually has rapid growth in sales, which requires investments in plant, equipment, and working capital. The financial staff must help determine the most efficient sales growth rate and help decide on the specific assets to acquire and the best way to finance those assets. For example, should the firm finance with debt or equity, and if debt is used, should it be long term or short term? Ultimately, a financial manager must convey that there's a big difference between profitable and unprofitable growth, no matter how fast sales are increasing.

3. *Coordination and control.* The financial staff must interact with other officers and employees to ensure that the firm's operating and financing plans are implemented as efficiently as possible. All business decisions have financial implications, and all managers—financial and otherwise—need to understand this principle. For example, marketing decisions affect sales growth, which in turn affects investment and working capital requirements. Thus, marketing decision makers must be able to understand how their actions affect (and are affected by) factors such as the availability of funds, inventory policies, receivables policies, and plant capacity utilization.

4. *Dealing with the financial markets.* The financial staff must deal with the money and capital markets. Every firm affects and is affected by the general financial markets where funds are raised, where the firm's securities are traded, and where its investors are either rewarded or penalized. A firm's stock price is an informative indicator of how well the firm's operating and financing plans are working. This direct link between management decisions and stock prices provides the firm with useful feedback in assessing the merits of the corporation's overall strategy.

In summary, financial managers make decisions regarding which assets their firms should invest in, how those assets should be financed, and how the firm should manage its existing resources and future opportunities. If these responsibilities are performed well, financial managers help maximize the value of their firms and also maximize the long-run welfare of other corporate stakeholders, such as customers who buy products from the corporation, suppliers who provide productive inputs for the firm, and employees who work for the company.

MANAGEMENT DECISIONS AND SHAREHOLDER VALUE
Understanding Value

A firm's financing decision always reflects some view about the current status and future outlook of the capital markets. For example, suppose a firm chooses to finance a major expansion program by issuing debt. A financial manager must consider the terms of the debt issue and decide that it is fairly priced. But that decision requires a theory or an understanding of how bonds are priced in the capital markets. The financial manager must ask whether the firm's stockholders would be made better or worse off by the additional debt used to finance the firm's operating activities. That decision requires a theory or an understanding of how corporate borrowing affects the value of the firm's shares.

The investment decision cannot be completely separated from capital market conditions either. A firm acting in its stockholders' interest should invest in those assets that increase the value of their stake in the firm. But that requires a theory of how common stocks are valued, and how that value changes when managers make decisions.

Understanding how the capital markets function is the same thing as understanding how investors value financial assets. New theories during the last two decades have been developed to explain how investors price bonds and stocks. These theories have worked well in the sense that they seem to provide fairly accurate explanations of the link between financial managers' decisions and changes in financial security prices.

Time and Uncertainty

The astute financial manager must understand how to adequately assess the impact of time and uncertainty on his or her decisions. Firms often have the opportunity to invest in assets that generate little or no cash flow in the short run and that expose the firm and its stockholders to considerable risk. Research and development expenses are a good example of this type of investment. The investment, if undertaken, may have to be financed by debt that cannot be fully repaid for many years. The firm cannot simply ignore that such choices involve difficult trade-offs—someone has to decide whether the opportunity is worth more than its costs and whether the additional debt burden can be safely borne. An improper assessment of the costs and benefits of such decisions can create financial hardship for the corporation, or even bankruptcy.

Understanding the Value of Information

Information is an unusual and valuable commodity throughout the world of business. In financial markets, the right information can be worth millions—but only if other investors do not have the same information at the same time. Suppose, for example, you learn that one company will imminently make a takeover offer to acquire another company at a price which significantly exceeds that company's current market price. Such information is potentially worth a tremendous amount of money. Unfortunately, fiduciary responsibilities and legal restrictions preclude the selective dissemination of valuable information prior to complete public disclosure. Because financial markets are efficient, as soon as important financial information is revealed, it travels instantly to New York, London, Tokyo, and all the other major financial centers.

Companies spend considerable time and money providing information to investors. If they did not do so, investors would be skeptical and unsure of a firm's future prospects. They would have to expend personal resources trying to collect information for themselves, and they would be unwilling to pay as much for the firm's shares. This would increase the company's cost of obtaining the financing it needs for its investment decisions. This would reduce a firm's ability to invest profitably, hurting society as a result.

As the saying goes, talk is cheap. Should investors trust the information given out by companies? The answer is: not always. But institutions have been created to reduce this credibility problem. Sometimes the information is certified by a firm of accountants or investment bankers, who put their reputations on the line when they certify a company's financial reports and statements. Sometimes managers send a message of confidence by "putting their money where their mouth is." For example, you will find it easier to raise money for a new business if you are investing a large fraction of your own net worth in the company.

Many financial decisions take on extra importance because they convey or signal information to investors. For example, the decision to reduce the cash dividends paid out to shareholders usually signals trouble for the firm. The stock price may fall sharply when the dividend cut is announced, not because of the dividend cut per se, but because the cut portends poor performance in the future.

How Do Managers Maximize Share Price?

What types of decisions and actions should management take in order to maximize the stock price of his or her firm? First, consider the potential link between stock prices and profit. Does *profit maximization* result in stock-price maximization? If so, then a manager can simply concentrate his or her effort on the tangible objective of profit maximization. Investors in the financial markets can then be relied upon to price the company's stock appropriately. In order to answer this question, we must consider the relationship and distinction between total corporate profits and *earnings per share (EPS)*.

For example, suppose IBM had 50 million shares outstanding and earned $200 million, or $4 per share. If you owned 50 shares of the stock, your share of the total profits would be $200. Now suppose IBM sold another 50 million shares and invested the funds received in assets that produced $50 million of income. Total income would rise to $250 million, but earnings per share would decline from $4 to $250/100 = $2.50. Now your proportional share of the firm's earnings would be $250, far below the anticipated $400. You (and other current stockholders) would incur what is known as *earnings dilution,* despite the fact that total corporate profits had risen. Therefore, other things held constant, this example suggests that if management is interested in the welfare of its current stockholders, it should perhaps concentrate on maximizing earnings per share rather than total corporate profits. If we refer to our firm-as-a-pie analogy, although the pie has grown larger in this example, the new shareholders receive a disproportionately large piece.

Next, we consider the question of whether maximization of expected earnings per share will always maximize stockholder welfare. Should management also consider other factors in its decision? Let's consider the *timings of the earnings.* Suppose IBM had one project that would increase earnings per share by $0.20 per year for five years, or $1 in total. Management would like to compare this project against an alternative project, which would have no effect on earnings for four years but would increase earnings by $1.25 in the fifth year. Because management must choose between these two alternatives, such projects are referred to as mutually exclusive. Which project is more beneficial for shareholders? In other words, is $0.20 per year for five years better or worse than $1.25 in year 5? The answer depends on which project adds the most to the value of the stock, which in turn depends on the time value of money to investors. Thus, timing is an important reason to concentrate on wealth as measured by the price of the stock rather than on earnings alone. Therefore, managers need an accurate, straightforward method for assessing the impact of time on the value of the firm's stock price.

Another issue relates to risk associated with investment projects. Suppose one project is expected to increase earnings per share by $1, while another is expected to raise earnings by $1.20 per share. Now let's suppose that the first project is not very risky. It is expected that if the project is undertaken, earnings will almost certainly rise by about $1 per share. However, the other project is considered quite risky by management and shareholders, so while our best estimate is that earnings will increase by $1.20 per share, we must realistically consider and weigh the possibility that there may be no earnings increase at all, or even a reduction in overall corporate earnings. Depending on how averse stockholders are to risk, the first project might be preferable to the second. Therefore, managers need a methodology which allows them to accurately assess the trade-off between the expected returns and risks associated with alternative investment decisions.

It turns out that the riskiness inherent in a firm's projected earnings per share also depends on how the firm is financed. Many firms go bankrupt every year, and the greater the use of debt, the greater the threat of bankruptcy. *Consequently, while the use of debt financing may increase projected EPS, debt also increases the riskiness of projected future earnings.* Therefore, managers must be able to assess whether the additional financial risk created for the firm's shareholders by the use of higher levels of debt creates a sufficient reward opportunity. The increase in EPS may be more than offset by the higher level of risk.

If a firm is profitable, management must decide whether it should retain earnings and reinvest them in the firm, or pay dividends to the firm's stockholders. Dividends return cash to shareholders, while retentions will increase future profits and thereby create the opportunity for higher dividends in the future. Stockholders like cash dividends, but they also like the future growth in EPS that results from reinvesting earnings profitably back into the business. A financial manager must decide exactly how much of the current earnings to pay out as dividends rather than to retain and reinvest—that is called the *dividend policy decision*. The optimal dividend policy is the one that maximizes the firm's stock price.

This discussion suggests that the firm's stock price depends on the following factors:

1. Projected earnings per share
2. Timing of the earnings stream
3. Riskiness of the projected earnings
4. Use of debt
5. Dividend policy

Every significant corporate decision by management should be evaluated in terms of its effect on these factors and, hence, on the price of the firm's stock. For example, suppose General Mills' restaurant division is considering developing a new line of eateries. If management decides to implement this new policy, management must first assess whether it can be expected to increase EPS. Is there a chance that operating costs will exceed estimates, that prices and customer patronage will fall below projections, and that EPS will be reduced because the new restaurant line was introduced? How long will it take for the new restaurant division to show a profit? How should the capital required to finance construction and invest in equipment be raised? If debt is used, by how much will this increase General Mills' riskiness? Should General Mills reduce its current dividends and use the cash thus saved to finance the project, or should it maintain its dividends and finance the additional restaurants with external capital? Financial management provides a framework that is designed to help managers answer questions like these, plus many more.

A BASIC METHODOLOGY FOR MEASURING VALUE

Financial managers must be knowledgeable about how value is determined for both *financial assets* (such as stocks and bonds) and *real assets* (such as projects, business units, or even whole companies). In both cases, value depends directly on the cash flows the assets are expected to produce. The process of valuing streams of future cash flows is called *discounted cash flow (DCF) analysis.* The DCF methodology is a widely used framework with many applications in corporate finance. Some common applications include estimating a firm's cost of capital, assessing the valuation effects of issuing different types of securities, determining the value of new investment projects, and estimating the value of takeover targets.

The fundamental underlying rationale for discounted cash flow analysis is the *time value of money.* A dollar in hand today is worth more than a dollar due some time in the future, because a dollar received today can be invested and thus will be worth more than a dollar in the future. The DCF methodology tells financial managers how much additional value would be gained or lost by changing the timing of cash flows from an investment.

The actual process of performing a discounted cash flow analysis can be broken down into four steps.

1. *Estimate the future cash flows.* Estimating future cash flows for some assets, such as bonds, is relatively easy. In that case, since the asset's cash flows are contractually fixed, the promised flows will be realized unless the issuer defaults. Estimating cash flows for other classes of assets can be extremely difficult. This is due to the fact that cash flows from other assets are more difficult to estimate accurately. For example, when Microsoft made the decision to develop its new Windows 95 software, it had to estimate research and development costs, and the future revenue and operating cost cash flows, all over a multiple-year project life. Cash flow estimation under such conditions is obviously challenging, and highly accurate forecasts are quite difficult to come by.

2. *Assess the riskiness of the flows.* When cash flows are being estimated, a single scenario that uses one set of estimates is usually not sufficient. Rather, the inherent uncertainty in the cash flows must also be considered in the analysis.

3. *Incorporate the risk assessment into the analysis.* The effect of risk on asset values can be included in the analysis in either of two ways: (1) by the certainty equivalent (CE) approach or (2) by the risk-adjusted discount rate (RADR) approach. In the CE approach, the expected cash flows are reduced or adjusted downward to account for risk. The higher the risk of the project's cash flows, the lower the risk-adjusted, or certainty equivalent, cash flow. In the RADR approach, the discount rate rather than the cash flow is adjusted for risk—the higher the risk of the project, the higher the discount rate. As a practical matter, the risk-adjusted discount rate will reflect risk from two sources: the riskiness of the project's cash flows (business risk) and the financial risk created by the way the project is funded (financial risk).

4. *Find the present value of the flows.* The final step is to find the present value of the cash flows. This step informs a financial manager about the expected value of a stream of future cash flows in today's dollars. Thus, the process of discounting eliminates the problem of comparing cash flows that occur at different times in the future.

The concept of opportunity cost plays an important role in DCF analysis. To illustrate, suppose a firm retains all of its earnings from the previous year and is now evaluating several investment alternatives. Should a cost be assigned to these retained earnings, or should the funds be considered as "free" capital? One line of reasoning might suggest that the funds have a zero cost—after all, the retained earnings have no apparent cost, since the firm already has access to those funds. However, an opportunity cost must be assigned to each alternative. By investing the retained earnings in one alternative, the firm forgoes the opportunity to invest those funds in any other alternative. Moreover, the firm's shareholders have not been given the opportunity to invest those funds elsewhere in alternative investments, since the firm retained all its earnings rather than returning them to shareholders as a cash dividend. Thus, there is a cost to the firm and its shareholders, and this cost should be incorporated into the investment analysis.

The discount rate applied in DCF investment analysis must reflect foregone opportunities, but which alternatives should be considered? The appropriate discount rate should reflect the return that could be earned by investing the funds in the best alternative investment opportunity of *similar risk*. However, it may be very difficult to estimate the returns available on comparable alternative real-asset investments. When Microsoft was setting the opportunity cost rate for its Windows 95 investment, the most logical choice was the return expected on other new software investments. However, such information is rarely available, so the expected rates of return on financial assets are usually used to set the opportunity cost rate for all investment decisions. For most projects, a firm will determine its cost of capital and use that rate as the opportunity cost for many of its investment decisions. The cost of capital is simply a weighted average of the returns that investors expect to receive on the firm's existing set of financial securities. New projects that have risks very different from the firm's existing projects are often evaluated using more advanced techniques, such as the method of comparables.

We see, then, that in any DCF analysis it is necessary to assign an opportunity cost discount rate. In general, that rate must reflect the following three factors:

1. *The riskiness of the cash flows.* The discount rate must reflect the risk inherent in the cash flows—the higher the risk, the higher the discount rate. For example, the discount rate used to evaluate corporate bonds will be higher than that used to evaluate Treasury bonds, and the rate applied to cash flows from a firm's common stock (dividends plus capital gains) will be higher than that applied to its bonds.

2. *The prevailing level of rates of return.* The discount rate must reflect the prevailing level of returns in the economy. Thus, in July 1996 the discount rate

applied to cash flows having the same level of risk as a three-month Treasury bill was 5.3 percent, but in May 1992 the rate was only 3.5 percent. Because of changes in expected inflation, in risk aversion, and in supply and demand conditions, the prevailing return on short-term Treasury securities rose by 180 basis points in four years.

3. *The timing of the cash flows.* The final consideration is the timing of the flows; that is, do the flows occur annually, quarterly, or over some other period? In general, most analyses are conducted in terms of annual discount rates, and in many situations the cash flows do occur annually. Under these circumstances, no adjustment to the annual discount rate is required. However, if the cash flows occur over some period other than annually—say, semiannually—then the discount rate must be adjusted to reflect this timing pattern.

RECENT INNOVATIONS IN APPLIED VALUE MEASUREMENT

In our previous discussion of the potential conflicts of interest between management and stockholders, we described how stockholders can encourage managers to maximize shareholder wealth through the use of incentive compensation systems. Several types of incentive-based compensation are commonly used in practice, including executive stock options and performance bonuses based on profitability goals. However, stock options can be designed to reward managers even when shareholder wealth is not materially enhanced, while performance bonuses based on accounting profitability may or may not be highly correlated with how well managers have done for their shareholders. For example, corporate managers may make decisions designed to increase accounting profits but which may not improve the corporation's overall cash flow. Such decisions would not be expected to increase share prices. Two new analytical approaches have been developed recently that focus attention directly on management's success or failure in maximizing shareholder wealth: market value added (MVA) and economic value added (EVA).

Market Valued Added (MVA)

As we have discussed throughout this chapter, the primary goal of any corporate manager should be shareholder wealth maximization. This goal obviously benefits shareholders, and it also ensures that scarce economic resources are allocated as efficiently as possible. Although this fundamental concept is widely accepted, it is easy to confuse the objective of maximiz-

ing the firm's total market value with the objective of
shareholder wealth maximization. A firm's total market
value can be increased by raising and investing as
much capital as possible, but such decisions are not
necessarily in the best interests of the firm's shareholders. For example, corporate managers may mistakenly
invest in poor projects in an effort to increase the size
of their firms. As we discussed previously, it is important to distinguish between profitable and unprofitable
growth. Shareholder wealth is maximized by maximizing the *difference* between the firm's market value of
the firm's equity and the amount of equity capital that
investors have supplied to the firm. This difference is
called *market value added* (*MVA*):

MVA = market value of equity − equity capital supplied

Note that MVA can also be defined in terms of total
capital supplied, including both debt and equity. Total
capital supplied would be relevant in those cases where
the objective is to measure changes in the total value
of the firm, not just its equity value. However, since
some forms of capital are not publicly traded (e.g.,
bank loans), it may not always be possible to obtain
accurate values for all of the firm's capital. Therefore,
MVA measures usually emphasize equity value.

To illustrate, consider General Electric. In 1995, its
total market value was $121 billion, while its investors
had supplied only $32 billion. Thus, General Electric's
MVA was $121 − $32 = $89 billion. This $89 billion
represents the difference between the cash that General
Electric's investors have put into the corporation since
its founding—including retained earnings—and the
value the shareholders would receive by selling the
business at its current market price. By maximizing
this difference, management maximizes the wealth of
its shareholders. Generally speaking, management has
created incremental value for its shareholders whenever the difference is positive and destroyed the value
of some of its shareholders' investment whenever the
difference is negative.

While the managers of General Electric have done a
remarkable job of increasing shareholder wealth,
Kmart's managers have done poorly. In 1995, Kmart's
total market value was $3 billion. However, investors
have supplied Kmart with $5 billion of capital, so
Kmart's MVA was a negative $2 billion. In effect, Kmart
has remaining only $0.60 of wealth for every dollar
investors put up, whereas General Electric has turned
each $1 of investment into $3.78.

There is a direct link between MVA and the net
present value (NPV) capital budgeting rule. The NPV
capital budgeting rule is a widely used DCF method
that compares the discounted value of an investment's
cash inflows and outflows. A positive value indicates

that the present value of the inflows exceeds the present value of the outflows; hence, the project would be considered acceptable. To illustrate, consider a company that decides to retain $5 million in earnings for investment in a project, but the present value of future cash flows from the project is only $3 million. Even though the project will cause the total market value of the company to be $3 million greater than if the earnings had been paid out as dividends, shareholders will have $2 million less wealth. This net reduction in shareholder value occurs because shareholders have been denied the opportunity to receive the $5 million and reinvest those funds in alternative investments that would have a market value of at least $5 million. With $5 million added to the capital invested in the company but only $3 million added to the company's total market value, the firm's MVA would fall by $2 million. Note, also, that the project would have an NPV of negative $2 million. Since NPV measures the amount that a project can be expected to add (or subtract) from MVA, managers can follow the NPV rule and should, at a minimum, avoid accepting negative NPV projects. This, in turn, would ensure that the firm's MVA continues to increase. Of course, those companies with the highest MVAs, such as General Electric, have done a spectacular job of identifying and investing in positive NPV projects. These lucrative investments have, in turn, caused investors to bid up the firm's stock price, thereby increasing its MVA.

Economic Value Added (EVA)

While MVA measures the aggregate effect of managerial actions and decisions on shareholder wealth since the inception of the company, *economic value added* (*EVA*) focuses on managerial effectiveness in a given year. Hence, MVA is a longer-term measure of a manager's historical performance, while EVA provides a timelier but short-term measure of value creation. The basic formula for EVA is:

$$\text{EVA} = \text{operating profit} - \text{cost of all capital}$$
$$= (\text{sales revenue} - \text{operating costs} - \text{taxes})$$
$$- (\text{total capital supplied} \times \text{cost of capital})$$

Operating profit is defined as sales revenues minus operating costs and taxes. Hence, it measures the total cash available from operations on an after-tax basis that is available to make payments to the corporation's providers of investment capital, while the cost of the capital is estimated as total capital times the weighted average cost of that capital. To illustrate, suppose a firm had $200 million of sales, $160 million of operating costs, and $20 million of taxes, so its operating profits as defined were $20 million. We'll assume these results are for the firm's 1995 fiscal year. Suppose also that the firm had $100 million of debt and equity capital, and the weighted average cost of that capital was 10 percent. The firm's 1995 EVA would thus be $10 million:

$$EVA = \$20 - \$100(0.10) = \$20 - \$10 = \$10 \text{ million}$$

EVA is an estimate of a business' true economic profit for the year, and it is usually significantly different from that firm's accounting profits. EVA represents the residual income that remains after the opportunity cost of the firm's entire capital base has been deducted, whereas accounting profit is calculated without recognizing a cost for equity capital. EVA depends on both operating efficiency and balance-sheet management: Without operating efficiency, operating profits will be low, and without efficient balance-sheet management, there will be too many assets and too much capital. This results in higher-than-necessary capital costs, which would lower a firm's EVA.

Note that EVA (but not MVA) can be calculated for individual business divisions as well as for the entire company. The cost of capital should reflect the risk of the business unit, either for the whole company or for an operating division. Note also that the specific calculation of EVA for a company is much more complex than we have presented here because many accounting issues, such as inventory valuation, depreciation, amortization of research and development costs, and lease financing must be adjusted properly when estimating a firm's true economic operating profit.

EVA is an intermediate measure of firm value that begins with the NPV of an individual project and ends with the firm's MVA. Each project's expected economic profitability, which is initially measured by its NPV, contributes to the firm's EVA for any given year. MVA is the present value of the EVAs that the firm is expected to produce in the future. Thus, the creation of good investment opportunities (positive NPV projects) creates the expectation of high EVAs, which investors recognize by bidding up the price of the firm's stock. This, in turn, creates a large MVA.

Although EVA is a timely and important topic for corporate managers today, the underlying concept is not new. Managers have always known that they need to earn more than the cost of capital. However, this basic premise is often lost because of a mistaken focus on accounting measures of profitability. EVA provides managers with a relatively straightforward and accurate way to assess the likely impact of a firm's investment, financing, and dividend decisions on the wealth of the firm's stockholders. Thus, EVA can be reinforced by using it as a tool to evaluate a manager's performance.

Using EVA as a Managerial Incentive

In the past few years, many highly successful firms, including Coca-Cola, AT&T, Quaker Oats, Briggs & Stratton, and CSX, have adopted incentive compensation systems based on EVA. The primary motivation is that EVA is linked both theoretically and empirically to shareholder wealth. For example, AT&T found an almost perfect positive correlation between its EVA and its stock price, whereas the correlation between accounting profits and stock prices was much lower. Thus, managers can focus on the tangible objective of accepting projects that have positive EVA. When executive compensation is tied to EVA, managers are given the proper incentive to adopt decisions and implement the set of actions that contributes the highest incremental value for the firm's shareholders. Moreover, what holds for AT&T holds for stocks in general—security analysts have found that stock prices track EVA far more closely than other measures, such as earnings per share, operating margin, or return on equity. Had analysts and investors used EVA as an evaluation tool in the 1980s, they might have foreseen that IBM's EVA was negative during most of the decade. This was a clear signal that IBM's managers were committing capital to projects that were not good investments for the firm's shareholders. Not surprisingly, IBM's stock price performed very poorly throughout the decade.

SUMMARY

Finance has become one of the most complex, challenging, and interesting topics in business today. During the 1990s, an increasing number of corporations have publicly and vocally advocated the merits of maximizing shareholder value. While this objective is praiseworthy, the modern financial manager needs to understand how to go about the process of actually achieving that goal. Rapid changes in competition, regulation, and the securities markets have made this objective seemingly more difficult. The material and methods outlined in this chapter provide the reader with important insights for managers about how to succeed in maximizing shareholder value.

FINANCE

Arbitrage Pricing Theory

Arbitrage describes the process of simultaneously buying a security, currency, or commodity on one market and selling it in another. Price differences between the two markets give the arbitrageur his or her profit. The arbitrage pricing theory is based upon the concept of arbitrage and describes how assets should be valued if there were no riskless arbitrage opportunities. When security markets are competitive and efficient, then opportunities to profit from arbitrage should be nonexistent.

Beta

This is a measure of the systematic risk, or market risk, of a particular security or portfolio. Systematic risk describes any risk that influences the value of a large number of assets. Beta measures a security's return over time relative to the overall market. (Note that market return is usually measured by Standard & Poor's 500 Composite Stock Price Index or the Dow Jones 30 Industrials.) The higher the beta, the riskier, or the more volatile, is the stock or portfolio. Beta is frequently used to analyze the risk of equity mutual funds by showing the volatility of a fund relative to the market as a whole (as measured by the Standard & Poor's 500 Index of the most widely held stocks). A mutual fund with a beta of 1.0 would have returns that match those of S&P 500. A mutual fund with a beta greater than 1.0 is more volatile, or riskier, than the market. A mutual fund with a beta less than 1.0 is not as volatile, or risky, as the market.

Bond Indenture

An indenture establishes the formal terms of a lending relationship between a borrower and a lender. It is a written agreement, and it outlines important terms such as the principal, the rate of interest, the maturity rate, and other restrictions that the borrower agrees to abide by.

Call Option

A call option is a security that gives the owner the right, but not the obligation, to buy a prespecified amount of an asset at a fixed price during some specified time period. Call options on many common stocks are actively traded in the United States.

Capital Asset Pricing Model (CAPM)

CAPM is part of the larger capital market theory that attempts to quantify investment risk. Under CAPM, systematic risk is measured by a statistical factor labeled *beta,* which is the mathematical expression of the relationship between the return on an individual security and the return on the market as a whole. The market return is measured by a market index, such as the Dow Jones Industrial Average or the Standard & Poor's 500 Composite Stock Price Index. In other words, beta measures the volatility of a given security against market averages. The CAPM states that the value of a financial security depends only on the statistical relationship between the security and the value of all securities that trade in the financial markets. Investors who purchase risky assets obtain an expected return that is higher than an investment in risk-free assets.

Capital Budgeting

Capital budgeting is the planning for the purchase and management of long-term assets in a corporation. A capital budget is usually prepared each year and contains a complete list of the firm's planned investment projects. Major corporations often prepare longer-term capital budgets, which detail the firm's expenditure plans several years into the future.

Capital Structure

This comprises the common stock, preferred stock, long-term debt, and retained earnings a company maintains in order to finance its assets. Thus, it can be considered as the mix of the different securities that a firm issues in order to finance its various investment projects. A firm's capital structure is often described in percentage (rather than dollar) terms, with each percentage reflecting the fraction of the firm's total financial obligations represented by each type of security.

Common Stock

Common stock refers to certificates that represent ownership to a corporation. Usually, common stock shareholders have the right to vote for the election of corporate directors. In privately held companies, they may also elect the corporate officers. Corporations may issue various classes of common stock—some with voting rights, some without. Holders of common stock normally do not have any right to receive dividends, although if a company's earnings permit, the board of directors may elect to declare a common stock dividend, either in cash or in additional shares. Common stock may be issued with a par value or with no par value. In either case, it is recorded in the stockholder's equity section of the balance sheet.

Cost of Capital

This is the rate of return available in the marketplace on investments comparable both in terms of risk and other investment characteristics, such as marketability and other qualitative factors. A more practical definition is the following: the expected rate of return an investor would require to be induced to purchase the rights to future streams of income as reflected in the business interest under consideration. Cost of capital is an integral part of the business valuation process. However, it is determined by the market and is totally out of management's control. Cost of capital represents the degree of perceived risk by potential investors: the lower the perceived risk, the lower the cost of capital.

Discounted Cash Flow

This refers to a method used to express a forecasted stream of future cash flows in terms of its present value, or its value in today's dollars. Discounted cash flow is the fundamental principle underlying business valuations and is used for various purposes:

- To calculate the expected future benefits to investors in either debt obligations or equity interests
- To determine the price of a partnership interest in a buyout agreement
- To value debt obligations for debt/equity swaps
- To value minority interests
- To designate the value of partial interests in an entrepreneurial business for divorce settlements
- To assess estate taxes

Many valuation methods are used by analysts, investors, appraisers, the IRS, and others, most of whom employ discounted cash flow as the primary tool. For certain types of companies, such as hotels and other real estate–based businesses, the internal rate of return method can effectively calculate the discount rate to be used in discounted cash flow analyses.

Dividend

The distribution of a company's earnings to its owners—the stockholders—is a dividend. Cash dividends are most common, although dividends can be issued in other forms such as stock or property.

Exchange Rates

Exchange rates are the prices at which one country's currency can be converted into that of another country. Although perceptions in the currency markets of the security of a country's economic base certainly affect exchange rate movement, fluctuations are less a function of specific currency market manipulations than the outcome of a whole conglomerate of economic forces experienced on a worldwide level, such as inflation rates, interest rates, political unrest, financial market aberrations, and commodity prices. Furthermore, currency rates respond wildly to major economic shocks: local wars, oil cartel maneuvers, natural disasters, and anticipated political and economic actions of the world powers. Within a globalized economy such as the United States, exchange rates play a critical role in virtually every aspect of financial management. Companies that import or export, or that compete against companies that import or export, should watch exchange rates closely and if necessary enter into futures currency contracts or trade in financial futures to maximize profit potential.

Financial Leverage

In accounting and finance, financial leverage refers to the amount of long-term debt that a company has in relation to its equity. The higher the ratio, the greater the leverage. Leverage is generally measured by a variation of the debt-to-equity ratio, which is calculated as follows:

$$\frac{\text{Long-term liabilities}}{\text{Total stockholders' equity}}$$

A company's optimal leverage depends on the stability of its earnings. A company with consistently high earnings can be more leveraged than a company with variable earnings, because it will consistently be more likely to make the required interest and principal payments.

Free Cash Flow

Free cash flow represents the amount of cash generated by the existing operations of a corporation that is not required for reinvestment in new projects in the firm. Free cash flow can be positive or negative for any corporation in a particular year. Ultimately, however, since this represents the amount that can be returned to stockholders, it must eventually be positive in order for the firm to sustain and increase its dividend payments.

Futures Contract

A futures contract is an obligation to purchase or sell an asset at an agreed-upon price on a specific future date. The buyer commits him- or herself to purchase the asset, and the seller commits him- or herself to sell the asset. Futures contracts are generally traded on organized exchanges, and changes in the value of the agreement are settled in cash each day. Futures contracts exist for currencies, stock indexes, commodities, and debt instruments.

Interest Rates

Interest rates concern the payment borrowers make for the use of the funds they borrow and the payment lenders demand for the use of the funds they lend (termed *interest*), expressed as a percentage of the principal (loan amount). This percentage is the interest rate. Interest rates typically are expressed in whole percentages and base points. A basis point is $\frac{1}{100}$ of a percentage point. There are four main components to market interest rates:

- The risk (or default) premium
- The maturity premium
- An inflation premium
- The "real" rate

The risk premium is a recognition that different classes of borrowers have greater or lesser risk of default. Interest rates are higher for riskier borrowers; they are lowest for the U.S. Treasury, which is considered a risk-free borrower. The difference in interest rate between any other borrower and the U.S. Treasury for the same maturity is called a *quality spread.* The *maturity premium* reflects the fact that, in general, a longer loan will have a higher interest rate than a shorter loan of the same quality. The *yield curve* shows the change in interest rates as maturities are extended for a given class of loans. The *inflation premium* is a recognition that inflation may erode the purchasing power of the funds lent. Thus, interest includes compensation for the inflation expected over the length of the loan. The remaining portion of interest rates reflects the real rate of interest that must be paid to induce the lender to forgo the use of funds. (Note that this is not simply the interest rate less current inflation, but rather interest rates less the average expected inflation over the length of the loan. Subtracting the current inflation rate provides an inflation-adjusted interest rate. Often, since the future interest rates are assumed to conform to an average of past rates, lenders use some such average as a proxy for expected inflation.)

Internal Rate of Return

This is the discount rate at which the net present value (the value of all future cash flows, in excess of the original investment, expressed in today's dollars) of an investment equals zero. Internal rate of return is frequently used by financial managers to decide whether to commit to an investment. In most cases, an investment opportunity is accepted when the internal rate of return is greater than the opportunity cost (the projected return on an investment of similar risk) of the capital required for the investment.

Lease

A lease is a contractual arrangement that allows one party the use of some specific assets for a specific time period in exchange for a payment, similar to a rental arrangement. The *lessee* is the party that receives the use of assets under a lease, and the *leasor* is the party that conveys the use of the assets. An operating lease is usually a short-term cancelable arrangement, whereas a financial (or capital) lease is a long-term noncancelable arrangement.

Long-Term Debt

Long-term debt is a debt obligation that has a maturity of more than one year from the date the obligation was incurred. The debt obligation commits the company to repay the amount borrowed and to make regular interest payments through the life of the loan. Failure by the borrower to make the required payments can result in bankruptcy.

Market Efficiency

An efficient market is a market in which the prices of the assets or securities fully reflect all available information. When new information arrives, whether favorable or unfavorable, prices adjust instantaneously. Investors who purchase assets or securities in an efficient market can expect to receive fair value for their investment.

Mergers and Acquisitions

These are processes of business combination. There are three forms of business combination:

- Statutory merger
- Statutory consolidation
- Acquisition

The differences between these three combinations is primarily a function of the legal nature of the resulting combined company. A statutory merger occurs when two separate companies combine in such a way that one of the companies will no longer exist. This combination is best expressed by $X + Y = X$. A statutory consolidation occurs when two or more separate companies combine in such a way that both companies no longer exist and a new company is formed. This type of combination is best expressed by $X + Y = XY$. An acquisition occurs when two separate companies combine in such as way that both keep their legal identities. This type of combination is best expressed by the equation $X + Y = X + Y$.

Net Present Value (NPV)

In corporate finance, this refers to the present value (the value of cash to be received in the future expressed in today's dollars) of an investment in excess of the initial amount invested. When an investment or project has a positive NPV, it should be pursued. When an investment has a negative NPV, it should not be accepted.

Operating Leverage

Operating leverage describes the degree to which a company's cost of operation is fixed as opposed to variable. Thus, it is a measure of how much a firm's profits can be expected to change when sales increase. Firms with a high degree of operating leverage will experience greater changes in profitability when sales change. Usually, companies with high operating leverage will maintain low levels of debt, or financial leverage.

Parity Conditions

A parity condition describes the relative value of one country's currency to that of another country's currency. The condition states how, for example, differences in inflation or interest rates between countries should affect the relative values of their currencies.

Portfolio

A portfolio is a combination of different securities or assets. A portfolio may consist of combinations of stocks, bonds, real estate, or any other asset held by an investor. By holding a collection of different assets, an investor's wealth will be less affected by adverse events that impact any one particular asset in the portfolio.

Preferred Stock

This is a type of capital stock that gives its holders preference over common stockholders in the distribution of earnings or rights to the assets of a company in the event of liquidation. Preferred stock usually pays an established dividend. For example, a 5 percent preferred stock pays a dividend that equals 5 percent of the total par value of outstanding shares. Preferred stocks generally do not have any voting rights. Preferred stock may also carry a variety of features. It may be callable by the company, dividends may be cumulative, common stock warrants may be attached, or it may be convertible to common stock under specific conditions, to mention only a few variations.

Price/Earnings (P/E) Ratio

This is a measure of a company's investment potential. Literally, a P/E ratio is how much a share is worth per dollar of earnings. The price/earnings ratio is calculated as follows:

$$\frac{\text{Market price per common share}}{\text{Primary earnings per common share}}$$

A company's P/E ratio depends on investors' perceptions of a company's potential. Factors such as risk, quality of management, growth potential, earnings history, and industry conditions all come into play.

Put Option

A put option is a right that is granted in exchange for an agreed-upon sum to sell property. If the right is not exercised within the specified time period, it expires and the holder forfeits the money. Options are used most frequently in securities transactions, although stock options are also used as incentive compensation for key managers. Instead of exercising options, most investors prefer to buy and sell them in the open market before expiration, cashing in on increases in trading value. One of the interesting features of trading in options is the amount of leverage option buyers enjoy. Buyers put up a relatively small amount of money to control a large amount of common shares, potentially leveraging sizable profits.

Risk Management

Many corporations and investors engage in activities designed to manage the risks they face. In the corporate world, managers seek to control business risks as well as financial and commodity price risks. As a result, managers often seek to use financial securities, such as options, futures, and swaps, to alter their risk exposure.

Risk Premium

A risk premium is the extra, or excess, return on a risky asset relative to the return on risk-free assets.

Thus, it describes the additional return that an investor can expect to obtain by accepting a greater amount of risk. Since there are many types of risky assets, each asset commands a different risk premium. As a general rule, the riskier a particular asset is, the greater the risk premium that investors will require in order to be an investor in that security.

Systematic Risk

Systematic risk is any risk that affects the value of a large number of assets, although each asset will have a different degree of sensitivity to the underlying risk. In financial markets, if investors maintain large, well-diversified portfolios, then asset prices will be affected only by this type of risk. Higher systematic risk will increase an investor's expected returns. Thus, systematic risk cannot be diversified away.

Tax Shields

A tax shield describes any reduction in a corporation's tax bill that can be brought about by management. Depreciation, for example, creates a tax shield because depreciation is a noncash expense that is deductible for income tax purposes. Similarly, managers can reduce their taxable income through the use of debt, because interest expense is deductible for income tax purposes (dividends, however, are not). Other types of tax shields are periodically available, such as investment tax credits.

Time Value of Money

The time value of money is the price or value placed on time. It is generally thought of as the opportunity cost associated with a particular investment. Money has positive time value associated with it, in the sense that a given amount of money is worth more than the certainty of having the exact same sum available at a later time. The reason is that any money received today can be reinvested to earn additional profits during the intervening time period.

Valuation Models

A valuation model describes the exercise of applying economic and financial principles in order to estimate the value of an asset. Discounted cash flow valuation models attempt to determine the value of an asset by estimating its stream of future cash flows and then discounting those future cash flows at a particular discount rate. Valuation models are used extensively in the field of finance by analysts, investment bankers, and corporate finance specialists.

Value Additivity

In an efficient market, the value of any two assets can be estimated as the sum of the values of the two individual assets. This is a variation on the theme that the whole must be equal to nothing more than the sum of the separate parts.

Working Capital

Working capital is measured as the difference between a company's current assets and its current liabilities. Thus, it is interpreted by some as a measure of a firm's liquidity, or its ability to pay its bills on a short-term basis. However, excess investment in working capital can be costly for a firm, as the rate of return on a company's working capital is likely to be lower than alternative long-term investment project returns. Thus, the maintenance of excessively high working capital creates too much liquidity and, hence, lowers overall returns.

MORE READINGS
Critical References—Books

Bartlett, Joseph W. *Equity Finance: Venture Capital, Buyouts, Restructuring and Reorganizations.* New York: Wiley, 1995.

 This is a very in-depth, comprehensive, three-volume text that explains and discusses the important aspects of any investment activity that involves billions of dollars. Early-stage investing, joint ventures, buyouts, restructurings, and pooled investment vehicles are thoroughly discussed.

Business International Corporation. *101 More Checklists for Global Financial Management: An Action Guide for Building a High-Performance Finance Function.* New York: The Corporation Publishers, 1992.

 This book offers 101 pointers on financial strategy, organizations, and treasury management systems, compiled from various Business International publications and representing the most current thought in treasury management.

Heath, Gibson. *Getting the Money You Need: Practical Solutions for Financing Your Small Business.* Chicago, Ill.: Irwin, 1995.

 This book explains numerous means for funding a small business with an overriding emphasis on community involvement and personal responsibility. Instead of challenging the leading financial loan sources, it explains how to work with them and get them to aid your project. The book also covers nonbank financing options, federal government sources, state programs, and microenterprise lending programs.

Livingstone, John Leslie. *The Portable MBA in Finance and Accounting.* New York: Wiley, 1992.

 This book covers an extensive range of the basic, key concepts in finance and accounting. It is presented in a very easy-to-read, how-to fashion with clear and helpful examples. The chapters were written by various academic and business experts in their given fields who have gained national recognition. It is a basic and broad source of information for anyone hoping to touch up on finance and accounting skills.

Smithson, Charles W. *Managing Financial Risk: A Guide to Derivative Products, Financial Engineering, and Value Maximization.* Burr Ridge, Ill.: Irwin Professional, 1995.

 This book deals largely with risk management. Risk management products are often viewed as the most complex and frustrating financial devices for the average investor. The purpose of this book is to simplify these products by showing them as what they truly are: combinations of the basic products with which most investors are familiar.

Critical References—Journals

America's Corporate Finance Directory. New Providence, N.J.: National Register.

This is a directory of major corporations with comprehensive listings of their financial functions. The directory focuses largely on U.S. public and private companies with assets over $100,000,000.

Business International Money Report. New York: The Economist Intelligence Unit.

This is a weekly newsletter that acts as a financial report for international executives.

CFO: The Magazine for Chief Financial Officers. Boston: CFO Publishing Corporation.

CFO is a monthly magazine that gives advice on financial tools, strategies, and risks for people in management positions. Its emphasis is on the actions and reactions of major corporations.

The Continental Bank Journal of Applied Corporate Finance. New York: Stern Stewart Management Services, Inc.

This journal is devoted to the evaluation and analysis of all aspects of corporate finance. Each journal consists of numerous papers that all cover one specific aspect of corporate finance. All of the works and papers are written by the leading academics and businesspeople in their given field.

Corporate Finance. London: Euromoney Publications PLC.

Corporate Finance is a monthly journal, with a magazine-type format, that analyzes and discusses the financial maneuvering of some of the world's top companies and corporate executives. All aspects of finance are discussed, along with how these aspects are utilized in different global economies.

The Corporate Finance Sourcebook. New York: McGraw-Hill.

This is a complete guide to the financial services and capital investment resources used by business communities worldwide. It provides the reader with sources for potential funds and sources for companies that can help manage their funds. There are nearly 4,000 entries in this comprehensive guide.

Corporate Finance: The IDD Review of Investment Banking. New York: Investment Dealer's Digest.

This is a biannual publication that is a leading source of financial information for investors. The first half of the review is broken down into industry categories, where information on all of the public offerings in the United States for the first half of the year is given (quarterly data is also provided). The second half provides a list of the market deals that took place in the United States during the last half of the year. The information shows how, and if, businesses are raising their funds.

Euromoney International Finance Yearbook. London: Euromoney Publications, 1987.

This journal is designed to be a thorough and complete reference source on international finance. The yearbook is divided into three parts. The first two parts act as an international forum for communication and analysis between top financial experts. The third part consists of vital financial statistics.

Financial Markets, Institutions and Instruments. Cambridge, Mass.: Blackwell Publishers.

Each journal consists of one paper written about a specific aspect of the financial market by leading authorities on the subject that are from either the academic community or business community, or have worked within both areas.

Global Finance. New York: Global Information, Inc.

This is a monthly magazine that covers the financial market and related issues at a global scale, dealing with raising and investing money in America, and how those aspects change in foreign markets.

Journal of Banking & Finance. Amsterdam: North Holland.

This is a monthly journal that discusses current issues in banking and finance within a global sphere. Each issue consists of numerous works written by various academics and business professionals.

Journal of Corporate Finance. Amsterdam: Elsevier Science.

This journal aims to publish original manuscripts that are concerned with the different functions necessary to govern corporate firms, including financial contracts, corporate governance structures, and business contracts. The journal is unique in that it deals with these issues solely in respect to the workings of a modern corporation. Each paper is written by a leading academic from the particular field being covered.

Journal of Empirical Finance. Amsterdam: North-Holland.

The *Journal of Empirical Finance* is meant to be an international forum for empirical researchers, focusing on research in the fields of econometrics and finance. Each issue contains academic papers analyzing authentic financial markets and dealing with topics such as asset pricing, bond markets, corporate finance, foreign exchange, and market microstructure.

Journal of Finance. New York.

The *Journal of Finance* is distributed five times a year and contains numerous, lengthy papers written by the leading academics and business professionals in finance. Each paper deals with current issues in global finance.

Midland Corporate Finance Journal: A Publication of Stern, Stewart, Putnam & Macklis, Ltd. New York: Stern, Stewart, Putnam & Macklis, Ltd.

This journal contains papers concerned with the prominent financial issues of the time, which are written by various academics from all over the country.

The Mitsubishi Finance Risk Directory. London: Risk Magazine, 1995.

This directory is a leading work in risk management. It contains a list of banks and brokers, a list of exchanges around the world, a list of support services that deal in derivatives, a glossary of potentially confusing terms, a country index (of which law firms, banks, exchanges, brokers, software companies are in each country), and a company index used to find all the information the book has on any given corporation.

Moody's Bank & Financial Manual: Banks, Insurance and Finance Companies, Investment Trusts, Real Estate. New York: Moody's Investors Service, Moody's Banks and Finance News.

This manual gives summaries of investment opportunities offered by banks, insurance companies, investment companies, unit investment trusts, and other financial opportunities. The manual is broken down by company, with the investment opportunities of each specific company blocked together. It also offers ratings of these opportunities through Moody's rating system.

International Business

The recent, striking changes in the political structure of nations around the world have been far-reaching in their impact. Nowhere have these changes had a more pronounced effect than in the business world. The current business landscape has changed from one where a few major players presided over the vast majority of all business transactions to one that is truly global in its inclusion. As walls fall and barriers are lifted, endless opportunities emerge in new markets for businesses equipped to take advantage of them.

This chapter will focus primarily on three topics. These include a discussion of the need for businesses to be able to compete in a global environment, the skills and characteristics required to be competitive in a global environment, and the new benefits and opportunities associated with taking on a global business perspective.

THE GLOBAL MARKETPLACE

In an earlier time, foreign markets were viewed by some national companies as new markets only: a new potential customer base that could be tapped or left untapped. Today, large companies realize that their very survival relies on being competitive worldwide.

The elimination of many barriers to entry into world markets has put increasing pressure on companies to compete globally. Companies must now compete for more than just a customer base. The supply of raw materials, technology, and distribution networks on a global level draws many companies into transnational transactions to remain competitive. A company must seek out the most beneficial relationships with suppliers and distributors, even when they are outside the company's home nation, because its competitors are doing so. A company must seek out the most profitable markets in which to conduct business, because its competitors are doing so. A company that is unwilling to compete on a global level, when that is clearly the trend in its industry, may very well lose its market share and its ability to compete in domestic markets as well.

With an impetus to remain competitive to stay alive, companies are realizing the need to expand operations and relationships on an international level. To do so, "managers must recognize the need for simultaneously achieving global efficiency, national responsiveness and the ability to develop and exploit knowledge on a worldwide basis."[1] However, companies must manage this expansion properly to find success in international markets.

THE COMPETITIVE ADVANTAGES NEEDED FOR GLOBAL COMPETITION

What does it mean for a country to be competitive on a global level? Michael Porter offers a comprehensive explanation to this question in his work, *The Competitive Advantage of Nations*.

Porter suggests that the only meaningful measure of a nation's competitiveness should be based on that nation's level of productivity, where productivity "depends on both the quality and the features of products and the efficiency with which they are produced" (p. 6).

To maintain a high level of productivity, nations must continually upgrade their methods through seeking out quality-improving practices and more efficient means of production. This quest leads many national companies into the international arena.

Porter also stipulates that for firms to undertake an appropriate competitive strategy, they must distinguish their areas of operation as either a part of a multidomestic industry or a global industry. In a multidomestic line of business, the service a company provides in a particular country is largely independent of the service it provides in other countries. In any service-based industry, the service must be customized to fit the needs of the customer base. Since the customer needs vary widely from country to country, the service a company provides must also vary. Because of this, there is little opportunity to recognize benefits from economies of scale, consolidation of tasks, or universal strategy application in multidomestic industries. Competitive advantages are necessarily confined to the individual countries in which a company competes.

Global industries, on the other hand, are affected in completely the opposite direction. Competition is truly worldwide, and a firm's competitive position in one country does affect its position in other countries. Further, a firm is able to draw on competitive advantages that not only span more than one country, but grow out of having a presence in more than one country. These competitive advantages include economies of scale, transfer of brand equity, and a more integrated, universal strategic approach.

Porter has developed a model, The Determinants of National Advantage, to summarize these concepts and depict their relationship to each other. Figure 6.1 displays this "national diamond" model. Porter defines the forces of *firm strategy, industry structure,* and *competitive behavior,* located in the top box in the diamond, as the prevailing conditions in a given nation, which govern how a company is created, organized, and managed. It also refers to how other, national rival companies compete with another national firm.

Factor conditions, captured in the box on the extreme left of the model, refer to a nation's available factors of production. These include access to raw materials, skilled labor, infrastructure, and technology. Diametrically opposite in the box on the right side of the model are *demand conditions.* This force refers to the nature of the demand, as expressed through customer identity and expectations, for the product or service a given industry provides. In the box located at the

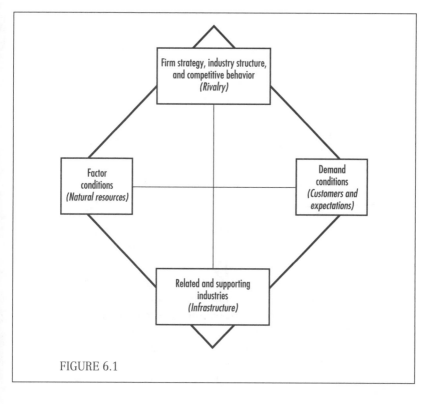

FIGURE 6.1

bottom of the model are *related and supporting industries*. This force refers to the significance of the presence, absence, and role of supplier industries and related industries that are internationally competitive.

Porter uses the diamond shape to emphasize the interactive nature of these forces in creating a national competitive advantage within a given industry. If a nation can manage its industries domestically in such a way that an environment focused on continuous improvement is fostered, the competitive advantages developed within a given industry will be sustainable on an international level.

BENEFITS AND OPPORTUNITIES ASSOCIATED WITH A GLOBAL APPROACH

Success in global business markets is attainable through more methods than just the sole expansion efforts of individual companies. Expansion into new markets is often quite successfully managed through the process of a *joint venture.*

Simply put, a joint venture happens when two or more parties agree to undertake a project together in which resources, liabilities, and profits will be shared. Joint ventures come in three forms:

1. *Contractual joint ventures:* Under this arrangement, the joint venture is not created as a separate legal corporate entity. It is an enterprise in the form of an unincorporated association, created to carry out clearly defined activities and to attain specific goals over a specific time period. There is a clear separation between the companies that agree to cooperate, by which each of them is responsible for its own liabilities.

2. *Equity joint ventures:* Under this arrangement, two partners agree to the formation of a legal corporation with limited liability and joint management. There is pooled equity in the corporation, from which an equity ratio is determined, as well as the profits and losses associated with the venture.

3. *Hybrid joint ventures:* Under this arrangement, partners agree to maintain the corporate status of a separate legal entity but may do without the limited liability option. Partners also agree to the specific responsibilities and time constraints described in the contractual joint venture.

Joint ventures are especially beneficial for companies that wish to expand into international markets. Companies from different nations that engage in a joint venture simultaneously establish business channels, relationships, and resources in a foreign country. Further, joint-venture partnerships have the potential to expand to other areas of operation, where two companies can share production capacity and distribution channels in their respective markets. This is an especially viable option when the partners in the original joint venture are not directly competing in the same markets.

Joint ventures also provide opportunities for entrepreneurial ventures, as one partner with resources can be matched with a partner with a viable product concept. Again, in these instances, the ability to cross international business borders is an extra benefit. Moreover, the introduction of a new innovation on an international level allows both partners to enjoy many competitive advantages that may prove to be sustainable over time and as markets expand.

SUMMARY

Prevailing trends of globalization make it imperative that nations, as well as the businesses they foster, develop the skills to compete on an international level. While this may seem an intimidating proposition for some companies, the benefits and opportunities associated with international expansion are numerous. Not only are there opportunities to improve on best practices in the areas of quality and efficiency, but there also exists enormous potential to discover and implement new technologies and innovations. These factors, operating in conjunction, will continue to create a global business climate that encourages higher standards for business products and practices across all nations.

CONCEPT **INTERNATIONAL BUSINESS***

Balance of Payments

This is a summary of the statement of international transactions between U.S. residents and residents of foreign nations. This serves as a measure of the United States' international trade and capital positions.

Balance of Trade

The net difference between the dollar value of a country's imports and exports over a period of time is the balance of trade. A country's current account reflects a currency drain when exports exceed imports. Although the balance of trade plays an important role in establishing national trade policies, it has little effect on a company's fortunes, other than as a long-term indicator of current stability.

Bank for International Settlements (BIS)

A consortium bank founded to coordinate the collection and rescheduling of German reparations after World War I, the BIS has survived as an international central bank for ten member countries. With consensus approval from its member central banks, the BIS sets standards for the global banking system.

Capital Flight

This term is used to describe the movement of capital out of or into a given market. Capital, by definition, is very mobile and has become even more mobile with the advent of instantaneous computer transfer ability on a worldwide basis.

Coproduction

This refers to a type of buyback countertrade generally used for the transfer of management experience or technology. In cases where equity interests are a part of a coproduction arrangement, both companies profit from the sale of the products. Aside from the gains made from the direct sale of the product, each partner sees several other benefits. The host partner gains new technology and management expertise, and the outside partner acquires a direct investment in a foreign country without the risk of starting a new business from scratch.

---

*Terms adapted from Paul A. Argenti, *The Portable MBA Desk Reference* (New York: Wiley, 1994), and Frederic S. Mishkin, *The Economics of Money, Banking, and Financial Markets* (Boston: Little, Brown, 1986). For an even more comprehensive list of terms, please see these two sources.

Countertrade

Countertrade involves the exchange of goods, services, and currency for other goods, services, and currency. An export financing tool, countertrade enables companies to sell to customers in countries that could not otherwise buy goods and services because of the absence of hard currency.

Debt/Equity Swaps

This refers to the exchange of debt securities for equity interests.

Development Banks

These are banks that function as coordinating and intermediary organizations to raise capital, attract investment, and provide technical assistance for the economic development of nonindustrialized countries.

Dumping

In international marketing, this refers to a situation in which a company charges less for a product than it originally cost or less than the company charges in its home market. This technique is used to eliminate a surplus or quickly gain market share in a new country or market, and it is usually considered an unfair practice.

Edge Act

The Edge Act is a federal law passed in 1919 that enables national banks to conduct foreign lending operations through federal or state-chartered subsidiaries called Edge Act corporations.

Eurobond

This is a corporate bond denominated in U.S. dollars or other hard currencies and sold to investors outside the country whose currency is used. Eurobonds have become an important source of debt capital for both large and small companies throughout the world. Normally, a Eurobond is syndicated by a consortium of international investment banks, providing wide exposure to investors in different countries.

Eurocurrency

This refers to a currency on deposit outside its country of origin. Such deposits are also known as *external currencies, international currencies,* or *xenocurrencies.*

Eurodollar

This refers to U.S. currency held on deposit in banks located outside the United States, mainly in Europe.

Eurodollars are commonly used for settling international transactions outside of the United States. Certain securities, debt as well as equity, are denominated in Eurodollars. This means that interest, principal repayments, or dividends are paid out of U.S. dollars deposited in foreign bank accounts.

European Community (EC)

This is an economic alliance, formed in 1957, designed to encourage trade and economic cooperation among its members. The EC is also called the European Economic Community and the Common Market.

Exchange Rates

This refers to the prices at which one country's currency can be converted into that of another country. Within a globalized economy such as the United States, exchange rates play a critical role in virtually every aspect of financial management. Companies that import or export or that compete against companies that import or export should watch interest rates closely and, if necessary, enter into futures currency contracts or trade in financial futures to maximize profit potential.

Export/Import Bank (Eximbank)

The Federal Import/Export Bank, whose primary function originally was to compensate U.S. exporters for subsidies granted competitors by foreign governments, Eximbank has reached far beyond this goal to become the primary source of export credit and guarantees for American companies. Except in very unusual circumstances, Eximbank will not support exports to communist countries nor finance the sale of military products or services. Moreover, to qualify for Eximbank assistance, companies must provide evidence that exported goods or services have at least 50 percent U.S. content.

Foreign Credit Insurance Association (FCIA)

An agent of the Export/Import Bank, FCIA provides exporters with insurance coverage against both commercial and political risk. The main goals of the FCIA are as follows: (1) protecting exporters against failure of foreign buyers to pay their credit obligations for commercial or political reasons, (2) encouraging exporters to offer foreign buyers competitive terms of payment, (3) supporting an exporter's prudent penetration of higher-risk foreign markets, and (4) giving exporters and their banks greater financial flexibility in handling overseas accounts receivable.

General Agreement of Tariffs and Trade (GATT)

A multilateral treaty, the basic aims of GATT are (1) to liberalize and promote world trade via multilateral trade negotiations, (2) to place world trade on a secure basis, and thereby (3) to contribute to global economic growth and development.

Global Marketing

This is the activity of a global corporation that seeks to achieve long-run, large-scale production efficiencies by producing standardized products of good value and long-term reliability for all consumers (or industrial users) in all segments of all markets; in addition, it refers to the marketing of a standardized product on a worldwide basis, with little allowance for, or acceptance of, regional or local differentiation of the marketing-mix strategies.

Globalization

This refers to the process of interlinking financial markets in different countries into a common, worldwide pool of funds to be accessed by both borrowers and lenders. Globalization came about as a result of the growth in international trade.

Industrial Policy

This is the course of action set by a government to influence the development of domestic industrial sectors in particular and the direction of national industrial growth in general.

Industrial Production

The output of U.S. factories, mines, and utilities is its industrial production. This output constitutes the production of things—the goods, portion of goods, and services. The Federal Reserve Board has measured industrial production since the 1920s. Industrial production is a coincident indicator of economic activity: It traces the behavior of the business cycle nearly exactly.

Keiretsu

A Japanese term, it refers to corporate conglomerates whose members cooperate with each other for strategic purposes within the international business environment.

Letter of Credit (LOC)

This is a popular bank instrument stating that a bank has granted the holder an amount of credit equal to the face amount of the LOC. A bank guarantees payment of its customer's draft up to a stated amount for a given period of time.

London Interbank Offered Rate (LIBOR)

This is the base lending rate that banks charge each other in the London Eurocurrency market. LIBOR is the European equivalent of the U.S. prime rate.

North American Free Trade Agreement (NAFTA)

This multilateral accord between the United States, Canada, and Mexico is also referred to as the North American Free Trade Zone (NAFTZ).

Offshore Financial Center

This is a location with banking facilities to accept deposits and make loans in currencies different from the currency's country of origin. Banks located in off-shore financial centers are exempt from the bank's home country banking regulations. All offshore financial centers, including those in the United States, offer tax preferences—usually, but not always, in the form of tax-free remittances of earnings to an offshore parent company.

Organization for Economic Development (OECD)

This international organization, established in 1961 in Paris, France, acts as a global forum to stimulate world trade and economic development. The OECD's membership consists of the world's developed countries: Australia, Austria, Belgium, Canada, Denmark, Finland, France, Greece, Iceland, Ireland, Italy, Japan, Luxembourg, the Netherlands, New Zealand, Norway, Portugal, Spain, Sweden, Switzerland, Turkey, the United Kingdom, and the United States.

Organization for Petroleum Exporting Countries (OPEC)

The most important international commodity group (ICG) in the world, OPEC has a significant impact on the world price of oil and, subsequently, on the balance of payments of every country; and it is the model of a successful international cartel.

Parallel Trade

This is a form of countertrade that involves the execution of two distinct and individually enforceable contracts: the first for the sale of goods by an exporter, the second for the purchase of the goods. Both contracts are requirements for insurance, and sometimes credit, for each shipment. Parallel trade agreements that involve cash transfers are also known as *counterpurchases.*

Regional Banks

This includes large banks such as Mellon, First Chicago, Norwest, and Crocker, that function regionally in a fashion similar to money center banks at the national level. Regional banks serve as corespondents for smaller local banks in the same way that money center banks act as corespondents for regional banks.

Tax Haven

A country with tax-preference laws for foreign companies and individuals is a tax haven. Three classes of jurisdictions are referred to as tax havens: those that (1) have no relevant taxes, (2) levy taxes only on internal taxable transactions but none at all or very low taxes on foreign source income, and (3) grant special tax privileges to certain types of companies or operations. The principal functions of tax havens are to avoid or postpone taxes, avoid exchange controls, and act as a shield against confiscation, nationalization, and other forms of expropriation.

Trade Credit

The credit granted to buyers of exported goods and services is trade credit.

Trade Deficit

This refers to an imbalance in merchandise trade that results in an excess of imports over exports.

Trade Finance

This refers to the financing of imports and exports.

MORE READINGS
Critical References

Bartlett, Christopher, and Sumantra Ghoshal. *Managing Across Borders: The Transnational Solution.* Cambridge, Mass.: Harvard Business School Press, 1989.

This book begins with a reclassification of business organizations as multinational, global, or international. It then defines the transnational corporation as a combination of these three, assigning to it specific characteristics from each business category. The rest of the book explains how a corporation can manage its functions, strategies, and practices to integrate the characteristics of the multinational, global, and international organizations in such a way that the corporation gains all the benefits these different business forms provide, without experiencing the drawbacks. Not nearly as pragmatic as other sources on the subject, this work offers a highly theoretical approach to managing across borders.

Harrigan, Kathryn Rudie. *Managing for Joint Venture Success.* Lexington, Mass.: Lexington Books, 1991.

Based on the fundamental acceptance of Porter's theory of national competitiveness, this book explains in detail the benefits of establishing a joint venture, particularly between firms from different nations, especially in terms of changing competitive conditions to create competitive advantages for both parties. The book provides advice on how to manage specific joint venture types successfully, identifying several common problems many joint-venture partners face and providing suggestions on how to structure a joint venture such that these potential problematic issues are addressed even before the venture itself is under way.

Porter, Michael. *The Competitive Advantage of Nations.* New York: Free Press, 1990.

What makes a nation competitive in the international arena? This book summarizes Porter's "important trading nations," which are Denmark, Germany, Italy, Japan, Korea, Singapore, Sweden, Switzerland, the United Kingdom, and the United States. Porter refutes the theory that one factor makes a nation competitive; rather, it is a series of factors working in tandem that enable a nation to become and remain competitive in the global business world. Porter defines these forces, as well as captures the dynamic interaction between them, in his national competitiveness model, which serves as a basis for the work of many other international business scholars and is referred to frequently as a fundamental framework for understanding the international business scene.

CHAPTER 7

Marketing

WHAT IS MARKETING?

According to the American Marketing Association, marketing is "the process of planning and executing the conception, pricing, promotion and distribution of ideas, goods and services to create changes that satisfy individual and organizational objectives." More simply put, marketing is an approach to doing business that focuses on identifying the customer's needs and preferences. Using this information, a company can shape the goods and services it provides, as well as the strategy it uses to bring these goods and services to the public, based on satisfying the customer.

Virtually all companies use some form of marketing techniques. Having a *market orientation,* however, means that marketing must exist as more than just a functional area within a company; it must be a pervasive concern throughout the company. This chapter will introduce many marketing terms, equations, and models and explain how they all fit together. It will focus on providing a clear understanding of how companies operate within a market-oriented framework. It will also explain how companies identify the customer's needs and preferences, create products, set prices, and promote these products so that they will be consumed.

IS MARKETING REALLY A SOFT DISCIPLINE?

There is a common perception, both inside and outside the business world, about marketing as a discipline and those who do it. When most people think of marketing, usually the five Ps—product, price, packaging, promotion, and positioning—come to mind. While all five are important, we will discuss the first two, product and price, at length in this chapter.

Just as these basic marketing concepts are rooted in customer perception and preference, so are many other more sophisticated marketing concepts. Since customer needs and preferences are central to marketing, and people perceive customer needs and preferences as ever changing and potentially capricious, marketing winds up with a reputation for being unscientific. This, however, is not the case.

While a discussion of the concept of the five Ps is a good place to begin any marketing project, the assessment surely does not end there. The practice of marketing requires a quantitative orientation. Marketers rely on statistical analyses as a source of information in many phases of the marketing process. Specifically, marketers use regression analyses to glean information about the strength of customer preferences and the power of marketing efforts in relation to the impact on sales. In addition, marketing managers also use the analyses of *mean, variance,* and *covariance* to draw conclusions about customer preferences. Lastly, it is common for marketing managers to use statistical sampling techniques to draw conclusions about an entire population of customers based on information obtained from a small sample of those customers.

The practice of marketing is also replete with its own series of equations. The equations you will see in this chapter will be mentioned and explained within their functional context. It is important, however, to recognize that, while the relationships expressed in the marketing equations exist, the aforementioned statistical analyses drive the specifics of the equations.

The important conclusion presented here is that marketing, as a practice, requires using both quantitative as well as qualitative skills. While many marketers may begin from positions of guessing what customers want, marketing does not end there. Those initial hypotheses must be tested rigorously before they are accepted and implemented. Thus, those who are attracted to marketing as a discipline because it appears to have a creative focus without a quantitative element should reconsider these assumptions.

THE CUSTOMER

It stands to reason that any detailed account of the marketing process should begin with a discussion of the customer or consumer. For the purpose of this chapter, these words will be used interchangeably. *Consumer* refers to any "individual or household that pur-

chases or acquires goods or services for personal use."[1]
Similarly, the population of all consumers is referred to
as the *consumer* or *mass market*. A consumer market
has four key characteristics. In a consumer market
there are a large number of buyers and sellers, a wide
geographic distribution, small individual purchases,
and a wide variety of products to choose from.[2]

Within a consumer market, many theories exist
about how a given customer makes a purchasing decision. One commonly accepted theory is that the buying
process consists of a series of five stages that a customer goes through: need recognition, alternative
search, alternative evaluation, purchase decision, and
postpurchase feelings.[3]

The customer begins the purchase cycle by recognizing that he or she has a need that is not being met. This
simply means that the customer becomes aware that he
or she wants a good or a service and makes a decision
to acquire that good or service.

No discussion of need recognition is complete without
referencing A. H. Maslow's work, *Motivation and Personality*. Basically, Maslow proposed that people experience a hierarchy of needs, whereby higher needs do not
engage until all earlier needs in the hierarchy have been
met. Maslow proposes the following hierarchy:

Physiological needs: This category refers to the
needs of the human body, such as food, water,
and sex.

Safety needs: This category refers to the need of
humans to be protected from physical harm and
unknown and potentially detrimental influences.
These needs engage once a person's physiological
needs have been met.

Social needs: This category refers to the need for
humans to interact socially in groups and to feel a
sense of connection with others in a given group.

Esteem needs: This category refers to the need for
humans to be recognized as important in other
people's lives. These feelings are the basis for
self-confidence and prestige.

Self-actualization needs: This category refers to
the need people have to recognize all of their
potential and to become everything they have the
potential to become.

Many marketing people believe that, within the population of the mass market, all of these needs are active
when the members of a group of consumers individually decide on a purchase. Hence, marketing efforts can
be focused on showing how a given product can
address these needs, making the product more attractive to the target consumer. For example, home security
systems can be marketed to appeal to one individual's

safety needs (I need protection from criminals), while appealing to another's esteem needs (I am important enough to my spouse that he or she would invest in a home security system).

Returning to the discussion of the five stages of the buying process, once a need has been identified and realized, the alternative search and alternative evaluation stages begin. In these stages, the consumer acquires information on available products that fulfill the identified need. The consumer then compares available products against each other. As an example, a first-year college student with dirty clothes might identify the need for laundry detergent for the first time in his or her life. Upon arriving in the detergent aisle at the local grocery store, the student is confronted with the different purchase options (Tide, Era, Bold, Cheer, etc.) and compares them (Do I care if it is fragrance free? Do I need detergent with bleach? How much did that one cost compared to this? What is the real difference between these two? What did we use at home?) until reaching a decision.

The alternative search and alternative evaluation stages tie directly into Michael Porter's concepts of *threat of substitutes* and *threat of new entrants,* explained in his "Competitive Forces within an Industry" model (see Chapter 9 for more on Porter). The same model managers use to develop corporate strategy also has a direct application in marketing a product. In this context, a company that makes a product that already exists in the market is constantly trying to establish or maintain a secure position for the product in the consumer market. In the alternative search and evaluation stages, a customer is trying to get information on his or her options and compare them. In the case of the laundry detergent example, the student is in the grocery store trying to decide. The concept of threat of new entrants appears if there is some new product on the market, WonderClean, that promises to clean clothes so well that the clothes develop a resistance to getting dirty again. If this feature is especially appealing to the student, he or she will purchase this product instead of one of the veteran products on the market (Tide or Era).

The threat of substitutes concept can come into play as well. Say, for example, that while the student is evaluating laundry choices, he or she notices a different kind of product on the shelf. This product is not laundry detergent at all, but a bag of small organic rocks. The rocks themselves are alleged to contain deionizing properties when submerged in water that cause dirt and other toxins to repel from clothing. In fact, according to the package, these rocks clean clothes better than any laundry detergent, and they never wear out. If the college student is persuaded to purchase these rocks, then he or she has chosen a substitute product that may eliminate the need to ever buy laundry detergent again.

The ideas captured in the Porter framework integrate the five stages with concerns about the market in which the company is doing business, as well as the external forces affecting that market. Using these frameworks in tandem allows marketing managers to account for many more industry factors when making marketing decisions about a product.

Finally, after evaluating which product will best satisfy his or her present need, the customer makes a purchase decision, or figures out which product to buy. The last stage, postpurchase feelings, is another area marketing professionals focus on in an attempt to manage. There are two key concepts on which companies with a market orientation focus, both of which relate directly to postpurchase feelings. These are the concepts of customer retention and customer satisfaction.

Customer retention stems from the idea that the success of a product hinges not on the initial sale to a customer, but on the repeated sale. Simply put, customers buy more over time and companies make the most profit when a customer base has a long-term commitment. Further, companies are becoming more aware that loyal customers are the best and one of the most credible sources of advertising. For some products and services, more than half of all new business is the result of word-of-mouth customer referrals. Hence, customer retention must be addressed from the perspective that a company should want to enter into a long-term relationship with every customer it has. A company should want to foster loyalty to its brands and a customer-oriented image. This leads directly to the second key concept.

Customer satisfaction is another critical concern of brand managers and other marketing professionals. Simply put, customer satisfaction relates to how happy a customer is with a product or service, both in the product's performance as well as in the company's delivery of the product to the market. One commonly used measure of customer satisfaction is the *gap model*. The gap model is based on the following equation:

$$\text{Customer satisfaction} = \text{delivery} - \text{expectations}$$

where *delivery* refers to the delivery of the product or service to the market and *expectations* refers to the customer's expectations about that product or service. This construct allows for managerial intervention from two directions. Beyond the operational functions involved in bringing a product or service to the market, marketing people can manage the customer's perceptions of delivery, or the quality of the product or service the customer has received, through tracking the customer's perceptions.

Similarly, a customer's expectations can be managed as well. This kind of emphasis reduces the proclivity of marketing professionals to overpromise or to allow customers to build expectations that are unrealistic. Based on these two fundamental precepts, the gap model, depicted in Figure 7.1, identifies the major components operating within a customer/provider relationship in an effort to identify where satisfaction is breaking down.

The gap model stipulates that a customer has two sources from which he or she builds expectations about a product or service. Internally, a customer's expectations are based on personal needs; past experience with the product, service, or company; and word-of-mouth communications from other customers. Externally, the customer also receives information from the company about its products or services. The model identifies Gap 1 as the difference between what a company's management perceives customer expectations to be and what, in fact, the customer's service expectations really are. Gap 2 occurs when there is a difference between management perception of customer expectations and the quality specifications the company communicates to the customer regarding its products or services. Gap 3 occurs when there are differences between the quality specifications and actual service delivery. Gap 4 occurs when service delivery is not in line with what was promised through external commu-

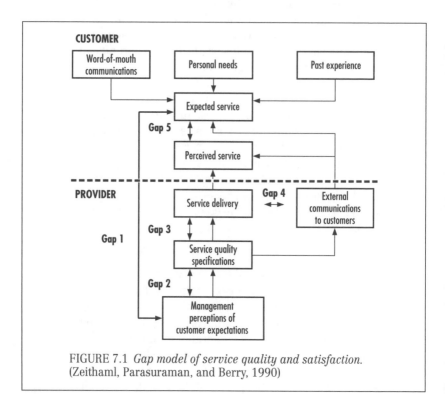

FIGURE 7.1 *Gap model of service quality and satisfaction.* (Zeithaml, Parasuraman, and Berry, 1990)

nications to customers. Gap 5 occurs when there is a difference between the expected service and the perceived service from the point of view of the customer.

The value of the gap model is twofold. The model is designed so specifically that it can monitor the production process at all its critical points, enabling managers to improve service empirically. Moreover, the model also accommodates customer perceptions, enabling a manager to identify customer perceptions and correct unfavorable ones occurring at any point in the process. Once a specific gap type is identified, management can take steps to close that gap and build customer satisfaction.

One more powerful measure marketing professionals use to identify and focus on customer needs and preferences is the practice of breaking customer bases down into smaller markets based on shared personal statistics. This practice is called *market segmentation.* Market segmentation can be done based on age, sex, race, religion, geographic location, income, sexual preference, profession, and educational background, just to name a few. The idea behind segmentation is that customers within these smaller populations share needs that are more easily identifiable and therefore easier to target through new product development and specific marketing efforts.

A cigar manufacturer, for example, may choose to run an advertisement for his or her product in *Golf Digest,* based on the idea that those who golf and therefore read golf magazines also smoke cigars and can afford to smoke expensive cigars. The cigar manufacturer would probably not run an ad in *Prevention* magazine, or *Health and Fitness,* because people who read these magazines generally do not smoke.

THE PRODUCT

With a basic understanding of what a customer is and how customers make decisions, the next important consideration is how marketing professionals use this information to develop products and services and entice customers to buy them.

There are many tools and skills that marketing managers use to solve these problems. Some of the models used in marketing are also used in corporate strategy, like those of Michael Porter and the Boston Consulting Group. As those models are covered in detail in Chapter 9, we will not mention them here. We will, however, focus on two traditional models used frequently in marketing: the *product life cycle* and *the perceptual map.*

The Product Life Cycle

Figure 7.2 is a representation of the product life cycle. The primary purpose of the product life cycle is to

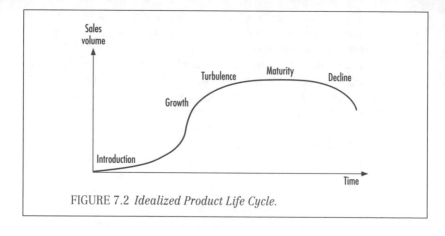

FIGURE 7.2 *Idealized Product Life Cycle.*

relate sales volumes for a given product to the amount
of time the product is available on the market and
thereby identify stages a product goes through across
these measures. Keep in mind that the efforts of marketing professionals can have a significant impact on
shaping the sales behavior of any given product. Further, any market segment can have its own independent life cycle for a given category. Still, the product life
cycle model serves as an excellent basis to chart the
development of a product within its market.

Traditionally, the product life cycle charts the following five stages: introduction, early growth, late growth,
maturity, and decline. During a product's introduction,
consumers may require a great deal of information
about the product if they are going to include it as an
alternative when making decisions. Marketers work to
achieve top-of-mind status with a product, meaning
simply that when a consumer thinks of a product category, a particular brand comes to the top of the consumer's mind associated with that product. In the soft
drink category, for example, three top-of-mind choices
might be Coke, Pepsi, and Sprite.

If the product is designed to meet a need not being
met by any other product on the market, advertising
efforts must focus on helping the customer to become
aware of a need for the product before any selling of
the product will be successful. Conversely, if a new
product is within a market where the need for the
product class and form has already been defined, managers will focus advertising and marketing efforts on
differentiating their products from those already on the
market.

Product differentiation requires that marketing
managers be aware of the difference between the features of a product or service and the benefits of that
product or service. In this context, a *product feature* is
simply a characteristic that the product or service may
have. This could range from weight to color to functionality. A *product benefit,* however, rests on the cus-

tomers' perceptions of how a given product feature will benefit them. How much a product weighs may be a feature, but being lightweight in the eyes of the customer may be a benefit. Close attention must be paid to discern exactly which of a product's features are perceived as benefits if new products are going to compete in well-established markets.

The second stage in the product life cycle is early growth. The transition from the introduction phase to the early-growth phase is usually marked by an increase in the rate of sales for a product. This can enable a manufacturer to pass on the savings he or she receives from the economies of scale yielded from a higher volume of sales. It may also prompt a shift in the marketing effort away from general demand creation through need recognition toward a more concentrated effort on product differentiation. Typically, increased sales during this period are thought to be from market expansion rather than from stealing competitors' market share. Hence, the perceived threat of the new product or service by its competitors is minimal in the early-growth stage.

The late-growth stage is signaled by a decline in the rate of sales growth, but not a decline in sales themselves. Market segments become more easily identifiable in the late-growth stage, prompting product modification efforts to cater to these segments and maintain market share. Competitors tend to launch their strongest efforts to retain sales growth and their market share during this period. Price also becomes a major basis for competition, in addition to product variations.

In the maturity stage, the product has been on the market long enough to develop a strong and loyal customer base. Most sales in the maturity stage are to this base of repeat users. As a result, sales remain steady and are affected more by changes in the purchasing ability of the customer base to buy the product than any addition of new customers to the base. There is very little product modification in the maturity stage. Most marketing efforts are focused on packaging and promotions for the product rather than changing the product itself.

The maturity stage is also marked by the phenomenon of *turbulence,* or the clear emergence of the dominant industry players and the elimination of more minor players who could not sell enough volume to achieve the economies of scale needed to stay competitive within the market. For the same reason, it is quite difficult for a new player to enter into a mature market. Distribution channels also become a major focal point for continued success in a mature market, as the more widely available a product is, the easier it is to purchase.

The final stage in the product life cycle is decline. During this stage, product sales begin to drop off, and the rate at which they decrease is directly related to the cause that precipitated the onset of the decline stage. If a new substitute product enters the market and renders the original product obsolete, product sales might decrease more sharply. Consider, as an illustration, the case of music CDs replacing LP records. If, however, there are gradual changes in the original customer need, this condition might bring about a slower decrease in sales.

Once the decline stage is under way, however, micro-economic factors can precipitate an even more rapid deterioration. If demand for a product decreases, an excess supply can cause prices to drop. In addition, a decrease in demand also eliminates the economies-of-scale benefits the product once enjoyed, again making it less profitable. Since all managers battle with scarce resources, it is far more likely that a product in the decline stage will receive fewer marketing and promotion dollars so that a profitable product can be funded. The combination of all these factors can increase the swiftness of the decline phase.

The product life cycle allows managers to read external signals to discern what phase a product is in. Having some insight into where a product is on the life cycle enables marketing professionals to manage the current phase more effectively, as well as plan ahead for upcoming phases. For these reasons and many others, the product life cycle is one of the most common and most long-lived tools used in marketing today.

The Perceptual Map

The perceptual map is another tool that marketing professionals use to focus on consumer needs and opinions with respect to a given product. Perceptual maps are great tools for providing a visual representation of where specific products fall within a category, based on measures of what attributes a customer is seeking in a product class.

Perceptual maps are usually drawn on a simple X- and Y-axis structure, where either two or four dimensions of consumers' perceptions of a product's attributes can be captured. Information on consumer perceptions and preferences is obtained through marketing research and marketing survey techniques. Statistical analyses, like the ones mentioned earlier, are conducted on the data to create results that are more scientific and more easily used for predictive purposes. Once the dimensions of perception have been identified, a marketing person can identify all products his or her company offers in relation to these dimensions, as well as assess the competition's product lines.

Figure 7.3 is an example of the perceptual map of the passenger automobile market. The X axis represents the perceived inverse connection between youth, responsibility, and functionality on the part of customers. The right side of the X axis denotes the most extreme perception that people equate sports cars with youthfulness because they are less functional and practical, and functionality and practicality are adult concerns. Marketing executives can use this information to promote sports cars as inspiring youthful feelings in their owners, thus appealing to those who may feel pressured by adult concerns and perceive that purchasing a sports car will make them feel young and carefree again.

The left side of the X axis denotes the other extreme customer sentiment, that a car with a higher degree of functionality and less sportiness is the more responsible adult choice. Marketing professionals address these perceptions by appealing to a customer's sense of conservation, often through emphasizing a family orientation when presenting a car through advertising.

The Y axis represents the price variable associated with buying a car. The top of the Y axis represents luxury automobiles, known to be very expensive. The bottom of the Y axis represents economy-class automobiles, known to be least expensive.

Marketers understand, through customer surveys, that these are the considerations most people weigh before buying a car. Most people want some combination of sportiness, luxury, functionality, and value for the dollars being spent. The combinations of these features that people choose, as represented by the cars they choose to buy after expressing their portfolio of preferences, are plotted on the X and Y axes.

Using a perceptual map yields many benefits for the marketing person. It clues the marketing person in to

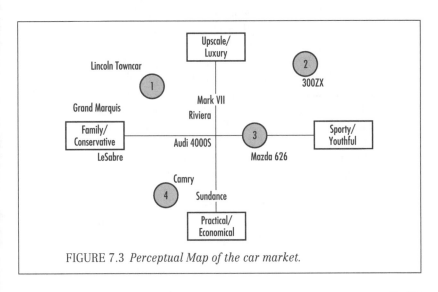

FIGURE 7.3 *Perceptual Map of the car market.*

customer perceptions and misperceptions about a product. It facilitates successful product positioning, as the marketing person is now aware of what needs and preferences the customer is looking to satisfy and can use this information to highlight the features and benefits of his or her product that address the customer's concerns.

The perceptual map can also identify new product possibilities for a company, as it highlights what areas of the market are being covered already and how successful these products are in the eyes of the consumer. A perceptual map can also prevent a company from making too many products within the same class, avoiding cannibalization within a single company's product line. Finally, the perceptual map is another tool that ensures that marketers stay well acquainted with the needs and desires of their target markets.

Pricing Influences Sales

One key criterion for determining the success and longevity of a product is how well it sells. Second only to the actual features and benefits of the product itself, the price of the product has the greatest influence on how it will sell in the marketplace.

There are many strategies that marketing professionals use to determine the price of a product. One of the basic tenets of microeconomics is that a product should be sold at whatever price results when the marginal revenue for the product is equal to the marginal cost of the product (see Chapter 3 for a more detailed explanation). There are, however, other strategies to determine a product's price.

Fundamentally, a product's price will almost always be related to its cost. Since there is a cost benefit, or a reduction in cost, when goods can be produced in volume, marketers aim to take advantage of these cost benefits, known as *economies of scale*. Of the four pricing strategies we will discuss, three accommodate economies-of-scale considerations.

A second important economic concept that affects pricing is the idea of *elasticity of demand*. Elasticity of demand is a numerical predictive measure of how sensitive a product's sales volumes might be to changes in that product's price. Specifically, the elasticity of demand for a product is equal to the value of the marginal change in a product's sales brought on by a change in price, divided by the actual marginal change in price.

Given these two considerations, marketers generally choose from one of the following four pricing strategies or they create some successive combination of these strategies.

Penetration Pricing

Penetration is a pricing strategy marketers use when they are introducing a new product into a market. In a penetration strategy, marketers set the price of an item as low as possible. The idea behind this kind of strategy is that a low price will generate the greatest possible volume of sales for that product. A penetration strategy is generally used in cases where the product being introduced is a commodity-type product, like sugar, and does not have much in the way of features or benefits to distinguish it from the competition. Thus, consumers will probably make their purchase decisions based on considerations of price. Further, a higher market share in commodity-type products allows the manufacturer to benefit from the economies of scale gained from increased production levels.

Perceived Value Pricing

Unlike the penetration strategy, the *perceived value* pricing strategy does not link the price of an item with the cost of producing it. Perceived value is a pricing strategy in which marketers set the price of an item based on how valuable the customer believes the item to be and, hence, how much the customer will pay for it. This is a common strategy for luxury goods like prestige fragrances. The $65 price of a 3.5-ounce bottle of Calvin Klein cologne is in no way linked to the $4.50 it cost to manufacture the product.

Skimming Pricing

Skimming, like perceived value pricing, is another pricing strategy in which the price of a product is not directly related to the cost of producing the product. In a skimming strategy, marketers set the price of the new product as high as the market will allow. This allows marketers to identify the population segment of the consumers who do not hold price as one of the key criteria for making a purchase decision. In this case, the elasticity of demand would be a small value.

Once the population segment that is not price sensitive has been saturated, or the product has reached almost all those consumers who were ever going to buy it, marketers progress to incorporate a different pricing strategy. In an effort to compete in population segments where the price can be manipulated to appeal to other segments that are price sensitive, marketers adjust the price of a product to address higher elasticities of demand. One example of this phenomenon is the retail clothing industry. When clothes are originally available for purchase, they are available at full retail prices. Those consumers with a low elasticity of demand buy what they like with little regard for price. Once enough time has elapsed for the merchant to believe that all those in that population segment have been accommodated, the merchant puts the clothes on sale, reducing the price by degrees until it is low enough to meet the requirements of those who desire the clothes but have a higher elasticity of demand.

Target Return Pricing

The last pricing strategy of the four is *target return* pricing. Some companies measure the success or failure of a product based on the relationship of how much revenue, or in some cases profit, a product generates in relation to how much it cost to make the product. This measure is called *return on investment,* or ROI. A target return pricing strategy is commonly used within an ROI framework, as it allows the price of an item to be set with predetermined revenue and return figures in mind. The choice to use this strategy depends less on the product category and more on the general philosophy of the company making the product.

The strategy a firm uses to price a good or service can and does vary from firm to firm and from product to product within a firm. Clearly, there is a whole host of considerations a marketing professional must account for before choosing a strategy. What is always true is that, aside from the features and quality of the product itself, price is the single most powerful variable in determining the success or demise of a product.

SUMMARY

Many leading firms see marketing as one of the most effective weapons for competing in today's business world. To have a market orientation, a firm must know its customers and be committed to serving their needs as they emerge and change in all aspects of its operations. This is no small task.

The marketing professional must integrate scientific skills with human perception and intuition talents in order to be successful. In this chapter, we outlined some of the basic tools available to marketing professionals to achieve this end, as well as highlighted some of the more important considerations marketers must balance. Ultimately, the true test of a marketing professional is his or her ability to understand the consumer base and manage to satisfy consistently the ever changing consumer needs.

 **MARKETING**

Advertising

Advertising includes any printed or broadcast message sent and paid for by an identified organization to a target market via television, radio, newspapers, magazines, direct mail, billboards, and transit cards.

Advertising Frequency

This refers to the number of times an average prospect is exposed to an advertisement within a specific time period.

Area of Dominant Influence (ADI)

The ADI is a geographic area made up of all counties that receive signals from radio and television stations in a particular market.

Attributes/Features

The descriptive characteristics of a product are its attributes or features.

Augmented Product

An augmented product is one with attributes in addition to those needed to serve its core function that differentiate it from other products available in its class.

Available Market

This refers to the collection of those consumers who have an interest in a particular product or service, access to it, and the funds to pay for it.

Benefits

A benefit is the perceived use or value of a product characteristic to a consumer.

Brand

A brand is a name, term, symbol, or design that is intended to identify clearly and differentiate a seller's product from the products of his or her competitors.

Brand Awareness

This is a measure of consumer knowledge that a particular brand exists.

Brand Extension

This is a marketing strategy that takes the brand name of one product category and extends it to another for purposes of acquired credibility and recognition for the new product category.

Cannibalism

This refers to the reduction of sales in one product caused by the introduction of another product, where both products are made by the same company.

Cold Call

This refers to a personal selling technique in which a salesperson approaches a customer with little or no warning.

Commodity

A commodity is a highly standardized product or service, like gold or corn.

Comparison Advertising

This is an advertising strategy in which a company presents its product as significantly better than a competitor's product.

Core Product

The primary and essential function that a good or service is providing to a consumer is the core product. For example, fundamentally, people buy houses to have shelter, but this may not be the only reason a consumer has to buy a house.

Covariance

A measure of influence of one dependent variable to another, covariance represents the weighted correlation between two dependent variables.

Customer

Any individual, household, or company representative that acts as the buyer of goods and services offered to the mass market is a customer.

Direct Marketing

This is a marketing tool designed to elicit immediate action from the consumer through direct customer contact.

Economic Value to Customer

Economic value to customer = EVCx = (life-cycle costs of a competitor's product in relation to that of a home firm) – (start-up costs for the home firm's product) – (postpurchase costs for the home firm's product) + (incremental value of the home firm's product).

Elasticity of Demand

This is a measure of how sensitive sales volumes of a product are to changes in that product's price, equal to the marginal change in sales, divided by the marginal change in price.

Experience Law

This is a law of marketing stating that the unit cost of value added to a standard product, measured in constant currency, declines by a constant percentage each time the accumulated product doubles, such that: $Cq = Cn\,(q/n) - b$. This is one of the underlying precepts of economies of scale, in that quality becomes less expensive when the product is made in volume.

Focus Group Interview

This is an interview conducted with 8 to 12 people who represent a target market for a product, in which the group is asked specific questions related to a product and its use.

GAP Model of Service, Quality, and Satisfaction

This model is designed to identify misperceptions or shortcomings in the relationship between the consumer and the service provider in such a way that these gaps can be corrected and customer satisfaction can be improved.

Generic Product

A generic product is an unbranded, inexpensive, plainly packaged version of a common consumer product, usually of standard or slightly substandard quality compared to its branded counterparts.

Ghost Shopper

A ghost shopper is a marketing specialist, posing as a regular consumer, who is hired to monitor and evaluate the presentation skills and sales abilities of the store's salespersons.

Marketing Mix

This comprises the marketing tools and techniques a company uses to achieve its goals relative to a specific target market audience.

Marketing Myopia

This is a phenomenon experienced when a company becomes so involved in the actual process of selling its product that it loses sight of the true nature and purpose of the product itself. When a company focuses more on selling a product than on the product itself, an outstanding opportunity for competitors to steal market share is created.

Marketing Orientation

A corporation's strategy rests on its marketing effort. It becomes the business philosophy, not just a functional area. Corporations focus goals around managing customer retention and satisfaction through product definition, characteristics, and interfunctional integration throughout the company. Having a market orientation necessitates "the organization-wide generation, dissemination and responsiveness to market intelligence."[4] Alternative orientations a corporation can have include sales, finance, R&D, or manufacturing.

Market Segmentation

This refers to the process of breaking up the mass market into discernible subgroups, by geography, behavior, or demography.

Market Share

Market share is the total number of units sold or dollars earned by one product or company in relation to the total number of products sold or dollars earned in an entire product class.

Mass Marketing

This includes the mass production, distribution, and promotion of one product for all buyers.

Mean

A numerical average, equal to the sum of terms in a given series divided by the number of terms in that series is the mean, also called the *expected value*.

Penetration Pricing

This refers to a pricing strategy that dictates that the price of an item being introduced into a market should be set as low as possible to generate the greatest possible sales volume for that product.

Perceived Value Pricing

This refers to a pricing strategy that dictates that the price of a given item should be set based on the customer's perception of the value of that item, not on the seller's costs.

Point-of-Purchase Advertising

This is a method of advertising designed to trigger impulse purchases through the use of eye-catching, attractive displays at the locations where customers actually pay for a product.

Product

A good or service a company makes in quantity to sell on the open market is a product.

Product Life Cycle

Key terms include:

1. *Product class*—At the most generic level, this term refers to all products from all competing producers that serve the same functional purposes in roughly the same manner, despite smaller differences in appearance and performance,[5] for example, all passenger cars manufactured in the world today.

2. *Product form*—A lesser generic level, this term refers to all products within a group that are more similar in customer perception and use than all items in a product class. Using the passenger car example, a product form within this product class would be luxury passenger cars.

3. *Brand*—This term refers to several items in a product form produced by the same organization or company. Mercedes Benz is a brand within the product form of luxury automobiles.

4. *Model*—The least generic classification, this term refers to a specific and individual item produced by an organization or company. A 300 E Class Sedan is a specific model produced under the brand of Mercedes Benz within the product form of luxury automobiles within the product class of passenger cars.

Product Mix

The portfolio of products that a given company produces for market consumption is the product mix.

Pull Strategy

This refers to a marketing approach in which a manufacturer promotes a product directly to consumers in the hope that the consumers will then request the product from distribution-channel members.

Push Strategy

This refers to a marketing approach in which a manufacturer uses its sales force and trade promotions to sell a product actively to wholesalers and retailers, who in turn aggressively sell the product to consumers.

Regression Analysis

This is a statistical tool used to discern the relationship between a dependent variable, such as sales, to one or more independent variables, such as marketing spending, advertising spending, and promotional spending.

Relationship Marketing

This approach to marketing emphasizes the importance of personal relationship building between consumers, suppliers, and distributors inclusively, and marketing professionals with all parties.

Repeat Purchase Rate

This is the number of times a consumer purchases the same product within a specific time interval.

Response Rate

This is the percentage of responses generated by a direct-marketing campaign.

Skimming Pricing

This pricing strategy dictates that the price of an item being introduced into a market be as high as possible, thereby identifying the segment of consumers that is not price sensitive. Once that segment has been saturated, the price can be manipulated to appeal to other segments that are price sensitive.

Strategic Marketing

This refers to a company's marketing methodology, based on the formulation of how marketing efforts tie in to achieving the overall goals of the company through identifying specific marketing strategies to meet those goals.

Tangible Product

The physical attributes of a product constitute a tangible product.

Target Market

This is the collection or population of customers or consumers that a company has in mind as the primary audience for its goods or services and to whom the company gears its marketing efforts to sell the good or service.

Target Return Pricing

This pricing strategy dictates that the price of an item being introduced into a market be determined based on a calculation of return on investment, or that sales for the product reflect some predetermined return on the capital required to bring the product to the market.

Telemarketing

This is a tool used in direct marketing in which a consumer either calls or is called by a seller, listens to a sales pitch and description of a product, and then decides whether to place an order.

Trademark

This is the legally recognized right of a seller to the exclusive use of an identifying symbol or brand.

Variance

A measure of dispersion, the variance represents the average distance from any given observation in a series to the mean of that series, in units squared.

MORE READINGS
Critical References—Articles

Allan, Gerald B, and John S. Hammond III. "Notes on the Use of Experience Curves in Competitive Decision Making." Case study published by Harvard Case Clearing House. Boston: Harvard Business School, 1975: 1–12.

This article synthesizes basic ideas concerning experience curves and their effective use in competitive analysis, based partly on results of the publications of The Boston Consulting Group. The article indicates that firms whose marketing and pricing strategies are geared to accumulating experience much faster than their competitors can often achieve significant cost advantages. This cost reduction applies not only to direct labor cost, but also to an extended concept called the *experience effect.* The experience curve is a result of broadening the learning curve concept and implies that the cost of doing any repetitive task decreases as experience increases. The source and competitive implications of the experience effect are developed in the article.

Capon, Noel. "The Product Life Cycle" in *AMA Management Handbook.* 3d ed. Edited by John J. Hampton. New York: AMACOM, 1994.

This book provides an explanation of the product life cycle, which describes a given product's sales trajectory over time, from introduction to decline.

Kohli, Ajay K., and Bernard J. Jaworski. "Market Orientation: The Construct, Research Propositions and Managerial Implications." *Journal of Marketing.* Vol. 54 (April 1990): 1–18.

A synthesis of knowledge regarding the development of a framework for understanding market orientation is presented. *Market orientation* means the implementation of the marketing concept. The underlying purpose of the authors is to identify the market orientation construct's domain and then establish a foundation for future research by constructing an integrated framework that includes antecedents and consequences of a market orientation. In order to develop this framework, the authors reference writings in marketing literature from the past 35 years as well as incorporate 62 field interviews with managers in a diversity of organizations.

Critical References—Books

Aaker, J. *Managing Brand Equity.* London: Free Press, 1991.

The book distinguishes brands from products and explores factors that are inherent in the management of brand equity. Aaker indicates that, while a product can be reproduced by a competitor, a successful brand is a distinguishing name or symbol. Factors inherent in brand equity are developed and discussed in an informative manner and supported with examples.

Kotler, Philip. *Marketing Management: Analysis, Planning, Implementation and Control.* 9th ed. Upper Saddle River, N.J.: Prentice-Hall, 1997.

This is a comprehensive marketing management text utilized by various top business schools. The book is structured in five parts: understanding marketing management, analyzing marketing opportunities, developing marketing strategies, planning marketing programs, and managing the marketing effort. Hence, the text has an informative structure, as it first presents marketing management and then analyzes marketing and its development, planning, and management.

Peter, J. Paul, and James Donnelly. *A Preface to Marketing Management.* 6th ed. Burr Ridge, Ill.: Irwin, 1994, pp. 56–73.

The book addresses specific elements that are integral to marketing management. The book effectively presents components of marketing management and clearly develops an explanation of each of these elements.

Webster, F. E. *Market-Driven Management.* New York: Wiley, 1994.

This book combines cutting-edge research (from the founder of the industrial marketing area) with the latest marketing advances in a wide range of industries worldwide. It offers a new approach to integrating the marketing concept with all phases of corporate strategy, structure, culture, as well as other functions such as R&D, finance, human resources, and corporate communications.

Organizational Behavior

Defined as "the field of study that investigates the impact that individuals, groups and structure have on behavior within organizations, for the purpose of applying such knowledge toward improving an organization's effectiveness," organizational behavior gives the manager the information and knowledge needed to manage his or her workforce effectively. Often mistaken as a "soft" (and therefore less relevant) area of interest by MBA students more focused on learning the latest financial modeling techniques, the importance of this field can be clearly seen when we consider that the largest part of most companies' costs comes from their labor forces, and that the success of every initiative undertaken in an organization depends totally on the willingness of the workforce to implement it. The strategic use of a company's human resources has never been more critical, but it is hard to manage something you do not understand. Organizational behavior is the key to understanding why people behave the way they do in the workplace.

Organizational behavior covers human behavior in organizations—a huge field. However, it is usually broken down into three main areas, based on the level of analysis: individual-level elements (managing individuals), group-level elements (managing teams), and elements of organizational structure (managing the organization).

INDIVIDUAL LEVEL OF ANALYSIS— MANAGING INDIVIDUALS

The study of individual aspects of human behavior has its roots in the field of psychology. From an organizational perspective, we are interested in explanation and prediction to help us manage productivity and commitment. The core of every organizational behavior course includes coverage of personality and attitudes, decision making, motivation, leadership, and power.

Personality and Attitude

Managers often blame personality conflicts for problems or they say of employees that "they just don't have the right attitude." This is an easy way out for most managers—we can't do anything about personality or attitudes (other than tell a person to change them), so we can feel secure in the knowledge that the low productivity is not our fault and that our employees would be effective if only they made the effort. However, good managers can use personality differences to enhance the creativity and work of a division; good managers can set things up so that people working for them have positive, constructive attitudes. Yes, there are personality conflicts and bad attitudes out there—the key is how well do you manage them? To manage something, you need to understand it.

Personality

People differ along many attributes, and these differences in attributes make up their personalities. Sixteen *traits* have been found to be generally steady and constant sources of behavior: extroversion, intelligence, emotional stability, dominance, conscientiousness, risk aversion, sensitivity, trust, creativity, directness, confidence, need for control, ability to relax, group dependency, timidity, and seriousness. Thinking about each of these traits in turn, it is easy to see that people who are strong in some traits will behave differently to people who are not so strong. In organizational behavior, several other attributes have been shown to be related to behavior in the workplace. These are self-esteem, locus of control, achievement orientation, Machiavellianism, self-monitoring, risk taking, and authoritarianism.

Why does all this matter? It matters because most of us tend to think that other people are like us and do the same things for the same reasons. Most managers manage people using this principle. And yet, this does not work in the workplace. How many times have you expected one behavior from a person and actually seen something very different? This is where the difference in personality comes into play. If you are a manager who happens to have high self-esteem, you may expect your employees to be similar to yourself—and manage them accordingly. However, if one of your subordinates has low self-esteem, criticism from you could have a more powerful effect on that person than you expect. You may think you are giving a mild reprimand, but the employee hears major, negative feedback: the person's response is unlikely to be the one you expect. By understanding the differences among your employees, you can adapt your management style to be effective. With high self-esteem people you can give direct, blunt, and negative feedback; to your low self-esteem employees you may want to soft-pedal and coach to get the same effect. Suddenly an incomprehensible response becomes a manageable behavior, once you understand its source.

One final point about personality: There is a lot of discussion about how much personality influences behavior, especially in the workplace. The big answer is that it depends. If a person is in what is called a *strong* situation, where the situational cues are very powerful (for example, the traffic light is red), then we can predict their behavior regardless of personality most of the time (they will stop). However, if the situation is *weak,* and the cues are ambiguous or unclear (for example, the light is out), then their behavior becomes more a result of their personalities (more aggressive people will tend to drive through; more timid people will hesitate or stop.). It is usually in the ambiguous, weaker situations that personality begins to have a direct effect on workplace behavior. This has implications for managers: Systems, guidelines, and behavioral rules can all create strong situations, minimizing the impact of personal differences in the workplace and leading to predictable behaviors.

Attitudes

What about those employees who have a bad attitude? Most of us believe that attitudes are pretty set and that our attitudes control our behavior. That makes intuitive sense. However, research into cognitive dissonance has shown that attitudes are a lot more changeable than we used to think and that, in a lot of cases, our behavior controls our attitudes. This means that you can change people's attitudes by changing their behavior!

A simple example of this is giving money to charity. It has been shown that after people donate money to a charity, their attitude toward that charity is consistently more positive than it was before the donation. The act of giving money leads to a change in attitude. If you think about this, it does make sense: I have a certain image of myself—which may include disliking a certain charity. If I give money to that charity, I now have what the researchers call *dissonance*—I've just done something that goes against my attitudes and, psychologically, I feel uncomfortable. To resolve this dissonance I can do one of several things: I can negate the donation by saying I was forced to give, I can stop giving to the charity, or I can change my attitude by saying, "Well, the charity isn't that bad after all."

A knowledge of cognitive dissonance leads the manager to focus not on changing the attitude but on changing the behavior—which will then lead to a change in attitude. How do you change behavior? We'll talk more about that in the section on motivation, after we explore individual decision making.

Decision Making

Many managerial decision-making systems are based on the *rational optimizing model:* that people determine the need for a decision, identify the decision criteria, allocate weights to the criteria, develop the alternatives, evaluate the alternatives, and then select the best alternative in a rational, fact-based manner. As early as the 1950s, the validity of this principle was challenged by March and Simon, who saw that many decisions were, in fact, based on irrational processes and premises. Intuitively, we know that very few people are perfectly rational in their decisions—we make a lot of choices based on emotion, on avoiding risk, on not losing face, and so on—so it is hardly surprising to discover that similar, nonrational elements enter into decision making in the workplace. Some elements that we will look at in this section include escalating commitment, heuristics, selective perception, misunderstanding of probability, anchoring, and framing.

Escalating Commitment

"Escalating commitment" is an example of nonrational decision making. Let's say you have already invested a million dollars in a project—and it still isn't making money for your company. The rational thing to do is write off that money and start investing in a more profitable project. However, a lot of people would not make that decision. With thoughts like "We've spent so much on it now, we have to keep going," "It's bound to come good soon," or "If we back off after spending this much, we'll look foolish," good money can be thrown after bad. The most frequently cited example of escalating commitment is President Lyndon Johnson's decisions during the Vietnam War: Despite clear information showing that bombing North Vietnam was having no effect on ending the war, his decision was to increase the rate of bombing. As a manager, it is important that you avoid the temptation to prove your original decisions are right by throwing good resources into bad projects.

Heuristics

The other big influence on decision making that is often misunderstood and so not dealt with is the effect of heuristics. Heuristics are rules of thumb that people evolve to help deal with the myriad of decisions they face in their everyday lives. If we went through the full, rational, optimizing decision-making model for every decision we make, most of us would never get out of bed in the morning. We have developed numerous shortcuts that help us make decisions quickly and, usually, effectively. However, while these shortcuts originally helped us survive against predators and now make our everyday lives easier, these heuristics can work against us in the workplace. The classic heuristic we use is stereotypes: By basing our understanding of a whole group of people on one or two individuals we know or stories we have heard, we are able to make quick decisions about others. However, the accuracy of those decisions is unlikely to be very high. It is important, as a manager, to be aware of the shortcuts you tend to use and use them only when it doesn't affect the quality of the decision.

Selective Perception

Selective perception is another shortcut we use. Generally when we make a decision, we already have an option in mind. This implicit favorite then influences how we go about the decision-making process. If I favor flextime, I am likely to collect lots of examples of where it has been effective and had positive results. I am unlikely to collect information on cases where it hasn't worked. In some situations, I may not even see or hear things that contradict my preferred view, and I certainly won't go actively looking for disconfirming evidence—facts that may prove me wrong. Yet every scientist knows that the only way to prove something is to disprove it. You can never prove that all swans are white, as it is impossible for you to look at all swans, past, present, and future. You can, however, *disprove* the statement. One observation of a black swan proves that not all swans are white.

In the workplace, if we suspect someone of poor performance, we will watch the person closely—and, sure enough, we'll see evidence that he or she is a poor performer, but how often do we actively look for the disconfirming evidence? Maybe that poor performance was a one-off, and the person is generally a good performer, but we will never know, because we are not looking for that information.

Misunderstanding of Probabilities

Misunderstanding of probabilities also leads to nonrational decisions. Let's take an example of a flight instructor, with two students. One of the students makes a very poor landing. The instructor punishes the student and threatens him with suspension if he "doesn't get his act together." On the next flight, this student does much better. The second student lands perfectly on her first attempt. The instructor praises her and holds her up as an example to the class. Yet, the next time around, her landing is much worse. The instructor then, from the evidence, assumes that praise makes people lazy, they don't try as hard, and punishment and threats are more effective in training pilots. What this instructor is forgetting is that he is basing all his assumptions on a sample of just one flight—and that, generally, performance regresses to the mean: On average, I may have a performance of, say, 6/10. I may have a "lucky" day, when I perform at 9/10, but this doesn't mean that 9/10 is now my standard performance. My next performance is far more likely to be closer to 6/10 than 9/10, whatever the instructor does. The only thing the instructor can do is train me so that, over time, my average performance improves.

Anchoring

All good salespeople know that anchoring can work for or against you in decision making. Try this experiment: Ask two groups of ten people how much they would pay a trainee secretary. Tell the first group of ten that you think the pay should be $10,000, but tell the second group of ten that you think the pay should be $30,000. If you average the responses of the two groups, you will see that the second group's average is significantly higher than the first group's. Their decision was influenced by the amount you stated: the amount of the *anchor* was higher, so the amount of their average decision was higher. Marketers use this all the time when they offer discounts off recommended prices—people buy more than they would if the article was the same price but not discounted because they think they are getting a bargain compared with the higher anchor price.

Anchoring doesn't just happen with numbers; it also happens with first impressions and reputations. Most people make judgments about others within a few minutes of meeting them—and these first impressions then act as anchors for future behavior and attitudes toward those people. In addition, if you hear about people from others, what you hear can influence the way you behave to them when you meet them—your impression of them is influenced and anchored by what you have heard about them. This, combined with the selective perception we talked about earlier, shows how important it is to have a good reputation in the workplace.

Framing

Framing is a matter of how information is presented. Think about this phrase: "Our cookies are 90 percent fat free." Now think about it after reframing: "Our cookies are 10 percent fat." Simply reframing how the information is presented leads to a very different feeling about the product and, probably, a different decision.

Other things that organizational behavior has shown to be a part of decision making are a tendency to "satisfice" (take the first workable option rather than seeking out the optimal alternative), a tendency to be risk averse (if you frame something in terms of losses, the decision is likely to go against you; if you frame it in terms of gains, you will get a positive decision); the halo effect (the tendency to assume that, because someone has a good reputation in one area, the person is right here, too); and the effect of history (if the last decision a person made was right, we may assume the next one will be right, too, or, if we have historically been good in one area, we may assume that we will continue to be good there without applying the full rational model to the decision).

Recently, the concept of *bounded rationality* has developed: that human beings are capable of being rational within limits. As a manager, the use of reframing, seeking out disconfirming evidence and being aware of the factors influencing decision makers, can increase the rationality and effectiveness of your decisions.

Motivation

Like finance, operations, and so many other MBA subjects, the study of organizational behavior involves equations. As a manager, the first equation you need to know is:

$$\text{Performance} = \text{ability} \times \text{effort}$$

Before you can even start talking about effort, you need to make sure your employees have the skills and knowledge they need to do the job well. Without this, it doesn't matter how motivated they are, you still won't get high productivity because your people are unable to perform any more effectively. First, solve the ability part of the equation; then you are ready to move on to the effort, or motivation, element. If the ability part of the equation is the can-do element, then motivation is the will-do part: Motivation can be described as the "will to work and exert effort even when there is resistance."

The simplest way to motivate people is to expect them to be motivated! The self-fulfilling prophecy works here as well as anywhere else: If you expect something of someone, your behavior reflects that expectation and the person begins to behave that way. Our own behavior as managers can affect the behavior and performance of our employees.

Apart from this, there are many ways of looking at motivation that are useful to a manager. These fall into four main categories: needs theories, task theories, reinforcement theory, and calculative theories.

Needs Theories

Early work on motivation focused on drives or needs that people have and how, if work helps fulfill these needs, then people will exert more effort. Maslow's hierarchy of needs and McClelland's needs theory both take this approach. One thing all the needs-based theories have in common is that, to use them effectively, you need to know what your employees needs are.

Task Theories

The *job characteristics model* shows that work design can have an effect on how motivated people are. If a job has skill variety, task identity, and task significance, allows autonomy, and provides feedback, then employees are likely to feel the work is meaningful, feel responsible, and have knowledge of the outcomes of their work. This, in turn, leads to greater internal motivation, high-quality work performance, and greater satisfaction. This model has led to the redesign of work in many organizations—and its principles underlie the replacement of assembly-line manufacture with other, more integrated approaches.

Related to the task, yet motivating in a different way, is the use of goal setting. Research has shown that setting high but achievable goals encourages people to exert effort in trying to achieve them. One word of warning: Goals work only if the people trying to reach them accept them, so either you need their participation in setting the goals or you need to do a good selling job to persuade them why the goals are relevant and reasonable. Remember: Goals should be SMART: specific, measurable, attainable, relevant, and timely.

Reinforcement Theory

The basic principle of reinforcement theory is that behavior is a function of its consequences. If I think a certain behavior will lead to pleasant consequences, I am more likely to choose it. If I think a certain behavior will lead to unpleasant consequences, I am less likely to choose it.

Rewards and punishment are based on reinforcement theory and an understanding of the theory could help explain why some of your rewards and punishments are not having the desired effects. If, as a manager, you can make sure that when people work hard, the consequences are pleasant for them, then you are likely to have motivated employees. An example would be to simply acknowledge good performance and say thank you, or to give pay for good performance. Conversely, if people have done a poor job, and you don't want them to repeat it, you need to make sure that any pleasant consequences are withdrawn—don't say thank you for bad work.

This is not as straightforward as it seems. What if someone came to you with what you think is a good idea, and you say, "Great idea, write it up in more detail and I'll take it to the board." Some of you might think this is a pleasant consequence. But what if the person with the idea is already snowed under with work. The last thing he or she might want is another project to tackle, so, for this person, the consequence is not pleasant. What ends up happening? The person stops coming to you with ideas. By "punishing" the idea-generating behavior, by creating negative consequences for the employee, you have inadvertently stopped a behavior you may have wanted to encourage. For some people, punishment can be attractive, as it guarantees attention and, often, notoriety. Thinking through the perception and consequences of the reinforcement is critical if you want to be an effective manager.

One more aspect of reinforcement that is critical is timing. For punishment to be effective, it must be specific and immediate. However, for encouraging a behavior, intermittent reinforcement has the strongest effect. Gambling offers the best demonstration of this: If you won every time you gambled, or every fifth time (a fixed schedule of reinforcement), you would probably not find gambling as exciting as not knowing when you will win but winning occasionally and unpredictably.

As a manager, if you want people to develop a particular behavior, you can get them started with training and positive reinforcement every time you see them use that behavior. However, as we all know, if you constantly reinforce, people get satiated, and the thank-yous and well-dones lose their power. This is when you switch to intermittent reinforcement to keep the behavior going.

Reinforcement theory looks at motivation as a reflex—like Pavlov's dog, we are the victims of our conditioning. There are approaches to motivation that explicitly take into account human thought processes and cognitive reasoning. These can be called *calculative theories*.

Calculative Theories

These theories assume that motivation is the outcome of a calculated (although often subconscious) process that people go through when presented with a situation.

In *equity theory,* people calculate their inputs and outputs and compare them to those of others. For example, if I think I am working harder than my colleague, yet I'm being paid the same, I may well reduce my inputs (effort) until I think we are equitable. This has implications for organizations using fixed pay scales for jobs—how do you encourage people to perform better? Many companies respond with incentive schemes or performance-related pay, but these have their own problems, as we'll see when we look at reward systems in the section on organization-level elements. Equity theory can often explain why some people who used to be highflyers crash. There comes a point when they realize that although they are working harder and smarter, their returns are the same as those of other people who are just passing the time at the office, so why bother?

Expectancy theory is another calculative way of looking at motivation. The second equation you need to know is:

$$F = E * I * V$$

F (the force of motivation) is equal to *E* (*expectancy,* or the belief that exerting the effort will lead to performance) times *I* (instrumentality, or the belief that the performance will lead to an outcome) times *V* (valence, or the value given to the outcome). The importance of expectancy theory is that it shows that there are several places where motivation can break down:

1. Does my effort lead to performance? I might be working flat out, but the equipment I'm using is just not good enough to do the job.

2. Does the performance actually lead to a desired outcome? I could be the best service technician you have ever had in the company, but, however well I do my job, the customers complain that it takes too long to repair a machine because we don't have enough technicians to cover the territory, so I never get a good performance report—I end up demotivated.

3. How important is the outcome to me? I might be performing well—and it might really be possible for me to win the end-of-year sales bonus—but the amount is so small relative to my salary and my peers will tease me for winning, that it just isn't worth the effort.

At each stage there could be personal or organizational reasons for the breakdown in motivation. One lesson from expectancy theory is that it is as important (and often easier) to remove the demotivators as to improve the motivators. You can pay a person as much as you like, but if any one of the three steps breaks down, you will not get any more motivation for your money.

Leadership

The definition of leadership is neither complete, nor yet agreed upon. For most people, leadership is one of those things that they can't describe, but they know it when they see it. For now, we're going to use the definition of leadership as "the ability to influence people or groups toward one or more goals." From this definition, it seems that leadership belongs in the next section, at the group level of analysis. However, the history of leadership began with a very individual-level look at what constitutes a leader. So that's where we'll start as well. In the research, there are three main types of theory: trait theories, behavioral theories, and contingency theories.

Trait Theories

Early research into leadership focused on whether leaders and nonleaders had certain personality attributes. Are leaders born? Are there certain characteristics that leaders have and followers don't? This would make life easy; we would be able to identify leaders early on and make sure they took the leadership positions, a definite help for most companies. However, the research proved disappointing; while there are certain traits that most leaders show (including a high degree of ambition, high energy level, the desire to lead, honesty and integrity, self-confidence, intelligence, job-related knowledge, and a high degree of self-monitoring), the correlations between these traits and leadership are low. The trait approach also overlooks the role of followers and the role of the situation (remember we said that behavior depends on the situation), and it does not make clear the causality: Does confidence lead to being a leader, or does being a leader lead to confidence?

Behavioral Theories

In an advance on trait theories, researchers moved on to explore whether leaders displayed certain types of behavior that made them effective. This was of particular interest to trainers, since if we could discover the key types of behavior, then we could train everybody to be leaders by teaching them the appropriate behavior. The most famous studies in this area were the Ohio State studies, the University of Michigan studies, and Blake and Mouton's managerial grid. All three of these studies showed that, to be effective, it was important for leaders to manage both the task and people elements of the job. However, another thing these approaches had in common was that, while they provided a conceptual framework that is useful for many managers, they do not give us any answers we can directly apply to the workplace, as they do not take the situation or rest of the group into account.

Contingency Theories

Called *contingency* theories because these theories say that the effectiveness of a behavior depends on the situation you are in, these are the theories most managers find most useful in the workplace. Five main theories here include: Fiedler's model, Hersey and Blanchard's situational theory, leader-member exchange theory, path-goal theory, and the leader-participation model (Vroom-Yetton). In all these models the effectiveness of various leadership styles depends on characteristics of the followers (their maturity, for example) as well as aspects of the situation. The key lesson is that the most effective leaders are able to *flex* their leadership style to match the group and the situation.

Any discussion of leadership would not be complete without looking at substitutes for leadership. In some situations, there are factors that define the requirements so clearly that leadership becomes superfluous. For example, professional associations often act as substitutes by providing universally accepted codes of conduct and standards of performance.

Power and Influence

Leadership has been defined as the ability to influence a group toward a goal; power is the ability to influence, period. There are three main areas to look at when we think about power: the source of the power, the role of dependency, and politics.

Where Does Power Come From?

French and Raven are credited with the early attempts to describe where power comes from. They developed a list of five sources of power within organizations: *coercive power,* which depends on fear; *reward power,* from the ability to give out things of value; *expert power,* or influence because you have special skills or knowledge; *legitimate power,* which you have because of your position in the company; and *referent power,* or power you have because people admire and respect you. As a manager, think about where your power comes from. Coercive power relies on the fact that people fear you, and reward power is effective only so long as people value the rewards you have to offer. Legitimate power relies on your rank in the company hierarchy, and recent events such as white-collar downsizing have shown how quickly that can change for any level of management. Expert power lasts as long as no one else knows as much as you. Referent power is the only source that seems maintainable—and referent power is the one source that seems to rely on interpersonal skills and an understanding of other people.

How can you use your power bases? By using power *tactics.* Tactics for influencing others include reason (use of facts and data); friendliness (use of social connections and appeal); coalition (getting support of others); bargaining (negotiating exchanges of favors); assertiveness (being direct, open, and firm in your needs); higher authority (gaining support of upper levels for your plans), and sanctions (using organizational rewards and punishments to induce compliance). Again, like the bases, the different tactics have different levels of acceptability, as well as some negative consequences that need to be thought through before you act.

The Role of Dependency

The key to power: The greater a person's dependency on you, the more power you have over that person. Think about this: At first glance, a CEO seems like a very powerful person. However, CEOs are almost totally dependent on other people, so, in fact, their level of power is not very high. If you as a manager are dependent on other people's performance for your own performance review, then these other people have power over you, whether they know it or not. Dependency can increase if the resource you control is important, scarce, and nonsubstitutable. So, you can work to increase your power by either increasing other people's dependency on you or reducing your dependency on others.

Politics

Often framed as negative, politics are a natural part of any organization. Having accepted that, what is a working definition of politics, and when are politics functional or dysfunctional for an organization? Political behavior can be defined as "activities not required in your formal role, but that influence, or try to influence activities and resource distributions within the company." Such behavior can be in the interests of the company, or it can be in direct opposition to what is best for the organization. Then it becomes dysfunctional political behavior. Organizations are a social structure of human beings, with limited resources—and these factors combine to make political behavior almost inevitable. Political behavior tends to increase as resources become more constrained, and if the situations facing the company are more ambiguous, rational, optimizing decision making can be made difficult.

Other, individual factors can contribute to political behavior. People who score high on a characteristic called *Machiavellianism* are more likely to show political behavior than people who score low on this scale. In addition, people who are self-monitors to a greater degree show a tendency to politick. An extreme form of politicking, where people try to control the image others have of them, is called *impression management,* in which most of a person's energy and time goes to managing impressions rather than doing work.

Much politicking is aimed at self-protection as much as at self-promotion, and defensive behaviors are often seen in organizations with high levels of political behavior. Defensive behaviors include working to rule, passing the buck, playing dumb, stalling, scapegoating, escalating of commitment, and protecting turf and territory.

Although politics can be useful, more often they are dysfunctional for the organization. As a manager, be aware of why politicking increases, what political behavior looks like, and how to handle it when you see it.

GROUP LEVEL OF ANALYSIS

It has been said that psychologists do not study groups because it's too hard, whereas organizational behavior researchers study groups because they have no choice. How many people in any organization truly work alone? To some extent, every employee interacts with others and, increasingly, companies are looking to teams, self-managed or otherwise, to increase creativity and/or productivity. At this level of analysis, organizational behavior includes social influences, organizational factors influencing groups, and the group itself.

Social Influences

There is no doubt that most people are influenced by other people around them. If my colleagues all think the job is great, I am more likely to think so, too—after all, they can't all be wrong, can they? The *social information processing* model argues that employees adopt attitudes and behaviors in response to social cues given by other people, including other employees, family, friends, and customers. Subtle comments about autonomy and job challenge have been shown to influence motivation and satisfaction levels of employees, so the social influence is very strong. This becomes particularly important when we start looking at what happens in groups.

In groups, one of the most powerful social influences is the drive to conformity. Most group members want to be accepted by the other people in the group, and to do this, many of us go along with group norms and decisions that we would otherwise disagree with. A classic example of group pressures toward conformity is the Asch experiments (see the key concepts section for details), in which 35 percent of people gave the wrong answer rather than disagree with the rest of their group! This social pressure to conformity is important in that it can lead to suppression of differences and disagreements, resulting in *groupthink,* where everyone goes along with a bad decision because no one wants to disagree. Pressure to conform is even greater when authority figures are involved.

Social influences in groups are usually in the form of *norms.* Norms are acceptable standards of behavior that are shared—and enforced—by group members. A simple norm might be that we all arrive to meetings on time. If you are late, the group enforces its norm by starting without you or by commenting on your lateness. Most norms are implicit; few groups actively discuss their norms. However, there is some evidence to suggest that they should do so, if only to capture and deal with the norms that push for conformity rather than allowing disagreement and discussion of alternatives.

There are some people in groups who seem to go against the social influences of the group. First, there are the "social loafers," people who, because they are in a group where their individual contribution cannot be measured, sit back and let the rest of the group do the work. The level of loafing is directly tied to accountability and, in groups where it is clear to all members who is contributing what and there are sanctions against loafing, loafing is less of a problem.

Second, there are people who will continue to challenge the status quo and disagree, regardless of group pressure for agreement and conformity. These brave souls, who can ultimately play a role in leading the group to a high-quality outcome, often suffer a dire fate; they are labeled as "institutionalized deviants" and anything they say is dismissed as "coming from the person who always disagrees" rather than being examined as a sensible and important comment. This institutionalization is the group's way of not dealing with the lack of consensus, and it enables the group to take an easy path.

As a manager, there are two messages here: If you are managing a group, you need to encourage disagreement and make sure that if someone challenges the agreed state of affairs that person is actively encouraged and not closed down; as a group member, you need to make sure you don't end up an institutionalized deviant.

How can you avoid this fate? There are several suggestions in the research. First, build up your credibility with the group through contributing early on; second, be constructive with your suggestions, where possible, building on other people's rather than knocking them down; and third, build coalitions with other people in the group so that when you disagree, you are not alone.

A word of caution: Minorities in groups tend to be institutionalized more than other group members, so if you are the only engineer, the only woman, the only man—or the only anything—in your group, you will have to take extra care in managing your role, for the group to be effective.

Organizational Factors Influencing Groups

To understand groups, it is important to realize that a group is part of a larger system—the organization—and so can be influenced by organizational factors. Richard Hackman's work with teams in organizations has shown that organizational factors can explain a lot of group effectiveness. First, does the team have a clear and engaging direction? Do the members know what they are trying to achieve and are they interested in achieving it? This links directly to the larger picture of *organizational strategy*. Without a clear organizational strategy, it is unlikely that a team will have a clear and engaging direction.

Second, does the team have the *organizational context* to do a good job? This includes organizational reward and information systems, as well as resource availability. A team, like an individual, has to see a clear link between performance and rewards (it's the expectancy theory all over again), and has to have the information it needs to do the job in a timely fashion (getting sales figures a month after the event may be interesting, but it is of little use in planning tactics for the team). Many companies make the mistake of setting up teams to work on a project and not allocating resources. What kind of resources? Time, for one! How many times do we set up special project teams and expect them to keep on with their regular jobs at the same time? Time, physical space, money are all resources needed to keep a group functioning effectively.

Third, does the organization have the coaching skills to develop the teams? Not every one of us can naturally work well in a team—we need to learn the teamwork as much as the technical side of our jobs. One major industrial company spent a lot of money putting its top managers through a high-level strategy development course, expecting that when they returned from the course, these managers would lead their own divisions' teams to developing strategies. However, the divisional teams produced very low quality decisions and failed to produce any usable strategies. What had happened? The teams knew what they were supposed to do but had no idea how to work toward their objectives as teams. It is one thing to tell someone to "manage conflict"—but how is that done? Management coaching is critical for the success of teams in organizations.

Over and above these factors that Hackman found, there are others. Does the organizational culture support teamwork? If you put a team together, but every time the team members get together they are criticized by their managers because they are away from their desks, the team is unlikely to be successful.

One last thing an organization can do to help groups be effective is to design the task so that it is interdependent. If the task can be done by individuals, then the time taken by group meetings and so on will lead to lower levels of performance (imagine an assembly line operation that held meetings every week to discuss objectives; this would be unnecessary and costly). However, if the task is redesigned to be interdependent (Volvo's team-based car manufacture or Xerox's teams of service technicians, jointly responsible for servicing a huge territory), then the meetings and time spent in group sessions directly improve the quality and quantity of work produced by the group.

The Group Itself

Characteristics of the group itself have a direct impact on the group's behavior and performance. Specifically, group composition, patterns over time, and interaction patterns all have an effect.

Group Composition

A lot of research has been done into the effects of group composition on performance. A basic requirement for the group is that it have the mix of skills, knowledge, and resources to do the task. If the group has to do financial analyses, make sure the group members have the knowledge and skill to perform the necessary calculations.

One dimension that has been looked at a lot is whether the group is heterogeneous or homogeneous. Homogeneous groups seem to have the advantage of being able to reach decisions faster, but heterogeneous groups may offer the benefit of bringing more alternatives to the table and so generating better-quality decisions. Recent work in the area of top management teams has suggested that the benefits of homogeneity and heterogeneity are contingent on other things: If the external environment is turbulent and experiencing rapid change, then a top team that is homogeneous has advantages for the company; whereas, when the environment is stable, a top team that is heterogeneous is best.

From a manager's point of view, the risks of a homogeneous team are clear: groupthink and lack of breadth of options. However, to successfully manage a heterogeneous team, the members must be able to handle the heterogeneity to minimize the *process losses* and capitalize on the *process gains* of the group. This suggests that it is not the heterogeneity per se that is the issue; rather, it is a matter of how the group manages its members and their differences effectively.

As earlier discussions of institutionalized deviants suggested, being a minority in a group means your contribution is likely to be restricted. So, when you are putting a group together, it would seem to be a good idea to make sure that if minorities are to be included, there is more than one representative from each—for example, put two women in the group rather than one, two engineers rather than one. In this way, you are

more likely to get the benefit of these people's membership than if they were the sole representatives of their
"category."

Patterns over Time

In the 1960s, a five-stage model of how groups developed over time became popular. In this model, the first
stage is *forming,* a time of uncertainty and exploration
into group purpose, behavior, and structure; then
comes a *storming* stage, when large amounts of conflict
emerge about leadership, roles, and task. From this
stage, the group moves into the *norming* stage, when
close relationships develop and group cohesiveness
increases. The fourth stage is *performing,* during which
the group can get down to the business at hand and
begin producing output. The final stage, *adjourning,*
occurs when the immediate task is complete and before
the next project is received, or it involves wrapping up
a temporary group.

While this model is intuitively appealing, there is little evidence to show that it is what really happens in
groups. Its main usefulness is in reminding managers
that conflict is a necessary part of the evolution of
groups—a group with no conflict is unlikely to produce
high-quality work.

More recent work, which actually followed the life of
groups as they worked, has led to the development of
the *punctuated equilibrium* model of group development. This model suggests that, once formed, groups
settle into norms and behaviors very quickly and stay
in those patterns for a while. About halfway through
the project, the group members will experience a *midpoint* transition, when they are likely to rethink their
structure, norms, and processes. From this time on, the
new patterns stay in place until the project is complete.
The implications of this model are that, if you want to
intervene in a group's dynamics or work processes, you
have two chances: at the start and at the midpoint. A
manager can create midpoints by imposing deadlines
and asking for milestone reports and outputs.

Interaction Patterns

Managing groups is different from managing individuals in that you are not just dealing with people, but also
with how they interact. Key interactions a manager
needs to understand and help the team learn to handle
are conflict management, negotiations, giving feedback,
and sharing information. All these are elements of
interpersonal communication and, indeed, most team
members will tell you that the most important thing
teams need to learn is how to listen. But let's take a
quick look at the specifics of these group interactions.

Conflict management.   Research shows that a group
with a high degree of task-related conflict will perform

well, but a group with a high degree of relationship-based conflict will do poorly. Your teams need to be able to distinguish disagreement about how we do the task from disagreement about how we are getting along. It is also important to realize that not all of us handle conflict in the same way, so training in conflict skills such as listening and assertiveness usually helps groups be more effective.

Negotiations. Fisher and Ury's classic work on negotiating applies as much to intragroup interactions as it does to between-party negotiations. Groups that bog down in positional bargaining and try to "cut up the pie" tend not to do as well as groups that look for the interests of the different group members and use these to move toward integrative bargaining, creating new solutions.

A classic example of the difference between these two approaches is the story of the two people who wanted the last orange in the store. They quickly agreed to cut the orange in half, as that seemed fair. However, if each had asked why the other wanted the orange, they would have found out that, while one wanted the juice to drink, the other wanted the peel for a recipe. Both could, in fact, have had 100 percent of what they wanted, if they had taken the time to learn each others' interests in the orange. Groups that search for win-win rather than win-lose solutions to disagreements are likely to last longer.

Giving feedback. There are times in every group when one person doesn't agree with or like how another person is behaving. What if every time I try to put an idea forward, another person interrupts me? I'm going to be frustrated and probably end up being angry at the person—not good news for the group trying to do its job. The skill of giving feedback to people about their behavior in a low-conflict way is valuable to all groups. Effective feedback is immediate and specific and focuses on behavior, not judgmental statements. It also emphasizes the effect the behavior is having on the group's work performance. After all, if certain types of behavior bother you but they don't affect the work of the group, then it's more a matter of you learning to live with the behavior, isn't it?

Sharing information. One of the most important things in groups is sharing information. The main benefit of a group is the breadth of knowledge and experience it has available for problem solving. However, as earlier discussions have indicated, just because something is the sensible and rational thing to do, doesn't mean it always happens. Social influences, politics, conflict can all limit the amount and quality of information sharing that takes place. One tip is to centralize the information the group has so that everyone can see it—and make sure that the group norm is to encourage new information and see it as helpful rather than disruptive. One thing that often happens is that information is heard but misunderstood. Getting group members in the habit of paraphrasing information received is an easy and effective way of checking that the information received is the same as the information sent.

After all this discussion of the difficulties with groups, you may be wondering why organizations bother to utilize groups. The simple answer is that they do so to cut costs. An interdependent, supportive team is often more productive than a selection of individuals. Many companies are actively looking to teams to reduce management layers and increase productivity in all types of work.

As a manager, an important thing to remember about groups is that it is not who's in the group that matters so much as how they interact—and that could be a matter of group composition (ability, knowledge, functional expertise), organizational conditions (Is there a clear direction? Is the team rewarded for team performance rather than individual achievement? Are the resources available for the team to work effectively?), and coaching (Can the team members handle disagreements effectively? Do they have the interpersonal skills needed to work as a group?).

ORGANIZATIONAL LEVEL OF ANALYSIS

One mistake many managers make is to underestimate—or ignore completely—the effect that the structure and systems of the organization have on how people behave. Our discussions of individual and group behavior have probably given you lots of ideas as to how many aspects of an organization can have unintended consequences. (This section is shorter than the others, because we have already covered a lot of the material.) It is important as a manager to think in a systems way (holistically) before attributing performance problems to either the individual or group level.

Four main areas to think through are the structure of the organization, the culture of the organization, the management systems and practices operating in the organization, and change management.

The Structure of the Organization

Basic organizational structure has three components. The first is *complexity:* To what extent are activities broken up? The second is *formalization:* How much are rules and procedures used? And the third is *centralization:* To what extent is decision making kept at a central headquarters unit? All these factors have been shown to influence organizational behavior. A high degree of complexity means work is broken down and is, thus, easy to control and monitor, but this tends to lead to employees missing the big picture. A low degree of complexity, usually resulting in a "flat" organization, can give rise to a high degree of intrinsic motivation, but this places huge demands on communication and time. A high degree of formalization can lead to highly predictable behaviors (creating a consistently strong situation), but it can also reduce innovation and create intense pressures for conformity. A low degree of formalization allows innovation but makes it difficult to produce consistency or measure performance objectively. A high degree of centralization gives an organization tight controls and good information on the rest of the division, as well as ensuring that all divisions are working to a common strategy. However, the low degree of autonomy experienced by the divisions and employees may cause other problems for motivation and performance. A high degree of decentralization allows local responses to customers and a large amount of autonomy to divisional managers but reduces the control and influence that the central organization has for producing a consistent strategy across the board.

One classic way of looking at organizational structure is the *mechanistic/organic* dichotomy. A mechanistic structure is characterized by a high degree of complexity and formalization; a limited, mostly downward information network; and high-level decision making—the typical pyramid organization. An organic structure has a low degree of complexity and formalization; a comprehensive, free-flowing information network; and highly participative decision making. These two structures clearly have very different consequences for the behavior of the people working in them.

Almost all organizations are broken into work divisions. These work divisions are set up in many different ways—by function, by geographic location, by product, by process, by customer—or by a combination of any of these (a *matrix* structure). Which structure is best depends on what your company does and how it does its work. The thing to remember is that people will tend to identify with their in-group and that communication across divisions will need to be actively managed.

Informal systems evolve within each division, leading to other divisions being viewed as different and, therefore, not as valuable. As a manager, you need to be aware of this and be prepared to actively manage cross-divisional information flows, communications, and the interaction between the divisional cultures, especially when the tasks are highly interdependent.

The Culture of the Organization

For most people, organizational culture is something they cannot define, but they know it when they see it. It can perhaps be best understood as the set of informal rules, relationships, and norms that determine what is acceptable and unacceptable behavior within the organization. Organizational culture can often have a more powerful influence on behavior than the formal structures and systems. If you view the organization as a very large group, then all the factors we discussed in the section on group-level analysis can apply at the organizational level with respect to the informal systems in operation. An example of how the informal culture can undermine the intentions of your formal systems is the role that peer pressure plays in performance: However great the incentive pay, however good the reward system, if the culture has norms of low effort and low performance, then that is what you will get.

A manager needs to pay as much attention to the informal organization as to the formal structure and systems. Management by walking around, by listening, and by keeping in touch with the grapevine all help you to collect information on this element of the organization. Culture can be managed: Modeling and reinforcing certain types of behavior can set a different tone and, in many organizations, you will see many, very different subcultures operating, showing how different managers can develop different informal systems—regardless of whether they intend to.

Management Systems and Practices

Within an organization, the management systems also have consequences for organizational behavior. In particular, decision-making systems and human resource management systems have strong effects.

Decision-Making Systems:

How are decisions made in your company? Are they made on an ad hoc, intuitive basis, or are they based on facts and information? Are the decisions made from the top down, or is decision making participative? How are decisions evaluated? The answers to all these questions have effects on how people in your organization behave.

If company decisions are made on a nonrational basis, then your employees are likely to do the same. It is difficult to persuade people to follow a time-consuming, rational model if no one else in the company does it and there is little support for the time and effort it takes. In addition, how likely am I to put together a closely reasoned report to send to senior management, investing time and energy, if I know that management's decision is going to be based on intuition or politics?

Participation in decision making has been shown to improve motivation and job satisfaction and reduce turnover and absenteeism. Top-down directives may be quick and easy, but they may miss some critical points that only the people on the front line know. Don't get confused though: Participation does not mean democracy. Top management is still ultimately responsible for the decisions an organization makes.

Whether decisions are evaluated will also have an effect on how much effort people put into the decision in the first place—remember, motivation is related to the belief that effort leads to an outcome. If decisions aren't evaluated, then how can there be positive outcomes related to my effort?

Human Resource Management Systems

Recruitment and selection, career development, and reward and recognition systems have crucial impacts on motivation and performance.

Although much of what we have discussed in this chapter suggests that it is behavior that is important rather than personality, there is one area where personality assessment is used a lot: in recruitment. The important thing for both company and employees is that there is a *fit* between what the company needs and what the employee wants. If an employee is highly authoritarian, he or she is unlikely to feel comfortable and perform well in a flat organization. Recruiting and selecting the right people on the basis of skills, knowledge, and fit are critical to developing performance-enhancing cultures and a satisfied workforce.

Career development can act as a reward to most people, and a lack of opportunity to move upward and onward can be a huge demotivator for employees. It is also critical that promotions are seen as being based on performance rather than on politics. Political promotions are often seen by employees as being outside their control, whereas, if performance is the basis of promotion, then motivation to perform well is increased.

If you think back to most of the motivation theories, the outcomes of behavior are important to the effort exerted. If I get rewarded for a particular form of behavior, I'll probably keep doing it; if I'm punished, I'll stop (most of the time). Many reward systems are left over from a company's early days and do little to encourage the behavior the company wants to see in the workplace.

As a simple example, a piece-rate pay system should encourage people to work harder and produce more, but can end up with the people paying so much attention to quantity that quality suffers. Performance-based compensation sounds like a great idea—until you realize that everybody's efforts are focused on getting good reviews and making good impressions at review time, rather than producing high-quality work all year round. It is important to remember that rewards aren't just about money: Promotion opportunities, benefits, and many other aspects of the job can be perceived as rewards by employees. Many companies are capitalizing on this by using flexible benefit packages rather than standard reward systems.

One last point on rewards: If you have a team working on a team task (i.e., an interdependent task), then you need to make sure the rewards are also interdependent, or you will be encouraging individual competition rather than team support.

Change Management

One of the areas where the knowledge of organizational behavior is making its biggest contribution is that of change management. Understanding why people behave the way they do includes understanding why they resist change and how that resistance might be overcome. It has been said that there is nothing new about effective change management; it is simply effective management with a new name. This is, indeed, close to the truth. Applying the principles of organizational behavior, the role of needs, motivation, social influences, and structure and systems will usually result in effective change implementation.

SUMMARY

If you retain only three points from this chapter, they should be the following:

1. How people behave is contingent upon individual, group, and organizational factors. You need to explore and understand these to understand why a person is behaving a certain way.

2. Thinking things through is critical; otherwise, your actions may well have unintended, dysfunctional consequences.

3. Organizational behavior is the *systematic* study of human behavior in organizations—there is nothing soft about it; it is probably the hardest subject on the MBA curriculum to truly master. (Ask any manager.)

Finally, managing people without understanding organizational behavior is like trying to fly without understanding aerodynamics—it can be done, but it will never be done very well.

ORGANIZATIONAL BEHAVIOR

Ability

This refers to an individual's capacity to perform the tasks of a given job, involving an assessment of what a person is potentially capable of doing.

Anchoring

Anchoring is when a previous piece of information influences later decisions. For example, if the first price you are quoted is high, you are more likely to end up offering a higher price for a product than if the original number was lower. First impressions and reputations can also have anchoring effects.

Arbitration

Arbitration involves the use of a third party to decide between two sides deadlocked in negotiation. The arbitrator's decision can be binding or nonbinding, as previously agreed upon by the negotiating parties.

Asch Experiments

In these classic studies by Solomon Asch, groups of seven or eight people were put in a classroom and shown two cards by the experimenter. The first card had a single line on it; the second card had three lines, each of a different length. Ostensibly, the task was for each person in the group to say which of the three lines was the same length as the single line on the first card. The right answer was quite obvious and, under normal conditions, people choose the right answer more than 99 percent of the time. In these experiments, however, all but one of the group were confederates of the experimenter, and only one person was the true, unsuspecting subject of the experiment. In each case, the subject was the last person to say which line matched. One by one, the other group members gave the same, incorrect answer. In about 35 percent of the cases, the subject agreed with the rest of the group, even though the answer was obviously wrong. The Asch experiments showed that conformity pressures can lead individuals to make incorrect choices in the interest of going along with and remaining a member of a group.

Attitudes

Attitudes are evaluative statements, either favorable or unfavorable, reflecting how an individual feels about something. When I say "I like my job," I am expressing my attitude about work. Attitude may or may not be related to behavior and it is important to separate attitude and behavior in order to be an effective manager. Some job-related attitudes of particular interest to managers are job satisfaction, job involvement, and organizational commitment.

Attribution

When individuals observe behavior, they attempt to determine if it is internally or externally caused. *Internally caused* means we believe it to be under the personal control of the individual. For example, someone missed a deadline because the person is lazy. *Externally caused* means we believe the behavior is a result of outside causes. For example, someone missed the deadline because we have given the person too heavy a workload. This links to the *fundamental attribution error,* which is the tendency to underestimate the influence of internal factors concerning one's own behavior and overestimate the influence of internal factors when making judgments about other people's behavior. For example, if I do well on a project, I will attribute it to my own abilities. If I see someone else doing well on a project, I will attribute it to external factors such as luck or timing. Conversely, if I do poorly on a project, I will attribute it to external factors. If I see someone else doing poorly, I will likely attribute it to internal factors. This is commonly known as the *self-serving bias.*

Autonomy

Autonomy can be a characteristic of a person or of a job. In a person, autonomy is the need to have freedom and discretion in managing work and/or life decisions. In a job, it is the degree to which the task provides the freedom and discretion to an employee to decide how to perform the work.

Bounded Rationality

This is the concept that people try to follow a rational decision-making process but are constrained by their ability to handle complexity. They therefore act rationally within the bounds of their ability to process information and so on.

Brainstorming

This is an idea-generation process that specifically encourages any and all alternatives while withholding any criticism of those alternatives.

Bureaucracy

The word *bureaucracy* was first used by Max Weber to describe a type of organization characterized by division of labor, clearly defined hierarchy, detailed rules and regulations, and impersonal relationships. Originally described as an ideal type of organization, this theory was used as the design prototype for many of today's large organizations. The word *bureaucracy* is often used to represent only the negative characteristics of this type of organization.

Causality and Correlation

Often there may be a correlation between two events: That is, when event A happens, event B tends to happen. However, this does not mean that A causes B; causality is not the same as correlation. An example is that statistics show a correlation between the growth rate of grass and the consumption of gasoline. Does this mean that increased use of gasoline makes the grass grow? Unlikely. In fact, there is a separate, common, causal factor: Grass grows most in the spring and summer, when the weather is better. The amount of travel by families in the United States increases in the summer, hence, the greater gasoline consumption. The season is the causal factor. The message here is to make sure you are not mistaking correlation for causality: Be systematic.

Centralization

Concentrating decision making at a single point in the organization makes the organization more centralized.

Charismatic Leadership

Some leaders are attributed with extraordinary leadership abilities by their followers. These charismatic leaders tend to behave in similar ways: They have a compelling sense of vision or purpose, they can communicate that vision in terms their followers can identify with, they show consistency and focus in pursuit of that vision, and they know and capitalize on their own strengths (Warren Bennis has done much work in this area). It has been shown that such behavior can be learned and still have a great impact on group performance. People will exert extra effort for a charismatic leader, but it may not always be appropriate to be working toward an ideological goal. In a crisis, the charismatic leader can help an organization, but when the organization is stable again, the charismatic leader can become a liability, as the "clear vision" becomes an unjustifiable belief in the leader's own "rightness" and can be disruptive to the organization.

Coercion

Coercion refers to the use of force to get someone to do something. The force can be physical intimidation or use of sanctions ("You'll do this or else"). Once an accepted form of management ("Do the work or you will lose your job"), coercion has become less accepted by today's workforce and is more likely to lead to reactance and resistance than to performance.

Cognitive Dissonance

In the late 1950s, Leon Festinger proposed the theory of cognitive dissonance, which is the inconsistency that someone might see between two attitudes or between a behavior and an attitude. For example, if you hold the attitude that honesty is important and yet you take a sick day to go see your baseball team in the playoffs, you are likely to experience dissonance. Festinger proposed that people will seek out a state in which there is the lowest possible dissonance. To achieve this, people can do one of four things: They can change their behavior to match their attitudes ("I'll stop lying"), they can reduce the importance of the behavior ("Well, it didn't really impact the company, and it wasn't really lying"), they can change their attitudes ("Why's honesty so important anyway?"), or they can seek out offsetting elements ("Well, I did work all last weekend for the company, so I deserve this break"). People tend to change their attitudes only when they see events as something they had control over: If my boss gave me the tickets, I'd just blame her for everything and experience very little dissonance at all. Another important thing is that, if a person is rewarded for the dissonant behavior, you are unlikely to see attitude change; the dissonant behavior will be attributed to the reward rather than to any internal process.

Cognitive Processes

These are active thought processes people use to interpret the world and the information they receive. Reinforcement theory assumes that cognitive processes play no part in human behavior, whereas the calculative theories of motivation explicitly focus on cognitive processes.

Cohesiveness/Cohesion

The technical definition of cohesiveness is "a measure of the degree to which group members are attracted to each other and are motivated to stay in the group." There is some discussion as to whether the two elements of cohesiveness would be better addressed separately—that people can be motivated to stay in a group regardless of their attraction to the other members. Attraction does not necessarily mean liking. Group members can be cohesive and still not actively like each other in a social sense.

Collectivism

One of Hofstede's dimensions was the individualism/collectivism continuum. Collectivism is the degree to which a national culture or, in more recent usage, an individual believes that society should be based on a tight social framework in which people are responsible to and for other people for care and support. Someone with a great commitment to collectivism believes groups are the natural way that people work and live, and that group needs have priority over individual desires—the group comes first.

Commitment

Organizational commitment is an attitude reflecting how much an employee identifies with an organization and its goals and wants to remain a member of the organization. High levels of organizational commitment are related to low levels of absenteeism and turnover.

Conditioning

Classical conditioning is about learning a conditioned response. This response is built by associating a conditioned stimulus (e.g., the ringing of a bell) with an unconditioned stimulus (e.g., offering a plate of meat). A dog shown a plate of meat will salivate. If the bell is rung every time the meat is offered, the dog learns to associate the bell directly with food. From that point, simply ringing the bell causes the dog to salivate, even when there is no meat in view: The dog now has a conditioned response to the bell ringing. A simple human-related example of classical conditioning is always putting on your best suit for job interviews, when you also happen to be on your most professional behavior. Eventually, the act of putting on your best suit will lead you to be on your best behavior, regardless of whether you have an interview. Classical conditioning is essentially passive, an automatic response to stimuli. *Operant conditioning* involves cognitive processes. In operant conditioning, behavior is seen as a function of its consequences: People learn to behave a certain way to get something they want or avoid something they don't want. If Pavlov is the father of classical conditioning, then the father of operant conditioning is B. F. Skinner. A simple example of operant conditioning is a reward system: You work because you get money—a very pleasant consequence. It also works in reverse: If you work very hard and get no reward (or are actually "punished" by criticism from your peers), you are less likely to work hard again.

Contingency Approach

Organizational behavior relies on a contingency approach to management in both theory and practice.

It is the study of human beings in organizations, and human beings are very complex. Two people may act differently in the same situation, and the same person's behavior may change in different situations. For example, not everyone is motivated by money, although some people are. This complexity means that organizational behavior must reflect situational behavior or contingency conditions. We can say that behavior X leads to outcome Y but only under conditions Z (where X, Y, Z are the contingency variables). An example would be that an employee's effort leads to high productivity if the equipment is working at 100 percent efficiency. Hence, the state of the equipment becomes the contingency variable. I was once asked, "Are you a contingency theorist?" I replied, "It depends." This is the essence of organizational behavior.

Delphi technique

In this technique for group decision making, members separately compile their judgments. These judgments are pooled and circulated for discussion, then individually the judgments are redone. The process is iterated until agreement is reached. The emphasis on compiling judgments separately helps avoid groupthink. This method is frequently used to capture and clarify expert thinking on ambiguous matters.

Demographics

Originally the study of the distribution of populations along certain characteristics, this term is now used to cover individual differences such as age, education level, tenure in the organization, cultural background, gender, and race.

Dependency

This is the key to power: The greater a person's dependency on you, the more power you have over that person. Dependency can increase if the resource you control is important, scarce, and nonsubstitutable.

Devil's Advocate

This refers to an explicit role undertaken by a group member who actively questions and challenges the group's ideas, process, and decisions. Such active questioning helps reduce the risk of groupthink.

Dialectic Inquiry

This is a method for group decision making in which members are forced to debate both sides of an issue. Dialectic inquiry forces consideration of factors that might otherwise not be considered and then examined. It has been shown to reduce the potential of groupthink and enhance the quality of decision making.

Distributive Bargaining

This is an approach to negotiation that seeks to divide a fixed amount of resources.

Diversity

This refers to differences, usually along ethnic, racial, gender, or religious lines. A diverse workforce is usually seen as one with a wider range of members than a less diverse workforce. Learning to cope with a diverse workforce is an increasing challenge for most companies. Different social groups have different values, attitudes, and ideas for what is and is not appropriate workplace behavior. Motivating and managing across and within these differences is a relatively modern challenge for managers.

Divisional Structure

Some companies run as a number of separate, autonomous business units, coordinated by a central headquarters. This is a divisional structure.

Division of Labor

When a job is broken down into its component parts and each part is given to a different specialist, the labor has been divided. This is the basic principle of division of labor. Originally developed along with capitalism, this approach to work increased efficiency, led to work and method studies, and ultimately resulted in the assembly line manufacturing process. While the upside of division of labor is increased efficiency, the downside is often decreased effectiveness, as employees lose sight of the big picture and how their roles impact the company.

Downsizing

This is a euphemism for large-scale layoffs to reduce the workforce in an organization.

Drives

Much of the field of psychology rests on the principle that human beings have certain drives that they need to fulfill and that fulfilling these drives provides the force for most of our behavior.

Effectiveness and Efficiency

Effectiveness is doing the right thing; efficiency is doing it with a good balance of inputs to outputs. You can be

100 percent efficient, but still not get anywhere because you are doing the wrong thing (i.e., 0 percent effective).

Electronic Brainstorming

In this form of brainstorming, individuals enter their ideas via computer from geographically separate locations.

Empowerment

Empowerment is the outcome of processes, decisions, and procedures that increase employees' intrinsic motivation. Empowered employees perceive their work as meaningful and themselves as having responsibility and being able to influence their own and other people's activities. Empowerment is a popular buzzword, but achieving true empowerment requires a large investment in system and employee development.

Equity Theory

This theory proposes that individuals calculate their outcome/input ratio. Equity theory recognizes that motivation is not only the outcome of an absolute calculation but also of a relative calculation. If employees calculate that others are getting more outcome (salary, success) for the same input (effort), they perceive inequity. When people perceive an imbalance in their outcome/input ratio, tension is created, which provides a basis for motivation as people strive for perceived equity and fairness. Based on equity theory, in a situation of perceived inequity, employees can be predicted to make one of several choices. They can change their inputs (decrease effort), they can change their outcomes (increase productivity), or they can reframe the situation (distorting perceptions by changing the referent other). Equity theory is not limited to financial aspects. It has been shown that job titles as well as office space and selection for project groups may also function as outcomes for some employees in their equity equations.

Expectancy Theory

One of the most widely accepted theories of motivation supported by research evidence is Victor Vroom's expectancy theory. This theory argues that motivational force $F = E * I * V$. E is *expectancy*, that is, the expectation that performance will lead to the promised reward. I is *instrumentality*, or the expectation that effort will lead to performance. V is *valency*, or the reward/outcome valued. In other words, the strength of a person's motivation to exert effort on a task will depend on whether doing well on the task will lead to positive benefits (e.g., performance-based compensation), whether making the effort will result in achieving the performance level required (e.g., in some cases an individual might be working very hard but because of situational factors might not be able to meet the performance standards), or whether reward for reaching the performance level actually matters to the individual. Expectancy theory therefore shows that to effectively motivate people it is important to understand an individual's goals and three sets of linkages: (1) between effort and performance, (2) between performance and rewards, (3) between rewards and individual goal satisfaction. While more sophisticated models of motivation are available, most organizations find it hard enough to meet the requirements of this simple, three-factor equation. Expectancy theory is a powerful tool for managers trying to motivate employees.

Extrinsic

Extrinsic means "from outside." Extrinsic motivation refers to the desire to exert effort because of an external incentive, such as pay or recognition. There is some discussion as to whether external rewards can lead to a reduction in *intrinsic* motivation (such as a sense of achievement, satisfaction). In some cases, where the intrinsic motivation is a result of dissonance-resolving attitude change (e.g., I don't get paid much for this job, so I must like it to be still doing it), there is evidence that increasing the external rewards (pay) leads to a reduction in intrinsic motivation. In other cases, where the intrinsic motivation seems more a result of an internal need being met (e.g., a sense of achievement), then external rewards do not seem to have a significant effect.

Feedback

Feedback involves giving individuals direct and clear information about their effectiveness. Feedback can come from a person or from the job itself. If you as a manager are guiding feedback, it will be more effective if it is given immediately and if it is behavioral (rather than based on personality or attitudes), specific, and gives clear information on how to improve. For example, telling someone his or her work rate "sucks" is not feedback. Instead, say, "Last week your performance was down by 10 percent; I think it is because you were late on Tuesday and Wednesday, so I think you can correct this by being on time in future." Most often, it is a goofy idea to state your perception of the problem and ask the person concerned for suggestions as to how to improve the situation. People tend to be more committed to following through on their own suggestions than on those made by others.

Fiedler Contingency Model

This was the first comprehensive contingency model for leadership, proposing that effective groups depend upon a proper match between a leader style and situational context.

Flat Organization

An organization with the minimum number of management layers between policymakers and front-line workers is flat.

Flexible Benefits

This refers to programs in which employees tailor benefit packages to meet their individual needs by picking and choosing from a menu of benefit options.

Functional Silo

This phrase refers to the tendency of departments to become isolated from one another in a functionally structured organization.

Fundamental Attribution Error

See Attribution.

Goal-Setting Theory

Edwin Locke proposed that intentions to work toward a goal are major sources of work motivation. The theory states that specific and difficult goals lead to higher performance. Research has shown that the key to the effectiveness of goal setting is not necessarily whether employees participate in setting the goals, but rather that the goals are accepted and agreed upon by employees.

Groupthink

This refers to a condition whereby group pressures for conformity prevent the group from critically evaluating alternative viewpoints. The classic example of groupthink, the Bay of Pigs incident,[1] shows how a narrow focus and lack of analysis can lead to potentially disastrous decisions made by a group.

Halo Effect

This involves drawing a general impression of an individual based on a single characteristic. For example, if someone is well-dressed, you might assume the person is intelligent, even if there is no evidence for this characteristic.

Heuristics

Heuristic means "by trial and error." In organizational behavior, the phrase *heuristics* refers to the set of implicit biases and decision-making roles that individuals hold in their minds as a result of previous experience, misunderstanding of probability, and selective perception. These rules of thumb often lead to less-than-optimal decisions.

Hierarchy of Needs

Probably the most well-known theory of motivation, Maslow's hierarchy of needs suggests that every human being has a hierarchy of five needs. An individual moves progressively through this hierarchy, which, from lowest to highest, comprises physiological, safety, social, esteem, and self-actualization needs. According to Maslow, if you want to motivate someone, you need to first understand what level of the hierarchy that person is currently on and focus on meeting the needs at that level. The theory's intuitive logic and ease of understanding make it appealing to managers. However, research does not generally validate the theory.

Hygiene Factors

Hertzberg suggested that there are some factors that motivate people, leading to performance and job satisfaction, and there are other, separate factors that prevent dissatisfaction. These hygiene factors, such as company policy, relationship with supervisor, work conditions, and salary, will, when adequate, prevent dissatisfaction. However, they alone are not sufficient for leading to job satisfaction. Hertzberg's theory of separate motivation and hygiene factors has been criticized for his methodology and for ignoring situational factors. Nevertheless, it is widely read and demonstrates that satisfaction and dissatisfaction are not necessarily two ends of the same continuum.

Impression Management

In this process, individuals attempt to control the impressions that others form of them.

Integrative Bargaining

In this approach to negotiating, each side explores the interests of the other and seeks mutually satisfactory outcomes (i.e., collaborating rather than compromising).

Job Analysis

This involves developing a detailed description of the tasks involved in a job and ascertaining the knowledge, skills, and abilities necessary for an employee to perform the job successfully.

Job Characteristics Model

Hackman and Oldham's model identifies five job characteristics and their relationships to personal and work outcomes. Using the model, work can be redesigned to increase the level of motivation: the *motivating potential score*. There are five core job dimensions:

1. *Skill variety:*   Can the worker use a number of different skills and talents?
2. *Task identity:*   Does the worker complete a whole and identifiable piece of work?
3. *Task significance:*   Does the work have substantial consequences for the lives and work of other people?
4. *Autonomy:*   Does the worker have freedom, independence, and discretion in carrying out the work?
5. *Feedback:*   Do individuals receive direct and clear information about their effectiveness?

The first three characteristics increase the perceived meaningfulness of the work. Autonomy leads to increases in perceived personal responsibility. Feedback gives the individual knowledge of the actual results of the activities. These three *critical psychological states* (meaningfulness, responsibility, and knowledge) lead to the following personal and work outcomes: a high degree of internal work motivation, high-quality work performance, a high degree of satisfaction, and a low rate of absenteeism and turnover.

Job Description

This is a written statement of what a jobholder does, how the job is done, and why it is done. It includes a description of work environment and conditions of employment.

Job Design

This refers to the way the tasks are combined to form a complete job. Job *redesign* focuses on changing the task combination or the way the task is done to enhance motivation and/or productivity.

Job Enlargement

This refers to the horizontal expansion of jobs: It increases the diversity in overspecialized jobs but does little to instill challenge or meaning in the workers' activities.

Job Enrichment

This refers to the vertical expansion of jobs. Unlike rotation and enlargement, enrichment actively seeks to increase the meaningfulness, challenge, and skill variety of workers' activities.

Job Rotation

This refers to the periodic shifting of a worker from one task to another with similar skill requirements. While providing variety, which can increase motivation for some employees, job rotation does little to change the nature of the work itself.

Job Specification

This states the minimum acceptable qualifications that an employee must possess to perform the job successfully.

Leader-Participation Model

Victor Vroom and Phillip Yetton developed this model, which provides a set of rules to determine the form and amount of participative decision making in different situations.

Locus of Control

Some people see themselves as very much in control of their lives. Others see themselves as pawns of fate. If you believe you are in control, you are said to have an internal locus of control; the pawns are said to have an external locus of control.

Management by Objectives (MBO)

This management technique is based on goal-setting theory, in which employees are given specific measurable objectives to achieve. MBO has been shown to be successful when the goals are realistic, when there is top management commitment, and when feedback and rewards are contingent on goal accomplishment.

Managerial Grid

Blake and Mouton proposed a managerial grid extending the two-dimensional view of leadership style into a 9×9 matrix. Along one axis is concern for people. Along the other is concern for production. Blake and Mouton's findings suggested that managers perform best under a 9,9 style that is high in both concern for people and concern for production. This model does not take into account situational factors.

Matrix Structure

This organizational structure creates dual lines of authority (e.g., combining functional and departmental lines of organization).

Mechanistic Structure

This is an organizational structure characterized by a high degree of formalization, a high degree of complexity, and centralization.

Mediation

The use of a third party to facilitate a negotiated solution is mediation.

Motivation

Motivation is the willingness to exert high levels of effort toward organizational goals. It is usually conditioned by the efforts and ability to satisfy some individual need.

Nominal Group Technique

This is a group decision-making method in which individual members meet face to face, first to generate ideas individually and then to poll their judgments. Their decision is determined by the aggregate ranking of their ideas.

Norms

Norms are structural features of a group that represent group approvals for various behaviors. Norms can be explicitly agreed upon or can come about through tacit informal processes by which group members learn which behaviors are acceptable and unacceptable in the given group. Norms can be performance enhancing or performance disabling.

Ohio State Studies

These studies, undertaken at Ohio State University in the 1920s, identified two categories accounting for most leadership behavior as described by subordinates. The first behavior is *initiating structure:* the extent to which a leader defines and structures the roles of the group. The second behavior is *consideration:* the extent to which a leader develops job relationships based on mutual trust and respect for ideas and regard for feelings. This model does not take into account situational factors.

Organic Structure

This organizational structure is characterized by a low degree of formalization, a low degree of complexity, and decentralization.

Organizational Culture

This refers to a common perception held by the organization's members, or a system of shared meaning. For most people, organizational culture is something they cannot define, but they know it when they see it. It can perhaps be best understood as the set of informal rules, relationships, and norms that determine what is acceptable and unacceptable behavior within the organization. Organizational culture can often have a more powerful influence on behavior than the formal structures and systems.

Participative Management

This umbrella term encompasses management techniques in which employees share a significant degree of decision-making power with managers. These techniques include MBO, consultation committees, employee representation of policymaking bodies, group decision making, self-managed teams, and many other activities. Participative management draws on a number of motivation theories; for example, it is consistent with Theory Y, as it provides intrinsic motivation in line with Hertzberg's approach and meets the higher levels of Maslow's hierarchy of needs. It can also be seen to relate to employees' needs for achievement, power, and affiliation. Several European countries have firmly established principles of *industrial democracy* (France, Germany, Holland, Scandinavia), suggesting that the use of participative management techniques could be related to cultural values and beliefs about how organizations "should" work. More recently, here in America the use of self-managed teams to increase productivity and reduce costs has restored interest in participative management as an effective organizational management technique.

Performance Appraisal

This procedure is used in most organizations to evaluate employees' performance and decide on pay awards each year. In theory, performance appraisal is a valuable system for receiving information on obstacles to high-quality performance and for providing feedback to employees on their work, processes, and outcomes. In practice, many performance appraisal systems become politicized due the linkage of appraisal results and pay awards. More recently, in an effort to increase the value of the feedback element of the process, some organizations have moved to 360-degree feedback programs and peer appraisal systems.

Performance-Based Compensation

This refers to the practice of paying employees on the basis of performance measure. Instead of paying a person for time on the job, pay reflects productivity, quality, or some other aspect of the job, which can be effectively measured. Effectiveness of performance-based compensation depends, as theorists suggest, on two main factors: (1) Is the compensation valued? and (2) is the performance within the employee's control?

Personality Traits

These comprise characteristics that describe an individual's behavior over a range of situations. The consistency and frequency of the characteristic relates to the importance of the trait in describing the individual. For example, if someone is consistently outgoing in most situations, the person can be described as having the personality trait of an extrovert. The value of personality traits as predictors of employee behavior is limited because they ignore situational contexts. They may be valuable in explaining the behavior of individuals with extreme traits, but, in general, personality traits are dependent upon the situation in which the individual is an actor. A number of specific personality attributes have been isolated as having potential for predicting behavior in organizations. These include locus of control, achievement orientation, self-esteem, self-monitoring, and risk taking.

Political Behavior

This refers to behavior that is not required as part of one's formal role in the organization, but that influences, or attempts to influence, the distribution of advantages and disadvantages in the organization. Legitimate political behavior would be that which moves the organization toward fulfilling its goals (e.g., forming coalitions in meetings to make sure high-quality decisions are made). Illegitimate political behavior is that which effectively prevents the organization from reaching its goals, perhaps being aimed more at personal gain.

Positional Bargaining

In this approach to negotiation, each side takes a position, argues for it, and makes concessions to reach a compromise.

Power

Power is the capacity to influence the behavior of other people so they do things they would not otherwise do. The most important aspect of power is dependency. The greater a person's dependency on you, the more power you have in that relationship. For example, a machine operator might seem to have little power, but the organization is dependent on the operator to make the product it sells. Therefore, the machine operator has power within the organization. The most commonly referred to sources of power are:

1. *Coercive power*—power based on fear

2. *Reward power*—power to give positive benefits to people

3. *Position power*—power arising from a position in an organizational hierarchy or group

4. *Expert power*—influence based on special skills or knowledge

5. *Referent power*—influence held based on people's admiration and desire to model themselves after you

Like many things, power itself is neither good nor bad—it is how it is used by managers that makes the difference.

Punctuated Equilibrium Model

Connie Gersick's recent model of group development challenges the traditional forming/norming/storming/performing view of group development. Gersick's research showed that a group tends to follow a trajectory up to the midpoint of the project. At this midpoint, there is a concentrated set of changes in norms, processes, and behaviors within the group. After this midpoint, the group settles on a new trajectory. This model suggests, and subsequent research has indicated that interventions aimed at improving group effectiveness are most successfully made at the midpoint of a group's life. Managers can create midpoints through the setting of milestones and intermediate deadlines.

Rational Decision Making

This decision-making process is held up as the ideal way to make decisions. It assumes that the person making the decision is fully objective and logical and can make choices that are consistent and value maximizing. It also assumes that the decision maker has a clear goal and complete information and that there is a single, optimal solution. However, the method explicitly ignores the human factors in decision making, such as heuristics and organizational politics.

Reinforcement

There are four ways to shape behavior: positive reinforcement, negative reinforcement, punishment, and extinction. *Positive reinforcement* is following your response to a type of behavior with something pleasant—for example, praising an employee for a job well done. *Negative reinforcement* is avoiding something unpleasant as a result of response to a particular type of behavior. For example, if employees are missing deadlines, you could constantly call to remind them to complete their jobs in a timely manner. These calls are unpleasant to employees and they learn that by not picking up the phone they can avoid unpleasantness. *Punishment* is causing an unpleasant consequence to try to eliminate unwanted behavior—for example, suspending an employee without pay for arriving at work intoxicated. *Extinction* is the removal of any reinforcements currently maintaining a particular type of behavior. If you wish to discourage employees from asking questions at meetings, simply ignore them and they will soon stop asking questions. Positive reinforcement and punishment are the methods of shaping behavior that are most easily understood and most commonly applied by managers. Praising someone for doing well and punishing someone for doing badly are intuitively logical. However, negative reinforcement and extinction have a tremendous potential to effect an organization. Much apparently irrational behavior by employees can be seen, on analysis, to be the logical consequence of unintended negative reinforcement. Extinction also influences behavior in organizations. If, as a manager, you are too busy to act on many of your employees' ideas, over time your employees will learn not to generate ideas. You are extinguishing their idea-generating behavior.

Retrenchment

This refers to the refocusing of organizational forces and effort on core businesses and the divestment of peripheral interests.

Self-Esteem

This refers to an individual's degree of respect, liking, or valuing of him- or herself. It is the perception of self-worth. While this trait does vary for an individual in different situations, it has been found that most people have an underlying sense of self-esteem. Individuals with high self-esteem are more likely to attribute their successes internally and their failures externally, and have high expectations of achievement. Individuals with low self-esteem tend to attribute their successes externally and their failures internally. People with low self-esteem show more placidity of behavior, as they are more easily influenced by feedback than are people with high self-esteem.

Self-Fulfilling Prophecy

Research has shown that, if a manager is told that an employee has great potential, that employee will out-perform other people working for the manager. The expectation of high performance leads the manager to behave in ways that actually result in the employee performing well. This is known as the self-fulfilling prophecy. The self-fulfilling prophecy can lead to the *Pygmalion effect,* or the *golem effect,* when negative expectations lead to negative outcomes.

Self-Managed Teams

In these teams, the members themselves not only per-form the work, but also measure, monitor, and manage their performance.

Self-Monitoring

This personality trait reflects an individual's ability to adjust behavior to match situational factors. Individuals who exhibit a high degree of self-monitoring are very adaptable and responsive to internal cues.

Self-Serving Bias

See Attribution.

Situational Leadership Theory

A widely practiced leadership model developed by Paul Hersey and Ken Blanchard, this contingency theory focuses on followers and defines leadership effective-ness in terms of whether the leader is accepted or rejected. Situational leadership uses the same task and relationship dimensions. Depending on the maturity of the followers, the ability and willingness of people to take responsibility for their own behavior, leaders should use one of four specific styles: telling (high task, low relationship), selling (high task, high relationship), participating (low task, high relationship), or delegating (low task, low relationship).

Social Information Processing Model

Employees adopt attitudes and behaviors in response to the social cues of others with whom they have con-tact. This means that an employee's perception of the job or work environment often has more influence on his or her behavior than the manager's perceived reality.

Social Loafing

This refers to the tendency of some group members to exert less effort in a group situation than if they were working individually.

Span of Control

The number of subordinates that a manager can efficiently and effectively direct is the manager's span of control.

Stereotype

A stereotype is the tendency to judge someone based on the perception of the group to which that person belongs. For example, if I know a person is athletic I might stereotype the person as a "jock." This would then influence how I approach, interact with, and manage that person. Stereotypes are one of several shortcuts we use when evaluating other people, and they may or may not be accurate.

Task Interdependence

This refers to the extent to which a task requires people to work interdependently for successful completion. For example, making a car can be designed as a series of independent tasks (i.e., an assembly line). Alternatively, it can be designed as a highly interdependent task in which a group of people work together to produce a car (e.g., Volvo in Sweden). Research has shown that, for self-managed teams to be effective, their work needs to be designed as a highly interdependent task. Where task interdependence is high, reward interdependence should also be high.

Theory of Needs

David McClelland proposed that three needs are important in organizational settings for understanding motivation: (1) the need for achievement, which is the drive to excel and desire to do things better; (2) the need for power, which is the desire to be influential; and (3) the need for affiliation, which is the desire to be liked and accepted by others. McClelland proposed that individuals differ in which need is most important to them. Therefore, to effectively motivate employees, it is important to understand each individual's primary need and match the work and management style appropriately.

Theory X and Theory Y

Douglas McGregor suggested that managers hold two distinctive views of their employees and that these views have implications for how managers motivate their workers. Theory X assumes that employees dislike work, are lazy, dislike responsibility, and must be coerced to perform. Theory Y assumes that employees like work, are creative, seek responsibility, and can exercise self-direction. McGregor proposed that the Theory Y assumptions were more valid than those of Theory X. Therefore, participation, responsibility, and good group relations would maximize employee motivation.

Total Quality Management (TQM)

TQM is an organization-wide set of systems processes and management procedures aimed at high-quality performance. TQM, originally a clearly defined technique, now encompasses almost any quality improvement practices.

Trait Theories of Leadership

This refers to theories that sort personality, social, physical, or intellectual qualities that differentiate leaders from nonleaders. Six traits identified are ambition and energy, the desire to lead, honesty and integrity, self-confidence, intelligence, and job-relevant knowledge. Research shows only a modest correlation between these traits and effective leadership. The trait approach also overlooks the needs of followers and doesn't separate cause from effect (e.g., are leaders self-confident to start with or does leadership experience build self-confidence?).

Transactional Leader

One who guides or motivates followers toward goals by clarifying role and task requirements is a transactional leader.

Transformational Leader

One who excites and inspires followers through intellectual stimulation and charisma is a transformational leader.

Unity of Command

This is the principle that each subordinate should be responsible to only one manager.

Values

Values are basic convictions or beliefs that specific behaviors and outcomes are more desirable than others. Values are judgmental in that they include our ideas of what is right, good, or moral. Values are important in organizational behavior because they influence attitudes, motivations, and perceptions. An individual's belief as to what ought and ought not to be will influence their behavior in the workplace and what they see as acceptable and unacceptable management styles. For example, if you have a meritocratic value, (i.e., people should be paid on the basis of performance and not on the basis of time served), you are likely to evaluate a pay system based on seniority as wrong, bad, and unfair.

MORE READINGS
Critical References—Books

Argyris, Chris. *On Organizational Learning.* Cambridge, Mass.: Blackwell, 1993.

This book focuses on organizational learning, with emphasis on detecting and correcting errors that are or could be embarrassing to members of the organization. Each chapter has been published previously in a journal or book. The ideas presented in each chapter are illustrated with actual interventions that integrate the ideas into practice. The book is organized into four parts. Part 1 looks at organizational defenses, an important barrier to learning. Part 2 examines the barriers to organizational learning as they exist in several key managerial functions. Part 3 explores the human resources function, especially the common ideas and practices that are counterproductive to learning. Part 4 looks at how concepts for conducting research unintentionally reinforce organizational defenses.

Blake, Robert Rogers. *The Managerial Grid III: A New Look at the Classic That Has Boosted Productivity and Profits for Thousands of Corporations Worldwide.* Houston: Gulf Publishing, 1985.

This book creates an actual managerial grid with the vertical side charting the concerns for people (1 is low, 9 is high) and the horizontal side charting the concerns for productivity (1 is low and 9 is high). Points (1,1), (1,9), (9,1), (9,9), and (5,5) on the grid are each discussed in terms of motivation, managing conflict, behavioral elements, management practices, consequences, how to recognize the particular style of management being discussed, behavior, suggestions for change, and a summary. By reading about the different types of leadership, some with more emphasis on productivity and some with more emphasis on people, managers can figure out where they fit in and what changes need to be made to achieve the style of leadership that they desire.

Champy, James. *Reengineering Management: The Mandate for New Leadership.* New York: HarperBusiness, 1995.

Champy's first book, *Reengineering the Corporation,* focused on reengineering the doings of the workplace and caused a partial revolution in reengineering efforts. In this new book, Champy tries to further the revolution he began with a new tactic: reengineering the *manager.* It is a thorough, easy-to-read book that discusses why and how management needs to be changed. All of the aspects of management that are covered are done so with real-life examples of actual managers, their companies, and their tactics.

Hackman, J. Richard, ed. *Groups That Work (and Those That Don't): Creating Conditions for Effective Teamwork*. San Francisco: Jossey-Bass, 1990.
This book examines how work groups function. It links descriptive accounts of specific work groups with theoretical concepts, providing insights helpful to those who form, lead, serve as part of, or conduct research on work groups. It examines 27 diverse teams, grouping them into 7 categories: (1) top management, (2) task forces, (3) professional support groups, (4) performing groups, (5) human services teams, (6) customer service teams, and (7) production teams.

J. Richard Hackman, Edward E. Lawler III, and Lyman W. Porter. *Perspectives on Behavior in Organizations*. Edited by J. Richard Hackman. New York: McGraw-Hill, 1983.
This book discusses the behavior of organizations. Each section contains papers written by various scholars in the particular subject matter. The six broad and main sections covered are individuals and organizations, development of individual-organization relationships, design of work and reward systems, interpersonal and group processes, intergroup and structural factors, and leadership and organizational change.

Hackman, J. Richard and Greg R. Oldham. *Work Redesign*. Reading, Mass.: Addison-Wesley, 1980.
Many jobs are set up so that fun is not an option and productivity ceases. This book explains how to create a more inviting workplace by restructuring a person's job. An important part of this is understanding what work is appropriate for individuals and what work is appropriate for groups. Part 1 of the book deals specifically with people, their work, and how to change both of these aspects. Part 2 focuses on designing work for individuals, while part 3 focuses on designing work for groups. Hackman believes that the conditions necessary for effective teamwork are very different from those needed for effective individual work. Part 4 deals with implementation and change. Throughout, the book emphasizes the importance of thoroughly analyzing a work system before attempting to redesign it.

Handy, Charles B. *Understanding Organizations*. New York: Oxford University Press, 1993.

The book is broken down into two clear and helpful sections. The first describes the concepts of organizations ("Motivations to Work," "Roles and Interactions," "Leadership, Power and Influence," "Workings of Groups," and "Cultures of Organizations"). The second section focuses on the applications of these concepts ("The People of Organizations and Their Development," "The Work of the Organization—and Its Design, Politics and Change," "Being a Manager," and "The Future of Organizations"). The book can be applied to all organizations, ranging from schools to police forces to businesses.

Hersey, Paul. *Management of Organizational Behavior: Utilizing Human Resources.* Englewood Cliffs, N.J.: Prentice-Hall, 1988.

This management book focuses on motivation and the many facets of leadership. These include the impact of power, constructive discipline, and effective relationships. Illustrations and cases in the book are drawn from numerous organizations. The book creates a framework in which managers can mix their own managerial approach with a thorough understanding of human behavior and management theory.

Kanter, Rosabeth Moss. *The Change Masters: Innovation for Productivity in the American Corporation.* New York: Simon and Schuster, 1983.

This book focuses on the importance of people in making a corporation work. It explains how individual people can contribute to an entire corporation's success. It encourages the idea that a lot of little changes, made by individuals, can add up to produce a large change within a company. The book also stresses how environment is an important factor in fostering progressive thinking and stimulating ideas. The differences between those companies that nurture a creative environment and those that do not are discussed.

Katzenbach, Jon R. *The Wisdom of Teams: Creating High Performance Organizations.* Boston: Harvard Business School Press, 1993.

It has been said over and over again that teams perform better than individuals. Unfortunately, before this book, it was not yet obvious just how managers could utilize this fact to their advantage. This book shows managers how to get the most from their corporate teams. The book focuses on actual teams from within various corporations. It is broken down into three parts: part 1, "Understanding Teams" (why teams matter in the progress of corporations); part 2, "Becoming a

Team" (how and why teams perform well and what to do when they're not); part 3, "Exploiting the Potential" (how to get the most out of a team and how teams are vital to creating any major change within a corporation).

Kotter, John P. *The New Rules: How to Succeed in Today's Post-Corporate World.* New York: Free Press, 1995.

This book tracks the experiences of 115 Harvard MBAs from the class of 1974. It looks at each of their experiences to see how they have or have not adjusted to the rapidly changing workplace of the last 20 years. The book focuses on the importance of being aware of globalization, being flexible, and not relying on conventional career paths. It stresses moving away from big businesses and, instead, branching out on one's own into small business and entrepreneurship. Furthermore, it emphasizes the importance of not just managing, but leading, and doing so with a competitive drive and a desire to constantly learn and grow.

Lincoln, James R. *Culture, Control, and Commitment: A Study of Work Organizations and Work Attitudes in the United States and Japan.* New York: Cambridge University Press, 1990.

This book reports the design, conduct, and outcome of a survey of 51 Japanese and 55 American factories in 7 manufacturing industries. Using similar procedures for data collection and measurement instruments, the attitudes, values, and behaviors of Japanese and U.S. employees are compared, with an emphasis on those factors affecting employee commitment to the organization.

Lorsch, Jay W. *Handbook of Organizational Behavior.* Englewood Cliffs, N.J.: Prentice-Hall, 1987.

The objective of this book is to provide managers, students, and teachers of management with a brief, but thorough, set of references pertaining to the organizational behavior field. It centers on the way people actually behave in organizations and why they behave in that particular manner. The history and growth of the field is discussed in the first three sections ("General Overview," "Organizational Behavior and Underlying Disciplines," and "Organizational Behavior and Methodologies"). The last three sections deal with the many different uses and functions of organizational behavior in different settings ("Organizational Behavior at Various Systems Levels," "Managerial Issues," and "Organizational Behavior in Nonbusiness Settings").

Peters, Thomas J. *Liberation Management: Necessary Disorganization for the Nanosecond Nineties.* New York: Knopf, 1992.

This book throws out the traditional forms of organization and management. It is a lengthy text, which focuses on numerous companies that are thriving in the crazy '90s due to their flexibility and "disorganization" (CNN, EDS, and ABB are a few of those that are featured). The book discusses how so much of business today revolves around fashion and how many corporations are going for a softer image. Much of the book, and the companies it profiles, is about getting rid of central management altogether. It tells companies what they need to do, and change, to survive in the fast and frenzied '90s. The main point, as the author states, is that, "only a fickle, decentralized operation will survive in a fickle, decentralized global economy" (p. 9).

Pfeffer, Jeffrey. *Managing with Power: Politics and Influence in Organizations.* Boston: Harvard Business School Press, 1992.

This book deals with the control and use of power from a managerial perspective. It covers power in organizations, sources of power, strategies and tactics for employing power effectively, and power dynamics (how it is lost and how organizations change). It explains positive and negative uses of power and management with the use of real-life examples.

Sampson, Anthony. *Company Man.* London: Harper-Collins, 1995.

This book explains why the businessperson is a social individual and not just an economic entity. The "company man" (or woman) loses some of his (or her) generic qualities, as the book considers the complex and often challenging relationships involved with the profession and professional position, as well as the connection between lives at home and at the office. The book traces the history of the "company man" from the mid-twentieth-century conventions to the "company man" of the future. The book discusses the changes in Western business management as well and traces the dynamic role of business in society.

Steeples, Marion Mills. *The Corporate Guide to the Malcolm Baldrige National Quality Award: Proven Strategies for Building Quality into Your Organization.* Milwaukee, Wis.: ASQC Quality, 1992.

The book is a complete outline of what total quality management consists of within the framework of the Malcolm Baldrige National Quality

Award criteria. The book is made up of three major sections. The first explains the importance of quality in the workplace and the economic situations that led to the creation of the Baldrige Award. The second section attempts to clear up any confusion that might be caused by the seven Baldrige categories. The actual application is looked at and a case study is used for further clarification. The third section profiles winners of the award and how their devotion to quality has impacted their companies. The book is ideal for companies planning on applying for the award or for any company that wants to further its devotion to quality.

Steers, Richard M. *Introduction to Organizational Behavior.* Glenview, Ill.: Scott, Foresman, 1984.

This textbook is meant to introduce students to the fundamentals of organizational business. It is separated into five parts: the work setting, individual behavior, group behavior, people at work (use of applied topics), and predictions for the future. Throughout the text there are real-life examples from various workplaces, and case studies and exercises are given at the end of each chapter.

Wilkinson, Harry. *Influencing People in Organizations: Concepts and Cases.* Fort Worth, Tex.: Dryden, 1993.

This book is an organizational behavior textbook that is case-oriented and for graduate-level students, but is recommended for use in all types of organizations. The book is written in response to criticism from businesses toward MBA programs that neglect to teach their students about interpersonal skills. The book assumes that those people reading it have at least three years of job experience, have seen people functioning in organizations, aspire to be managers, and want to learn skills that will help improve their on-the-job performance.

Critical References—Journals

Academy of Management Executive. Ada, Ohio: The Academy of Management.

This quarterly publication contains academic papers that cover relevant issues in management for the near term. The academic papers are written specifically for managers as a primary audience. Each issue also contains book reviews.

Academy of Management Journal. Seattle: Pace University Press.

This journal, published six times a year, covers the study of management in a global forum. The divisions and interest groups of *Management Journal* are very broad, ranging from business policy and strategy to women in business. Each article contains only original, empirical research written by leading scholars.

The Academy of Management Review. Mississippi State University, Miss.: Academy of Management.

This is a quarterly publication that covers the organizational sciences in a global forum. The divisions and interest groups of AMR are very broad, ranging from business policy and strategy to women in business. Each topic is presented in purely theoretical, academic papers written by leading scholars. Along with the many different divisional topics discussed in each issue, academic books are also reviewed.

Administrative Science Quarterly. Ithaca, N.Y.: Johnson Graduate School of Management at Cornell University.

A quarterly journal for the further understanding of administration and how it works. Each issue contains articles that analyze administration and supply empirical investigation. There is also a book review section in each issue.

Human Resources Outlook. Edited by Audrey Freedman. New York: The Conference Board.

This outlook, published annually for human resources managers in business, identifies and discusses issues important to management in the near term.

Managing for the Future: Organizational Behavior & Processes. Cincinnati, Ohio: South-Western College.

This is a series of short booklets (called "Modules") put out by the Massachusetts Institute of Technology. Each booklet presents an overview of the specific subject matter, gives related exercises, and describes key terms relating to the subject matter. It also provides a collection of articles from various magazines that pertain to the subject at hand. Modules have focused on new organizational forms, making teams work, and the "new" organization, for example.

Strategic Management Journal. New York: Wiley.

This monthly journal covers relevant management strategy for the near term. Each issue contains articles written by leading academics in their fields.

Trends in Organizational Behavior. New York: Wiley, 1994.

These volumes consist of stand-alone chapters on leading trends in organizational behavior. Volume 1 contains chapters on the functional and dysfunctional linkages between organizations, with examples from the Exxon *Valdez* and Chernobyl incidents, the gray area between micro and macro organizational behavior, global companies and how they coordinate their activities, successful and unsuccessful corporate mergers, hypotheses about work and family, the role of personality assessments on personnel selections, the psychological contract in the employment relationship, and the changing work relationships in the 1990s. Volume 2 contains chapters on the current status of occupational stress management research and future research directions; implementing organizational change from an organizational justice perspective; organizational learning and the application of group collaborative software such as electronic mail and calendaring; new areas of job relocation research; the need for new models of entrepreneurial behavior in Eastern Europe and the former Soviet Union, focusing on such variables as personnel, organization, and society; a procedure to construct a diagnostic model of organizational behavior that enables identification of the causes of organizational ineffectiveness; and the major assumptions underlying cross-cultural organizational behavior research.

Strategic Management

The concept of business strategy stems from the need
of managers to be able to counter the effects of external
market forces while effectively managing their company's internal workings. Without a comprehensive,
executable corporate strategy, businesses are forced to
rely on crisis management to react to unforeseen
events. Table 9.1, which describes the key characteristics of crisis management, shows it is a less-than-
optimal management mode.

Crisis management, however, is not a manager's
only option. Managers who were forced to come up
with alternatives have made dramatic changes and

TABLE 9.1 CHARACTERISTICS OF CRISIS MANAGEMENT

- Crisis management requires a trade-off: expediency at the expense of efficiency.

- Crisis management necessitates that all available attention and resources be focused on the containment of one problem at a time.

- Crisis management tactics preclude management from doing the front-end planning—the exact planning that would avoid repetition of simi-lar future mistakes.

- Crisis management mode becomes self-perpetuating. Companies learn-ing to function well in crisis management mode tend to create crises so that they can continue to operate in the style that has become familiar.

developments in management philosophy and practice. Rather than merely reacting to forces that change the landscape of their businesses, managers have learned to anticipate and plan for these changes. Using such foresight mitigates the impact of negative forces while maximizing the opportunities created by positive ones.

When managers realized that they did not have to remain subject to the whim of unpredictable forces, they started to look for ways to manage their businesses such that success or failure was not wholly dictated by unforeseen events. Moreover, when they discovered that some of these events were, in fact, predictable, managers began to use this information to their advantage. They discovered that sometimes changes in a business landscape can create new opportunities for those who are ready to capitalize on them. As they developed the ability to predict, these managers developed the ability to manage.

If a company wants to move away from crisis management and develop a more useful management style, that company must engage in a few preparatory activities. The company's management must understand its own motivations for being in business and state explicitly what its goals are. The company must have an internal structure that delineates the flow of power and responsibility throughout the ranks. The company must also have a customized methodology for reaching the goals its management has set. Strategic management is the tool used to accomplish these objectives.

The strategic management process has two parts. The first part involves identifying what a company's common goals are and then creating a series of specific systems designed to direct all business activities toward these goals. The second part involves managing a successful implementation and inculcation of these systems throughout the corporation. Thus, we identify two major components of a corporate strategy: (1) the ideas and goals a company has, and (2) the method for achieving these goals. Management theorists still debate over what factors organizations should consider when developing a strategy, as well as what exactly constitutes a good strategy. This chapter introduces some of the ideas under discussion.

First, this chapter provides a brief historical overview of the concepts in the strategic management debate over the last 30 years. Then, through an examination of the contributions of several major management theorists, it identifies the basic components of a corporate strategy. In addition, the chapter explains some of the major methodologies associated with these theorists and concludes by summarizing the latest trends and wisdom on the topic.

HISTORICAL OVERVIEW OF STRATEGIC MANAGEMENT

Alfred Chandler

In 1962, Alfred Chandler, a noted researcher and management theorist, asserted the simple yet compelling idea that "structure follows strategy,"[1] in his work *Strategy and Structure.* According to Chandler, a corporation must focus its attention on defining a strategy before making any effort toward developing a structure, or this latter effort will be useless. Further, Chandler proposed that if an organization has invested in working out a comprehensive, meaningful corporate strategy, the corresponding corporate structure will emerge virtually on its own as a result.

While the test of time has proven the first of Chandler's assertions to be correct, it has also proven that a good strategy alone will not produce unique structural solutions to all of a corporation's problems by itself. Specific problems, including those related to implementation and the need for constant adaptation, require intense and individual attention to discover meaningful solutions.

While corporate strategy, organizational structure, and management practice are inextricably linked, the relationship is not simple, nor is it linear. This distinction is important for several reasons, some of which will be discussed in greater detail later in this chapter. In general, the crux of the matter is this. Corporations very often judge their performance based on how their competitors are performing. If a competitor is doing better, it is common practice for a company to invest time in finding out why. If the management of the second-place company believes it has identified a competitor's practice that is giving it the lead, the second-place company will attempt to emulate this practice. A stunning example of this exists with the recent American impetus to copy Japanese management practices. While copying competitor practices just for the sake of doing so is a bad idea in general (discussion to follow later), try to imagine the disastrous effects of misidentifying a competitor practice and still trying to emulate it! Unfortunately, American companies have made this mistake repeatedly.

Frequently, people make mistakes and misidentify strategies because they try to apply a direct rule where there is none. A perfect example of the misidentification error is illustrated by the labeling of decentralization as a hot management trend prevalent in the 1970s. This classification caused a structure to be labeled as a strategy. Once labeled a successful strategy, other corporations set out to adopt decentralization as a contrivance. In truth, widespread product diversification was the operating strategy. Decentralization was the structure that emerged when organizations followed this strategy.

Confusing structure with strategy is like confusing a car with a road map. A car can help you to get where you are going, but it cannot help you to decide how you should go. A sound organizational structure can assist in the fulfillment of the organization's goals, but it cannot define them. Historians and managers alike must pay careful attention to guard against repeating such mistakes in the future.

Frederick Taylor

Frederick Taylor is another premier management research authority. Taylor's ideas are responsible for shaping the research efforts of many management practitioners in recent history. Taylor's most famous assertion was that management was not a soft, unpredictable effort that businesspeople either had a natural talent for or did not. In fact, Taylor went far in the opposite direction. According to Taylor, management could be transformed into an exact science through studying business processes in the context of time and motion. Taylor theorized that by breaking down every activity a business undertakes into measurable increments, each component could be reworked to achieve maximum efficiency. These optimized components could then be reassembled into larger processes, creating a business whose every activity could operate under an optimal business scheme. This became the driving concept in many of the more recent management schemata, including the TQM ideas of W. Edwards Deming.

The contributions of Chandler and Taylor are mentioned to illustrate two points. Chandler's idea that structure follows strategy provides managers with a place to start in developing a plan for their businesses. Taylor's contributions on management efficiency theory provide the point of initiation for the modern-day application of mechanized, optimized management theory. Taken together, both communicate one central message shared by many other theorists in the field. For a firm to be successful, it must know where it wants to direct its energies and how these energies are best spent. A clear, well-pondered, implementable strategy is critical to a firm's continued health and well-being.

At this point, you should have a basic idea of what business strategy is, how the ideas behind it have developed over time, and why strategy is valuable. So now that you know what, how, and why there is such a thing as business strategy, the next most pressing question must be "Where or how do I get one?" The next chapter segment will introduce some of the major theorists in the area of strategy formation, as well as explain their contributions.

STRATEGY FORMATION: THREE WIDELY USED APPROACHES

Strategic management, as a topic for academic study, draws many experts and scholars whose work is noteworthy. For the purposes of this chapter, however, we cannot discuss them all. In this section we will focus on the three entities whose collective contributions provide the broadest overview of information on the topic.

Michael Porter

Michael Porter, a professor of strategic management at Harvard Business School, is viewed by many as the forefather of modern-day American business strategy. Porter is quite a prolific writer and we encourage you to read as much of his material as your time and interest permits. For the purposes of this chapter, however, we will focus on two of his major works, *Competitive Strategy* and *Competitive Advantage.* In these works, Porter focuses his discussion on the frameworks he has developed to identify and guide corporations through the process of developing a comprehensive business strategy.

Fundamentally, Porter stipulated that to succeed in business, an organization must establish these things:

- A good command of its own internal workings
- A comprehensive understanding of the industry in which it is functioning
- A working knowledge of what the competition is up to

Porter developed corresponding frameworks to facilitate managers' efforts in making these assessments.

The Formation of Competitive Strategy

Figures 9.1 and 9.2 illustrate the underlying concepts in Porter's approach to strategy formation, as outlined in *Competitive Strategy.* In Figure 9.1, the wheel is used as a metaphor for a corporation's structure. At the center of the wheel are the firm's goals and specific performance objectives. They serve as the basis for the structure and operations of each functional area. The spokes of the wheel represent the policies by which these goals and objectives are realized. The metaphor of the wheel belies the fact that all departments within an organization are integrally bound and must remain so if the wheel is to turn, or the organization is to function. A problem occurring in a specific department is a problem for the firm as a whole.

Figure 9.2 is a spatial representation of the four major factors governing the development of a competitive strategy. The diagram illustrates that, while these forces can be identified and examined independently, they also act, react, and interact with each other and with the firm's overall competitive strategy.

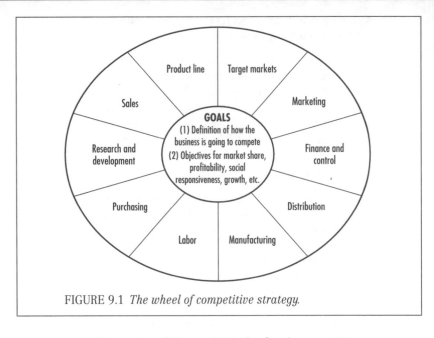

FIGURE 9.1 *The wheel of competitive strategy.*

At the center of Figure 9.2 is the firm's competitive strategy. While the title of the figure describes a formation process, a firm's competitive strategy does not simply emerge as the product of the collective influences identified in the figure. A firm must start out with a rough idea of its strategy. The model assists management in assessing the impact of four specific forces on the company's strategy, as is indicated by linking the corporate strategy box to the four forces by arrows of influence. Identifying these relationships enables management to go from a rough strategic concept to a polished, comprehensive strategy.

The four forces linked to the corporate strategy box are further divided into two categories. The left side of the figure represents the corporation's internal factors. The first force, the company's strengths and weaknesses, refers to a firm's financial, technological, and product resources, as well as to its human resources.

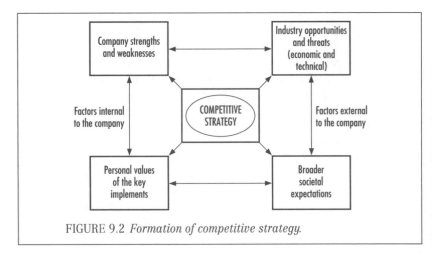

FIGURE 9.2 *Formation of competitive strategy.*

The second force, the personal values of the key implements, refers to the management style and belief systems of the firm's managers. A firm uses the combination of these resources to manage both its processes and people according to the established goals and objectives.

The firm's external factors appear on the right side of the figure. "Industry opportunities and threats" refers to the position and behavior of a firm's competitors. This factor dictates an industry's climate, as changes in the industry can give rise to both opportunities as well as risks. The second external force, broader societal expectations, refers to the societal norms to which the firm is subjected. Everything from government legislation to popular opinion qualifies as a societal norm. In sum, the right side of the figure captures the interaction of competitor behavior and society's projection of its own value systems, as well as how these two forces work together to impact the firm's competitive strategy.

The information presented in Figures 9.1 and 9.2, taken in conjunction, represent the basis for forming a useful competitive strategy, as summarized in the following four steps:

1. The organization must define itself clearly in terms of its basis for competing and its standards for measuring its success.

2. The organization must also develop policies that managers can use to successfully communicate this defining information to all operating parts of the firm.

3. Once self-defined, the firm must then identify and assess its internal strengths and weaknesses.

4. The firm must then evaluate these strengths and weaknesses, both in the context of the external competitive forces of its industry as well as society.

The Forces Driving Industry Competition

The previous models aid managers in obtaining a good command of the firm's internal workings. To accomplish the second of Porter's three objectives, managers should examine Figure 9.3, which identifies the primary factors, both internal and external to the firm, that shape the firm's business activities. It also captures the relationship operating between these factors. Most important, Porter conveys that all of these factors impact each other through their central impact on the industry itself.

Porter places industry competitors at the center of Figure 9.3. He uses the circular arrow, representing the dynamic of the rivalry among existing firms within the given industry, to capture the ever changing nature associated with this dynamic. Porter stipulates that the

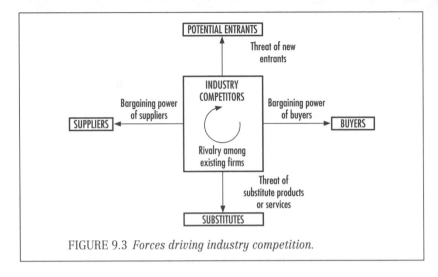

FIGURE 9.3 *Forces driving industry competition.*

firm's first order of business is to know and understand the positions of other firms already existing and competing within its industry. Simply put, a firm must be able to identify all of its competitors and should know what these competitors are up to within the industry.

Figure 9.3 also names and describes forces outside the realm of industry and their corresponding impact on each other as well as on the industry. For example, Porter uses the horizontal axis to capture the microeconomic effects of supply and demand. The left side of the axis, labeled as "bargaining power of suppliers," corresponds to the supply concept. The right side of the axis, labeled as "bargaining power of buyers," corresponds to the demand concept. Any activity from buyers, for example, will first impact at the center of the model, having an effect on the rivalry among existing firms. A change in the rivalry dynamic will prompt a change that will continue along the horizontal axis to impact suppliers. If the change in suppliers is dramatic, it may initiate the same line of activity described in the buyers example, only in the opposite direction.

By employing an axis instead of the typical supply and demand curve, Porter distinguishes between the theoretical concept of supply and demand and the actual entities doing the supplying and buying. He also differentiates between the market theory and the reality of the marketplace. According to market theory, a change in demand will produce an equal and opposite change reaction on supply, and vice versa. The Porter model does not require that suppliers and buyers act collaboratively. In reality, both suppliers and buyers can and do act independently of each other. Thus, the Porter model allows for a manager to assess the effects of any independent action, both on the firm as well as on the industry, without having to wait for the predicted market reaction to occur.

In the same vein, Porter uses the vertical axis to describe the relationship of change on two additional forces. The upper part of the vertical axis is home to the force of potential entrants. This concept represents the potential for firms to either enter or exit the industry mix. In other words, this force measures the likelihood that a manager will come to work on Monday and discover that a new competitor has moved in next door. The lower part of the vertical axis is dedicated to the force of substitute products. By substitute products, Porter means that firms must be aware of the development of new, related products or services that could replace the existing ones they now offer.

Similar to the relationship captured on the horizontal axis, the vertical axis displays the interactive effect that a change in one force can initiate on its partner force, as well as on the rivalry dynamic. The relationship captured on the vertical axis, however, is slightly more subtle. A change in the number of competitor firms in an industry does not precipitate an equal and opposite change in the number of substitute products available. Nor does the reverse hold true. Rather, a change in one force may create an attractive opportunity within the industry. Take the example of a new substitute product entering the industry. This event would surely change the rivalry dynamic because there is a new source of competition within the industry. This new source of competition may be more than some of the current players within the industry can endure, and these firms may be motivated to leave the industry. If one or more firms exit the industry, clearly this will change the rivalry dynamic again. The beauty of the Porter model is that it allows managers to evaluate changes independently, because it acknowledges that all changes need not happen simultaneously.

The Components of a Competitor Analysis

Once a firm has developed a clear, communicable self-concept and assessed itself in the context of its industry, the final consideration involves a detailed competitor analysis. Figure 9.4 provides managers with a framework to complete a successful and informative assessment of their industry competitors. Central to the model, and to the analysis, are four questions that compose what Porter deems a *competitor's response profile*. The questions, located in the center box of Figure 9.4, emphasize the need for managers to consider what moves a competitor might make on his or her own, as well as what moves a competitor might make in response to the manager's own moves.

To begin such an analysis, a manager should start by considering what a competitor's performance goals and objectives might be. For example, a product man-

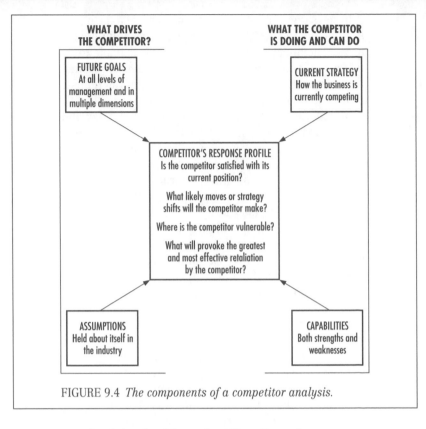

FIGURE 9.4 *The components of a competitor analysis.*

ager for Coke should wonder if Pepsi's performance goals for the year are to beat their prior year's earnings, or are they to outsell Coke at any cost? Clearly, these goals need not be identical.

Next, the manager should assess how close the competitor is to actually achieving these goals and what moves he or she might make to get there. (If Pepsi's goal *is* to outsell Coke, is Pepsi willing to engage in head-to-head combat to do so, as in the case of the nationally televised Pepsi Challenge?) Further, a manager should contemplate the competitor's weaknesses, both those the competitor may be aware of as well as those the competitor may be oblivious to. (Perhaps the brand manager at Pepsi does not know that you, the Coke brand manager, negotiated as part of your multibillion dollar advertising contract with the networks that Pepsi commercials that engage in head-to-head tactics can be aired only between the hours of 2 and 4 A.M.) Finally, the manager must evaluate, given the information ascertained from the previous considerations, how the competitor might react to a specific strategic move made by the manager's firm. (You must realize that the brand manager at Pepsi may be none too pleased upon discovering what you have done and may resort to strategic tactics of his or her own.)

Armed with this central information gleaned from the competitor response profile, a manager can work toward gaining a deeper understanding of the competitor's capabilities and motivations. To return to our study of Figure 9.4, focus your attention on the arrows emanating from the competitor response profile in the center box. On the left side of Figure 9.4 are the two forces stemming from considerations of what drives the competitor. Under this heading, Porter identifies the future goals of the competitor. These are a firm's goals as they have been communicated to all persons within the company. Porter also identifies assumptions the firm may have about itself and its position within the industry. These two forces, taken together, provide a skeletal archetype of the firm's industry motivation, its process for internal motivation, and its self-perception. These are all important factors in shaping the competitor's response profile.

The right side of Figure 9.4 is dedicated to forces that stem from an assessment of the behavior of the competitor. Specifically, the forces identified are the competitor's current strategy, or a status report of the basis on which the business is competing and how it is doing in the industry. In conjunction with current strategy is the consideration of the firm's capabilities, both in terms of its core competencies as well as in terms of its weak points.

Last, Porter emphasizes the interactive nature of the concerns driven by the right and left sides of the model on the center of the model. More specifically, any change in any of the four forces will impact the competitor's response profile directly. Moreover, a change in the competitor's response profile could prompt changes in any or all of the other forces.

Taken collectively, Porter's frameworks, the Formation of Competitive Strategy, the Forces Driving Industry Competition, and the Components of a Competitor Analysis, enable a firm to complete the three key assessments he deems vital to achieving and maintaining a competitive advantage in today's global business world.

The McKinsey Seven S Model

In addition to professional academics and theorists, another group develops diagnostic frameworks to examine corporate strategy—the management consultants.

The primary difference between academics and consultants is that all but the most famous academics are called upon to apply their theories to specific cases within an actual company. This is the domain of the management consultants. Conversely, it is unusual for the average management consultant to be commissioned to develop theoretical diagnostic models.

"Average," however, is probably the last adjective you would hear to describe a McKinsey management consultant. The following section will be devoted to explaining the McKinsey Seven S Framework, the product of a marriage between theory and practice.

McKinsey's primary objective in developing the Seven S framework was to put a new spin on management style and suggest that soft issues could and should be managed. Further, the use of the wheel, a format borrowed from Porter, also emphasizes the idea that a firm is the comprehensive, inextricable sum of its parts.

After the equivalent of conducting a Ph.D.-level research project on how America's best-run companies were managed, the best minds at McKinsey made two key findings. First, the consultants learned that a manager's effectiveness was determined by both the strategy and the structure of the organization. Their second discovery was that there was no linear relationship governing these three components, although they are interdependent. (Sound familiar? Sometimes conclusions gain more merit when they can be tested and retested.)

In reality, the management, structure, and strategy of an organization are related through a complex network of seven characteristic factors in the organization. Managers who try to run the firm as if it were a collection of several independent units soon learn about the spoke-and-hub concept of the wheel. A wheel is nothing more than a collection of spokes when there is no hub, and vice versa. Neither part alone can replicate the functions of a wheel. Similarly, an organization without common goals and strategy cannot function in the way it was intended. Sure, each unit can perform independent functions, but without a unifying force to bring the units together, they are merely spokes. Hence, McKinsey developed its wheel to illustrate this very point. Figure 9.5 provides you with all of the categories in a typical organization that must operate under a common goal.

The McKinsey study produced another interesting finding: Most successful organizations, regardless of line of business, had several practices in common. The McKinsey model incorporates these practices into eight characteristics.

1. *Maintain a bias for action.*   Successful companies are not afraid to make changes, even if that means making a mistake along the way.

2. *Learn from customers by staying close to them.* Successful firms maintain close relationships with their customer bases. In this way, firms can anticipate and plan for changes in customers' needs even before customers are aware of the change.

3. *Encourage autonomy and entrepreneurship in management by management.*   Management encourages others to find new and creative solutions to problems by allowing managers to challenge old rules

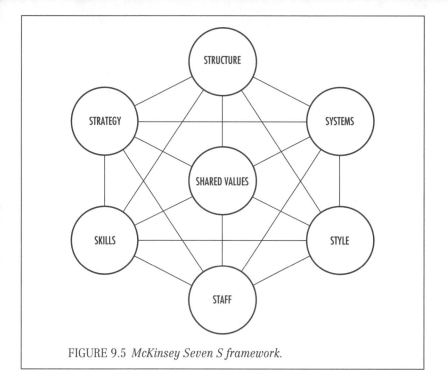

FIGURE 9.5 *McKinsey Seven S framework.*

and methods and then giving them the latitude to try new approaches.

4. *Respect contributions of all employees, especially those traditionally undervalued.* If managers want their staffs to buy into the goals of the firms, those who directly report to them must believe that the firms respect and value their individual contributions.

5. *Use a hands-on, highly visible management approach.* When management is present and involved in every aspect of the business, employees have more respect and include managers more in the everyday workings of the firm.

6. *Stick to the knitting: Know your core competency and stick with it.* Do not abandon your core competencies and core products in search of products or services that are glamorous today. Stick to what you are good at.

7. *Keep the organizational structure simple and staff only as much management as is required for bare minimum.* Creating many levels of middle and upper management only serves to create dissension within the ranks of a company.

8. *Allow core values to govern. Manage with loose and tight properties when respectively appropriate.* Trust in the fact that your staff knows and shares the core values of the company. Allow enough managerial latitude so that employees can try new ideas and methods. Provide enough managerial guidance so that everyone remains committed to the same goals.

The McKinsey wheel is an especially valuable tool for two reasons. Not only does the wheel reemphasize that all parts of an organization must work together to achieve common goals, it also provides specific areas and business activities to examine when diagnosing the health of a firm.

The Boston Consulting Group Matrix

While groups like McKinsey use an approach that focuses on the interdependence of a firm's parts, other consulting groups take a completely antithetical approach. On the other side of the strategic analysis process is the Boston Consulting Group (BCG). Unlike McKinsey, BCG believed that the best way to get an understanding of how a business was functioning was to break down the business into its smaller operating parts, commonly known as *standard business units,* or SBUs. SBU management became a very popular trend in the 1980s and drove managers away from considering their companies as integrated entities. Rather, managers began to view companies as a portfolio of SBUs. Which approach is the right approach? This is one of those issues still undergoing hot debate by management theorists.

Using the SBU approach, BCG designed a framework to assist companies using the same approach in classifying the performance of any specific product in relation to the overall performance of the firm. The framework, called the *BCG matrix,* identifies products or business units across two dimensions: market share and market growth. *Market share* refers to the percentage of sales one product earns in relation to the total market sales for all products in that category. For example, Tide may have 30 percent of the market share of the domestic laundry detergent market. *Market growth* refers to the potential for a product category to attract more consumer spending.

Figure 9.6 illustrates how these two forces work together to create four SBU categories. If a product or SBU is in a high-growth market with high market share, it is called a *star.* Products or businesses in this category usually require a good deal of capital investment from the company in order to capitalize on market-growth opportunities. Products that have a high market share in a low-market-growth business are called *cash cows.* Typically, companies can enjoy high revenues on these products without much additional investment or attention to maintain market share.

A product or business with a low market share in a low-growth industry is referred to as a *dog.* Products or SBUs in this category usually generate enough revenue to be self-supporting, but they are probably poor performers in relation to the other products or SBUs in the

		STAR	QUESTION MARKS
MARKET GROWTH	**HIGH**	High-share, high-growth businesses or products that generally need a lot of investment to secure their rapid growth.	Low share in high-growth markets that require investment just to hold their market position. The question is whether to put more cash into them to improve share, to phase them out, or to leave them alone.
		CASH COW	**DOG**
	LOW	High-share, low-growth businesses or products, usually well established, that do not need a lot of investment to maintain their market share.	Low share in low-growth market. They may have enough cash to support themselves, but they are in a position that is below average.
		HIGH	**LOW**
		MARKET SHARE	

FIGURE 9.6 *Boston Consulting Group market share matrix.*

firm. Lastly, there are those products or SBUs that have a low market share in a high-growth industry. These are called *question marks,* because they beg the most questions of management. Usually these products require investment to maintain their market shares in an industry, so management must decide if the investment is worth it.

In summary, all frameworks discussed represent traditional approaches to understanding and developing a business strategy. While these frameworks are widely recognized and accepted, recall that this chapter began by stating that strategic approaches were a topic of continuing debate. Therefore, the next section of this chapter provides summaries of two of the latest trends in strategic management today.

THE LATEST CONVENTIONAL WISDOM

Today's conventional wisdom comes from two strategy professors whose work has been appearing frequently in the *Harvard Business Review.* Gary Hamel and C. K. Prahalad are especially well known for two of their recent articles, "Strategic Intent"[2] and "Core Competence."[3] We will summarize the ideas laid out in both of these articles.

Strategic Intent

In this article, Prahalad and Hamel argue that companies need more than a formal model to define strategy. Companies need, as one of their self-defining goals, a desired leadership position within an industry. The authors insist that a company must develop "a competitive obsession with winning at all levels of the organization and then sustain that obsession over a ten to twenty year quest for global leadership." They must develop a strategic intent.

A famous example of a strategic intent was President Kennedy's initiative for the United States to be the first country to send a man to the moon. Although many people believed this to be an impossible feat, Kennedy maintained that it was imperative that we, as a nation, succeed to preserve our national identity. Americans, from the scientists at NASA to the American public in general, internalized this statement. Taxpayers did not complain about the allocation of money to NASA, while scientists worked around the clock to achieve "the impossible." When the goal was reached, it inspired unity and pride throughout the country.

Strategic intent is a long-term goal, and one that the business will stick to, even as the tides of business change. Equally as important, this strategy concept also includes an accompanying management process. Prahalad and Hamel suggest the following practices:

- Focusing of the organization's attention on the essence of winning
- Motivating people by communicating the value of the target
- Leaving room for individual and team contributions
- Sustaining enthusiasm by providing new operational definitions as circumstances change
- Using this intent consistently to guide resource allocations

While strategic intent requires commitment in terms of a long-term focus, it also enables a company to be flexible because it only requires the company to commit to plans for short-term action, leaving the company many opportunities to reevaluate and take advantage of new opportunities as they emerge.

Strategic intent also must be communicated in such a way that all members of a company buy into the idea and are committed to it personally. It must be inescapable. When Honda issued the strategic intent to beat GM's sales in the American markets in the late 1960s, it seemed like an impossible goal. Yet within 20 years, it was a reality, and it became a reality because every member of the Honda company force was committed to making it happen.

This kind of internalization, coupled with operational flexibility, allows for entrepreneurial management styles within the company—styles that can help a company overcome resource constraints by inspiring innovation and creativity toward achieving the same goal. Means are flexible, since the end has been determined and bought into by all. This style of management also requires flexibility to maximize short-term competitive advantages. The firm does not have to be married to one competitive advantage, but should be flexible enough to benefit from all.

The firm cannot be wed to typical evaluation schemes either. Instead of considering projects in terms of whether they yield benefits of either quality or cost, firms should be thinking in terms of quality and cost advantages. Firms should also engage in a collaborative style of management, in which the company encourages its staff to challenge all rules and realities that prohibit the company from achieving its goals and finding creative solutions.

The last critical part of a successful strategic intent initiative is that it must be perceived as a personal challenge made to every member of the company. This, in turn, will inspire a response of drive and determination to achieve the goal across all organizational levels.

For a strategic intent to work, managers must:

- *Create a sense of urgency.* Perpetuating a bias for action avoids crisis from inaction.

- *Develop a competitor focus at every level through widespread use of competitive intelligence.* Encourage employees to set personal benchmarks based on beating the best-in-class procedures of the firm's competitors.

- *Provide employees with the skills they need to work effectively.* Do not ever skimp on providing employees with as much training as they need or seek out.

- *Avoid competing initiatives by launching one challenge at a time.* Allowing enough time for a challenge to be absorbed and personalized by the staff before launching another will alleviate a sense of confusion and foster a more competitive environment.

- *Establish clear milestones and review mechanisms.* Managers must be sure to set specific goals and review processes in a timely fashion. Managers must also establish a clear and consistent rewards system.

- *Reciprocal responsibility.* Managers must share credit for every victory as well as share responsibility for every setback if the organization is to remain responsible and competitive.

- *Innovation rather than imitation.* Focus on developing and playing your own game well instead of trying to imitate someone else's game. Better to be a first-rate original than a second-rate imitation.

- *Creative management.* Rewrite the rules and use every tactic that will advance you toward your goal. Dump the rules of strategy that confine instead of advance the company toward the goal.

In a number of ways, the concepts described in "Strategic Intent" resemble those described in Porter and in the McKinsey wheel frameworks. In sum, the article is pushing for a style of management that focuses on harnessing the creative energy and entrepreneurial spirit of every employee within the firm toward attaining difficult but highly rewarding goals.

The Core Competence of the Corporation

In their second article, Prahalad and Hamel identify a very specific approach for managers to take when appraising a company's value and planning its future. According to these authors, it is becoming much more difficult for a company to survive in today's global business world. The old rules of management simply no longer apply. For a business to stay alive in an increasingly competitive environment, "the critical task for management is to create an organization capable of infusing products with irresistible functionality or, better yet, creating products which customers need but have not yet imagined."[4] Companies must be able to adjust to advancement in technology, emergence of new markets and shifts in old ones, and changes in customer preferences—quickly. No small feat.

Prahalad and Hamel advocate a management perspective that requires managers to abandon their vision of a company as a portfolio of businesses. Instead, the authors suggest viewing a company as a portfolio of core competences, or "complex harmonizations of individual technologies and production skills."[5]

Prahalad and Hamel define three tests a manager can apply to identify a company's core competences. First, a core competence should provide the company with potential access to a wide variety of markets. Second, a core competence should contribute in a significant and perceivable way to the customer benefits of the end product. Third, a core competence should be difficult for competitors to imitate. Last, core competences lead to core products, or the physical product of the core competence.

A perfect example of how these ideas fit together in the context of a real business is NEC. In 1980, NEC was primarily a computer company, earning revenues of $3.8 billion. By 1988, NEC's sales had grown to $21.89 billion. Instead of focusing on external markets and products, NEC kept an internal focus. It continued to develop its high-technology areas of expertise, along with applications for its new technologies. In the span of eight years, NEC took an expertise in technology and applied it to semiconductors, mainframe computers, and telecommunication products. While these were seemingly unrelated businesses at the time, NEC's application of its core competences in technology, as well as its core products in computers and office automation equipment, have earned NEC the honor of being the only company in the world that is a top-five revenue generator in telecommunication, semiconductors, and mainframe products.

Conceptualizing a company in terms of SBUs completely defies the core competence framework. According to the authors, the business unit approach violates the rules for managing according to core competence for the following reasons:

1. *Status.* In the SBU model, the SBU is autonomous. This defies the sharing principle of the CC model.

2. *Basis for competition.* The SBU has a product focus. The CC has a competence focus first, product focus second.

3. *Resource allocation.* The SBU is a discrete unit with a specific and independent capital allocation. The CC method requires a unified company perspective. Both capital and human resources are allocated on the basis of need.

4. *Impetus of top management.* The SBU manager focuses on optimizing sales and profit margins. The CC manager focuses on developing competencies and a strategic architecture within the company.

Which position is the correct position? Both sides can point to cases where businesses have enjoyed enormous success because they adopted one management theory or the other. Perhaps this is evidence to support the idea that strategy must be determined on a case-by-case basis. The important idea to conclude with is that a core competence style of management may require a major overhaul in the way a company currently does business to change the focus to the one described in the article. Yet an investment in such an overhaul may be exactly what a failing company needs.

Similarly, the article, "Strategic Intent," contradicts some of the "best practices" defined by our earlier theorists. Strategic management centers around changes and modification that allow a theory, organization, and manager to adapt to any given situation at hand. New theories develop as old ones no longer address current business issues. The nature of the commitment to accommodation for continuing adaptation to change lies at the very heart of strategic management.

STRATEGIC MANAGEMENT

Backward Integration

This refers to a strategy in which a company creates a competitive advantage by controlling the supply of the raw materials needed to make its products.

Business Strategy

This is the set of policies used to manage individual processes within a business, including decisions regarding individual products, services, suppliers, markets, and competitors.

Competitive Advantage

Any series of company practices or procedures that results in the company creating products or services that consistently surpass the products or services of its competitors constitutes a competitive advantage. It includes any business practice that gives a company an edge in the marketplace.

Components of a Competitor Analysis

This framework was developed by Michael Porter to assist managers in completing a successful and informative assessment of their industry competitors. The following forces are identified in the model:

1. *Competitor's response profile.* This is a list of questions that assist managers in considering what moves competitors might make on their own as well as what moves competitors might make in response to the manager's own moves.

2. *Future goals.* Under the heading of "What Drives the Competitors," this is a reference to the firm's goals as they have been communicated to all persons within the company.

3. *Assumptions.* Also under the heading of "What Drives the Competitor," this refers to facts or beliefs a competitor holds about itself and its position within an industry.

4. *Current strategy.* Under the heading of "What the Competitor Is Doing and Can Do," this refers to the status of how a business is competing and how it is performing within an industry.

5. *Capabilities.* Also under the heading of "What the Competitor Is Doing and Can Do" fall capabilities, or assessments of the competition's core competencies and weaknesses.

Core Competence

This is a specialty or area of expertise in a given company that exceeds or eludes its competitors and serves as the foundation for the company to grow or diversify into new product lines. Honda, for example, has a core competence in building high-performance engines.

Corporate Culture

This refers to a system of shared rules, beliefs, and values among members of a given company. Corporate cultures differ widely across companies. The corporate culture at IBM, for example, is far more formal in terms of dress, interoffice relationships, and office conduct than that of Microsoft.

Corporate Strategy

This refers to a method for managing a company's resources such that the company's strengths are maximized and its weaknesses minimized in relation to its competitors within the same market. A corporate strategy impacts a company's goals and objectives and the policies the company will form and follow to meet these goals and objectives.

Corporate Vision

This refers to the concept of what a business can be, beyond how it actually exists in the present, and the method for realizing the concept. For example, at the time they entered the American market, executives at Honda had a corporate vision that Honda would be the number-one-selling midsize car in America within 20 years of entering the market.

Crisis Management

This involves an unplanned effort and dedication of resources to solve an unanticipated problem or set of problems that threaten a company's status as a going concern.

Decentralization

In this organizational power structure, authority and decision-making responsibility are diffused throughout different levels of a company. Decentralization differs widely from the traditional functional organizational design where power rests with top management.

Five Forces Model

This framework, developed by Michael Porter, captures the dynamics of the prevailing environmental forces in which a company operates. These factors include:

1. *Rivalry among existing firms.* At the center of Porter's model is the current state of affairs within a market, before any external forces are considered. Porter contends that firms are always jockeying for position within a market and that the rivalry among firms takes on the form of a constant battle for market share.

2. *Threat of new entrants.* The first external driver, this force refers to the potential for new firms to enter an industry. Any time a new firm enters an industry, the competitive balance must be adjusted to account for changes in market share, new capacity, and new resources.

3. *Threat of substitutes.* Similar to the first external force, this force represents the potential changes in market equilibrium caused by the introduction of products that represent a viable alternative choice to the products currently available in the market and could reduce the size of the potential market by drawing sales away.

4. *Bargaining power of suppliers.* This force refers to the effect the supplier can have on determining the availability of materials and, consequently, on the supply and demand dynamics operating within a market.

5. *Bargaining power of buyers.* This force refers to the effect buyers can have on determining the demand for goods or services, thereby affecting the corresponding price for these goods and services.

Formation of a Competitive Strategy

This framework, developed by Michael Porter, provides a spatial representation of the five major factors governing the development of a competitive strategy. These factors include:

1. *Competitive strategy.* This is the plan a firm adopts to compete for market share within a given industry.

2. *Company strengths and weaknesses.* An internal force, this concept refers to a firm's financial, technological, product, and human resources.

3. *Personal values of key implements.* Also an internal force, this concept refers to the management style and belief system used by a firm's managers.

4. *Industry opportunities and threats.* Considered an external force, this concept refers to the position and behavior of a firm's competitors, and how competitors' behavior can give rise to risks and opportunities within an industry.

5. *Broader societal expectations.* Also considered an external force, this concept refers to the societal

norms, including legislation and popular opinion, that shape a company's behavior in the marketplace.

Forward Integration

This is a strategy in which a business expands its activities to include distribution or lines of business related to the selling of its core products.

Innovation

Any modernizing modification in a process or procedure that increases the efficiency of that process or procedure is an innovation. Information technology has been the catalyst for much of the innovation in American companies in the last ten years.

Leadership

Leadership entails the exercise of responsibility, influence, and authority over a group of people.

Management

Management is the administration of a process or those conducting a process to ensure that the process meets completion in the most efficient way possible.

Market Growth

This is the measured potential for a product category to attract more consumer spending.

Market Share

This is the percentage of sales one product earns in relation to total market sales for all products in that category.

McKinsey Seven S Model

This framework was developed by the consulting firm of McKinsey and company to chart the strategic relationships between forces existing in a company, where these forces determine a company's success or failure. The forces include: (1) strategy, (2) structure, (3) staff, (4) superordinate goals, (5) skills, (6) style, and (7) systems.

Mission Statement

This is a statement of why a given company is in business, what its objectives are, and what core values are guiding the company in achieving its objectives.

Reengineering

This involves reconceptualizing and restructuring business processes and practices with the intention of increasing efficiency, quality, and employee and customer satisfaction while reducing the costs associated with the procedure or practice.

Synergy

This is the concept that two or more different businesses, activities, or processes will, when working together, create an overall value greater than that of the sum of the parts, were they working separately.

Total Quality Management (TQM):

Developed by W. Edwards Deming, TQM is a series of business practices designed to monitor the quality of production throughout all its phases. TQM has its foundation in the concept that there is systematic and asystematic error inherent in every process and that each process should be controlled such that systematic error is minimized or eliminated, while asystematic error remains.

MORE READINGS
Critical References

Peters, Thomas J., and Robert H. Waterman, Jr. *In Search of Excellence: Lessons from America's Best-Run Companies.* New York: Warner, 1982.

The number-one bestseller in 1983, *In Search of Excellence* describes the eight basic strategic principles that the best-run companies utilize to foster continued success. The principles are: (1) a bias for action, (2) staying close to the customer, (3) autonomy and entrepreneurship, (4) productivity through people, (5) insisting executives stay in touch with the firm's essential business, (6) remaining with the business that the firm knows best, (7) few administrative layers and few people at the upper levels, (8) simultaneous loose-tight properties. The book develops each of the principles in depth, with theoretical support and extensive examples of successful companies.

Porter, Michael E. *Competitive Advantage: Creating and Sustaining Superior Performance.* New York: Free Press, 1985.

Competitive Strategy introduced techniques for industry and competitor analyses. *Competitive Advantage* further develops these concepts for exploration of additional complexities and then presents definitive guidelines for developing sound competitive strategies and instituting them within a firm. Porter describes how companies can create and then maintain a competitive advantage within a given industry by establishing an appropriate competitive range of focus. Value-chain analysis, which enables the manager to differentiate integral activities of a company in different functional business components for its product or service, is introduced. These business components, which include design, marketing, production, and distribution, are all linked through value-chain analysis, demonstrating the importance of considering all company activities in an integrated manner.

Porter, Michael E. *Competitive Strategy: Techniques for Analyzing Industries and Companies.* New York: Free Press, 1980.

This comprehensive book is about competitive strategy in business. Written for managers and other business professionals, the book assumes a conceptual approach, extending industrial organizational theory with case examples as support. The underlying premise is that significant benefits can be gained though an explicit process of strategy formulation as a coordinated effort among different functional business units. The book is divided into three parts. Part 1 develops the criteria for analyzing the structure of an industry and competitors. Part 2 applies the framework from part 1 to formulate competitive strategy for different types of business environments. Part 3 evaluates an array of business strategic decisions that challenge companies competing in a single industry.

Porter, Michael E. "How Competitive Forces Shape Strategy." Vol. 57, no. 2. *Harvard Business Review.* (March-April 1979).

A Harvard Business School faculty specialist in business strategy and industrial economics, Michael E. Porter develops a discussion concerning the identification and degree of business competition in industry. The level and source of competition is dependent on five forces: threat of new entrants, bargaining power of customers, bargaining power of suppliers, threat of substitute products or services, and jockeying for position among current rivals. The collaborative power of these forces determines the profit potential for an industry. Within an industry the bottom-line purpose of forming competitive strategy is to cope with and ideally outmaneuver competition. This is an excellent, concise source for understanding the forces that govern competition in an industry as well as for development of strategy to specifically address identified competitive forces.

The Job Search

People work for a variety of reasons, but most of us work because we're paid for it. Take the compensation out of the equation (and that comes in many forms) and you'd find a lot more people home with their kids, working on their lawns, or riding the surf off the coast of Hawaii. Because we're paid and because working means less time surfing off the coast of Hawaii, we try to maximize the compensation we receive for the amount of work we do.

This chapter walks you through some of the issues job seekers need to consider if they hope to find jobs that maximize the return for time spent at the office. Looking for a job is a struggle human beings have endured ever since the first time clock was punched; the differences between today's search and that of a search merely ten years ago rests largely in the tactics devised for the search and the tools available to manage those tactics. Orchestrating a job search is a skill that will not only improve each time it's exercised, but also one that is crucial in making the most of one's career.

This chapter deals less with the standard recruiting and job search issues as with some less frequently considered issues that often make the difference between being hired and not being hired.

WHY LOOK FOR A NEW JOB . . . OR ANY JOB?

If your goal is indeed to increase the size of your paychecks, the tactic that works the best requires that you change jobs. If you currently have a job, the chances for a *big* bonus or a significant raise—the kind that can really make a difference after all taxes have been taken out—are relatively slight (unless you're involved in a pre-IPO firm or you happen to be a rainmaker for an investment bank). The big increases in compensation come from changing jobs, not from staying with your current employer and banking 5 percent cost-of-living-allowance (COLA) raises year after year.

The observation that employers run the risk of losing their top performers to the highest bidder may—in fact, *should*—be alarming to employers reading this book. But it happens to be true. Individual loyalty to the firm is unfortunately a rarer and rarer occurrence, and it is premised more upon compensation than it is upon any sense of debt or longevity of relationship. The social contracts we once had with our employers are gone.

According to a 1992 Cornell University study, predictions for the future workplace include the belief that high levels of stress will prevail, organizations will be flatter, a greater percentage of annual salary will vary with corporate performance, and employees will have to take greater responsibility for their own careers.[1] These predictions are already ringing true. Massive layoffs coupled with growing populations and changing technologies create a hypercompetitive environment and force even corporate monoliths that used to be considered highly stable companies to adopt a nimble mode of operation. Additionally, not unlike the professional sporting business in which multimillion dollar, multiyear contracts are commonplace (and that's compensation based on potential, not performance), firms from the consulting industry—and even the financial services industries (two primary hiring industries for the top MBA programs in the country)—are paying significant bonuses for potential stars before the work even begins. This may range up to $60,000 in total first-year bonus compensation, in addition to base salaries hovering in the high $80,000s.

WHEN TO LOOK FOR A NEW JOB

Many people with jobs are often also people looking for jobs. They are using the foundation of their current workplace to benchmark their current situation, to maximize their return of invested labor. The best place to look for a job is from a job, and it's neither necessary nor recommended that you wait until you're out of work to start looking for work. You are much more attractive to an employer, at first glance, if you are already working. It tells the potential employer that another firm—preferably a name with market equity or even a competitor they'd enjoy accessing internal secrets from—has already bought into your capabilities. If you are out on the street looking for a job, you have to initially overcome the hurdle of what caused you to be put on the street. If you're just starting out in your career (having graduated from college or graduate school), you've got to overcome the chicken-and-the-egg dilemma: How can I get a good job without experience, and how can I get experience without a good job? We address the various answers to this question in this chapter.

STRATEGIC INFLECTION POINTS

Employees frequently think about changing jobs because of what Andy Grove, the CEO of Intel, calls "strategic inflection points" or the "times in the life of a business or a person when fundamentals are about to change. That change can mean an opportunity to raise yourself to new heights. But it may just as likely signal the beginning of the end."[2] You've heard of people who always have updated copies of their resumes available. You might consider such people paranoid, but what they are is opportunistic. Employees who understand their own strategic inflection points are the ones who are not only opportunistic but also the ones who understand their industry, their company, and their own skills. This knowledge enables them to anticipate change and how it may affect them. Consider the employee who never took the time to learn how to use a computer and is working for the company that just purchased a multimillion dollar computerized MRP system. Who has the advantage now—the young kid fresh out of college or the older employee who's been at the job, doing it the old way and probably doing it well, for 20 years? The odds-on favorite—regardless of whether it's fair—is often the young, trainable employee starting his or her career.

On a larger scale, consider the owners of Blockbuster Video, who built a multibillion dollar empire renting videocassettes. You can bet Blockbuster is fast approaching a strategic inflection point with the onset of digital satellites, telecommunication deregulation, and the prospect that consumers soon will be able to order any of thousands of movies over the telephone lines. How often will the suburban mom or dad be asked to run out to the video store to pick up the latest release when it's available for the same price simply by picking up the telephone?

Microsoft's recent response to the Internet is a good example of a positive response to a strategic inflection point. Late to the market, Microsoft understood the impact the Net would have on its business and it rallied to quickly capture the attention of a significant portion of the consumable market. Such revolutionary changes in the markets are occurring daily, and what makes us marketable is our ability to recognize and respond to such changes before they occur. This ability is linked largely to access to information. That is why extensive knowledge of the job market is vital.

WHAT DO I LOOK FOR IN A NEW JOB? DO I HAVE TO LIKE MY CO-WORKERS?

One of the first things you have to realize is that the office is not necessarily the place you'll go to make friends. Sure, it's great if you get along with your coworkers. If you do, there's a good chance your productivity, your longevity on the job, and your good feelings about your job will be greater than if you do not. But as Judith Martin (aka Miss Manners) says, "workers are not necessarily friends—they are a group of people who are thrown together at the whim of their employer."[3] Friendships aside, you do need to respect your coworkers and win their respect as well. You must trust their ability to do the same type of job you are doing day in and day out.

Finding a job that meets your qualifications in terms of pay, benefits, intellectual challenge, opportunity, vacation, and whatever else you deem important is clearly the pinnacle of employment success. But you need to be patient and perpetually aware of your own strategic inflection points. A short-term perspective leads to irrational market behavior, and few people get rich timing the market. Nobody can predict the future and not one person has been able to create a formula for guaranteed success that clearly defines a career-planning process leading to a prescribed end. Too many variables in the market, in the firm, in your personal life, and in areas that you have no influence over all contribute to render any ten-year career plan obsolete.

Five years, however, is a more workable number: long enough to factor in patience and transcend extended business cycles, but short enough to force the plan to be flexible. Developing a working career plan is not unlike writing a business plan. It cannot be a static document. It must live and respond to changing conditions as the market changes. And it must be referred to on a regular basis, not thrown into a box of records never to be seen again. This is often the document that was interesting enough to secure funding, convince a client to buy your product, or scare away the competition. It is almost sacrosanct.

LAUNDRY LIST

Establish your personal laundry list of requirements and expectations from your work and use the same criteria to rank your opportunities. What makes you tick?

Why are you working? Some people could not do without five weeks of vacation and will not consider jobs that won't allow them their beach time during the month of July. For that freedom they're willing to compromise weekends, salary, or intellectual challenge. All of these things could be construed as compensation—however, not the monetary variety.

Before you even start looking for a job you have to figure out what it is you are looking for in a job. And this is even before you consider function or industry. These are the core values you hold for yourself and for your employer. If you cannot answer these questions, then you should find a dark closet away from external influences (like the kids, the spouse, or the in-laws) and try to determine what really makes you happy, what you are willing to compromise, and what your absolutes are. Many of these questions are tough and easily passed over for want of a painless process. Some will need to be answered from sources within a firm that is less concerned with reciting the company marketing line and is more willing to let you in on its own real machinations and internal ethos. Adequate preparation on the front end will eliminate time-consuming frustrations during any search. Everybody's checklist will be different (see Figure 10.1).

RESUME WRITING FOR SUCCESS

I fully expect most readers of this book have already created a resume, and, if not, there are a number of great sources available that will walk a job seeker through the maze of often confusing information about writing a good resume. This is not one of those references. Coming up with the right resume is critical, and it should be the first step in any job search. Taking the time to do it right the first time and knowing the type of resume to use will save you considerable heartache when the time comes for you to actually hand your resume to an interviewer or submit it in response to a job opportunity. There is almost nothing worse than hearing about a job you'd like to apply for and not having a resume ready to submit. You find yourself staying up late at night attempting to construct a resume under extreme pressure—and most of us don't work well in those conditions.

There are a few things you need to know about your resume. The first is that a resume is meant to be a window into your working history. It is a historical sales document that presents your experiences in a positive way intended to create the need to meet you, to grant you an interview. A resume is not an autobiography and cannot—should not—be an attempt to disclose everything there is to know about you. Most of that stuff is not appropriate for a job interview and most

Company: ABC Corporation
Position: Chief Bottle Washer

Why do I want to work in this industry?
Why do I want to work for this firm?
Why would this firm want to hire me?
Do I like, respect, and trust the people I interviewed with?

Criteria	Job with ABC Corporation	
————————	Salary	Bottom line $60,000
————————	Bonus signing	Require $10,000
————————	Bonus starting	Require $5,000
————————	Bonus annual	Based on personal performance, division, or company as a whole?
————————	Job security	High, medium, low Why is this job available?
————————	Advancement/ firm	High, medium, low Why is this job available?
————————	Advancement/ industry	High, medium, low Where is this business going?
————————	Weekday hours	How long?
————————	Weekend hours	Yes or no, and how often? Are weekends necessary or just face time?
————————	Overtime	Yes or no My choice or theirs?
————————	Vacation	How long Do people actually take their vacations?
————————	Intellectual challenge	High, medium, low Will I be bored?
————————	Travel	a lot, a bit, none Do I like to travel and do I like where I'm going?
————————	Flexibility	A lot, a bit, none Do I like to travel and do I like where I'm going?
————————	Variety	High, medium, low Will I be bored?
————————	Social responsibility	High, medium, low Am I embarrassed to say I work here?

FIGURE 10.1 *Job requirement and expectation checklist.*

Criteria	Job with ABC Corporation	
————————	Workforce diversity	High, medium, low *Question:* Am I all alone? Is anybody?
————————	Environmentally friendly	High, medium, low *Question:* Will I be sued?
————————	Workplace	Teamwork or individual?
————————	Technology	Do I know it or can I learn it?
————————	Commute time	How long?
————————	Commute style	How done?
————————	Socializing	Do I like these people?
————————	Benefits	
————————	Health care	How much?
————————	Dental care	How much?
————————	Retirement	How much and when?
————————	Educational assistance	How much?

FIGURE 10.1 (*Continued*)

employers do not want to hear about unrelated issues. The resume should focus on your work experiences and say just enough to grab the employers' attention. Too many job seekers, especially at the senior level, ramble on and on in a resume and during an interview about truly interesting stuff—accomplishments and issues and skills that are, unfortunately, mostly or entirely unrelated to the job opportunity at hand. A resume alone will not get you a job, but it can provide the window of opportunity for the next stage. Do not think for a second that if you say it all on your resume you will have nothing left to discuss during your interview. There will always be things to discuss.

Granted, it's hard to write about yourself, and you'll likely find the exercise of writing your resume extremely frustrating because nobody, except our most obnoxious friends, really likes to tout his or her own successes. However, the work environment demands that you do just that. Since everybody is trying to find an advantage, you need to promote yourself better than the next candidate. You do that by being confident in your abilities and alerting the marketplace about your skills.

How can you best translate your skills and experience onto paper for inclusion in that most important document, the resume? By talking to people—talking to people you have worked with and for—and by asking them to describe you, the business you worked in, and your attendant job responsibilities. Your goals are to gain a complete perspective and to gain confidence. Sometimes you know exactly what you did but have trouble articulating your activities in a way you think appropriate for the resume. After taking notes, just summarize what you learned from these interviews. Don't try to make it presentable—just get the words on paper. Through this process you'll start to: (1) develop a keen understanding of what your work experiences have been and a familiarity with the best way to describe them, and (2) see ways to transform the casual scribbling into meaningful words that present well in a resume.

SOME OTHER THINGS TO THINK ABOUT
Career Objective: To Add or Not to Add?

The only reason to add a specific career objective is if the objective you state is the only one you'd consider. For example, if you know you want to be an investment manager in New York City to the exclusion of anything else, then go ahead and say so. You run into problems, however, when your resume slides across the desk of an informed recruiter who wonders why you've limited your options. There are a lot of jobs in different industries requiring similar career skills. Stating a defined career objective compromises your candidacy for such positions. If you cannot define a specific goal, you should not add a general goal simply to have a career objective stated. And if you state the goal as precisely as you should, it'll take up too much space on your resume. What more, for example, does the following tell me about you than what any other candidate may also be trying to convey:

> *Career Goal: To secure an entry-level position within a growing and dynamic firm that provides a cross-functional experience ultimately leading to increasing responsibility and a senior management position.*

No kidding! That is pretty much the same thing that everybody wants. Indeed, this career goal has laid out the *basic* strategy for the initial job search for the next 20 years. Career goals or objectives are meaningless unless they are very specific, short, and focused on the near term. Even then, however, stating a career objective is risky, because, once you submit your resume for a position, you no longer control where it goes. Therefore, you may be passed over for a position that somebody was kind enough to submit your resume for and that you would be eager to accept, because the career goal you have included on your resume does not fit the position.

Education

Your resume should have an education section. If you have recently left school and are not currently working, the education section should be at the top of your resume. Some argue that if you have an extremely prestigious education under your belt, the education section (including where you attended high school) should go first. However, that decision is best left to individual preference and your assessment of just how critical where you went to school will be for the position. If you know (or suspect) the recruiter attended the same small high school (or a comparable school), I would suggest adding that. Again, this is your resume and you need to be comfortable with what it says. If you were all-American everything in high school, were the class valedictorian, and were chosen to speak at graduation, I'd make mention of it on my resume, even though the information is old.

The education section should include the name of the college (not abbreviated), its location, the month and year you received (or expect to receive) your degree, the number of years you were there, the degree conferred, specific honors, relative course work, and any college-related, extracurricular activities that are pertinent to the position. "Keg Czar," while important to your fraternity brothers, is not appropriate for your resume.

Work Experience

This is where the rubber meets the road. The listings of prior work experiences will tell the employer the most important information about your candidacy. These sections should be honest and relate to the job you are applying for. Of course, you cannot re-create history, but you can change the perception of reality by constructing a resume that touts skills matched to the demands of the job that you seek. Consider that previous experience is only one part of your presentation. If we were measured only by what we've done, we'd all be caught in dead-end positions. Part of your success during an interview and on your resume is your interest and enthusiasm for the job and the company. I suspect most employers would rather hire an enthusiastic person who has shown a pattern of growing responsibility and experiences and is willing to learn to an experienced person who expresses no enthusiasm. Directly applicable work experience on your resume will help a lot. Similar experience will help somewhat and needs to be augmented by enthusiasm and a pattern of growth. If you offer limited or no work experience, your candidacy will require considerable enthusiasm and probably a few recommendations from senior people.

Consultant Alfred Mauer wrote about a new human resources paradigm.[4] And although the word *paradigm* is an overused buzzword, the perspective is interesting. Mauer wrote that the job market is changing and job seekers want the perfect match, but only the perfect match for the job. Industry is looking for experienced people who can hit the ground running with no additional training while adding significant value above and beyond their hiring costs. Mr. Mauer posits that, even at the highest level, "nobody hits the ground running at full speed. If they do, they're probably a nuisance. Every new employee needs some basic training."

Employers seeking an exact match for an exact task will spend more time and energy sourcing these employees than the firm that seeks the general athlete, with a tool box of skills offering adaptability and general traits that provide a foundation for learning while on the job. Job seekers need to promote their willingness to learn and their ability to acclimate well to different working conditions. That being said, the resume will not get you the job. Ultimately, that responsibility is yours in the interview and beyond. But a well-constructed resume might open a door to the right job with the right firm. All you need is the chance to pitch your case, and if you've done your research and prepared extensively, then that's all you can ask for and all you can reasonably expect.

RESUME TYPES

There is a variety of resume types, many of which you are no doubt familiar with. You should probably plan on using several types in your job search. The functional and chronological resumes are old standbys. Both work very well, largely because everybody uses them, they are portable, and they are easy to comprehend. Examples of each are shown in Figures 10.2 and 10.3. The variety that is probably somewhat less familiar is the electronic resume, either in text or in multimedia form, which is used to cast your candidacy across the Internet. The best Internet resumes are multimedia and they include sound, images, colors, animated sequences, and even video clips. Text over the Internet is boring and does not optimize the full potential of that vehicle.

A multimedia resume looks nothing like the text version of the resumes you are most familiar with. The way you package your candidacy is almost as important as the content of your candidacy, and the limitations rest only with your abilities to create. Assistance in doing so is easy to access and a number of self-help booklets with the appropriate software can be found in any good bookstore.

RESUME RED FLAGS

- *Check your spelling:* Too many people spend so much time on their resumes, they start to go blind to the text that's actually there. Read your resume

Jennifer Ruth Thomas
The Amos Tuck School · 514 Byrne Hall·Hanover, NH 03755 ·
(603)-646-7365 · E-mail:j.sotak@dartmouth.edu

EDUCATION

THE AMOS TUCK SCHOOL OF BUSINESS ADMINISTRATION, DARTMOUTH COLLEGE   Hanover, NH
Candidate for Master of Business Administration degree, 1997.
Prospective Student Host, Marketing Club; Organized Marketing
Career Panel.

UNIVERSITY OF MASSACHUSETTS   Amherst, MA
Bachelor of Business Administration in Marketing, Minor in
Economics, 1991.
Graduated cum laude. Economics Honor Society (Omicron Delta
Epsilon).

EXPERIENCE

1991–1995 **A. T. KEARNEY, Inc.**   New York, NY
Associate
Performed broad range of consulting services for Fortune 500
companies, including marketing-related consulting for leading
consumer products companies.
Managed client relationships and worked in joint client and
consultant teams in formulating recommendations for change.

- *Category Management Strategy:* Developed category
  management strategies and enhanced category position of a
  leading bottled-water manufacturer through improved trade
  presentation media. Assessed New Age beverage category market
  and its impact on bottled water. Developed a micromarketing tool
  for optimizing shelf space in retail locations.

- *Market Assessment:* Conducted customer, competitor, channel,
  and market expert interviews to assess competitive position of a
  leading home security equipment manufacturer. Performed
  extensive market research to project market growth and potential
  share expansion. Provided synthesized results to a major diversified
  conglomerate considering acquisition of the manufacturer.

1990, 1991 **JC PENNEY**   Garden City, NY
Assistant Merchandise Manager
Executed full range of merchandise management activities during
summer internships. Selected as regional champion for District Intern
Scholarship and qualified for nationwide competition.

- Managed sales team of ten full-time and eight part-time sales
  associates.

- Executed seasonal assortment planning, visual mechandising, and
  in-department promotions.

PERSONAL

- Enjoy volunteer work, YMCA Big Sister Program
- UMass Alumni Club Member (NY Metro Area)
- Conversational Italian and German, familiar with Russian

FIGURE 10.2 *Chronological resume.*

Shawn H. Smeallie

1 Topnotch Lane   home telephone: (617) 555-5555
Weeds, MA 03750   home fax: (617) 555-5555
                                         e-mail: Shawn H. Smeallie dartmouth.edu

DEMONSTRATED SKILL IN . . .

- Setting goals, determining objectives, and devising strategies toward the development of new business areas;
- Formulating and defining product concepts consistent with strategic marketing directives, developing business/marketing plans to develop and introduce same;
- Executing plans, mobilizing resources, and directing the development and marketing processes;
- Communicating and presenting concepts and plans to all interested stakeholders; building consensus, gaining agreement, and driving process.

SKILLS DEVELOPED WITH . . .

Leahy Clinic, Burlington, MA   1996–present
Development Director responsible for capital gift fund-raising for this academic medical center

- Managed all development activities of the Cancer Center and the Weiderecht Center for Clinical and Evaluative Studies.
- Developed marketing strategies to raise prospect/public awareness. Worked with physicians and individuals to increase private donations.
- Directed fund-raising efforts for new cancer center building ($20 million goal), fellowship programs, and research support.

St. Lawrence University, Canton, NY   1992–1994
As Associate Director, Major Gifts, managed the cultivation and solicitation of 250 major gift prospects in Midwest region, where $30 million was raised during the "Everybody Loves a Saint" campaign.

- Coordinated project activities related to targeted fund-raising.
- Traveled extensively with senior officers, deans and faculty, trustees.
- Enlisted, trained, and managed Chicago Volunteer Committee.

EDUCATION . . .

- Masters of Business Administration—The Amos Tuck School, Dartmouth College, 1996.
- Bachelor of Arts, Economics—MIT, 1992, Honors Program, Dean's List

PERSONAL

Single; avid fan of thoroughbred racing; four sons; attempting to be a decent downhill skier

FIGURE 10.3 *Functional resume.*

backward, word for word, and have a friend do the same. There is nothing more offputting in a resume than a typo.

- *Check your grammar:* If you use the passive voice, make sure all passages are consistent with this. Uniformity is critical. (And try not to use the passive voice.)

- *Check your data:* Do the phone numbers you list actually work? Is the reference you listed still working there? If not, try to find a current phone number.

- *Avoid being cute:* There exists a school of thought that your resume needs to be unique to capture the attention of the recruiters. There are plenty of anecdotal stories supporting times when a unique resume was successful. Nevertheless, a different-looking resume is usually nothing more than different and it will likely fail to be as cute to the recruiters as you thought it would be when you created it. Recruiters, reading hundreds of resumes, like to be able to look to a certain part of the resume for a certain type of information. They are creatures of habit. If you confuse them, they will not regard you any further. Give them the information where they expect it and leave your need to be an individual to another time.

- *Avoid buzzwords:* Buzzwords are some of the window dressings on a resume that sound nice to the uneducated, but are clearly red flags indicating foolishness to the well-trained eye. The Jargon Master Matrix (see sidebar) is a fine example of how matching various words creates intelligent-sounding phrases that are nothing more than a complicated way of saying very little. A *buzzword,* according to Webster's New Collegiate Dictionary, is "an important-sounding usually technical word or phrase often of little meaning used chiefly to impress laymen." Be careful of using buzzwords and refer to the matrix as an exercise in frivolity.

- *Resume length:* How long should a resume be? Academic resumes tend to be long. That may simply be the nature of academics, but more likely these resumes are long in order to list publications. At the early stage of one's career, a single-page resume is enough to convey the most important experiences of your working history. In the middle of your career, you'll be inclined to go to two pages. It probably won't be necessary, but you will be in the prime of your career and may feel obligated to put it all on paper. This urge will pass over a period of time. When you finally assume your position in the corporate boardroom, you'll resort to the minimalist approach and a single-page resume. It's at this point

Jargon Master Matrix

Pick three numbers and use them to choose a word from each column to create phrases. For instance, 11, 8, 7 gives you "value-based process model." This is useful terminology for anyone trying to sound important.

	Column 1	Column 2	Column 3
1	overarching	visionary	objectives
2	strategic	support	alternatives
3	special	customer-oriented	expectations
4	specific	stretch	mechanisms
5	core	planning	assessment
6	long-term	marketing	update
7	defined	service	model
8	technology-based	process	product
9	formal	fundamental	centralization
10	exceptional	sales	incentive
11	value-based	budget	initiatives
12	executive	operating	feedback
13	immediate	discretionary	infrastructure
14	interactive	tracking	proposition

that a single line often tells the whole story. In fact the higher you go, the less you'll need a resume. This is one of the advantages of success.

INTERVIEW

This is the single most important part of finding a job, because it's the time when you're able to respond to negativity, to pitch your case, to engage in dialogue. The interview is the true test of your powers of persuasion. And isn't that what business is all about? Regardless of what the proponents of the power of positive thought might otherwise suggest, going into an interview with the expectation that you will get the job will take you off the competitive edge that can serve you so well and may bring you to a level of complacency that will lead to the demise of your interview. There is almost nothing as bad as bombing the early part of an interview and having to struggle through the bulk of the remaining time knowing that there is no chance you will get the job. If this type of interview sounds horrendous, well . . . it is. Do everything possible to avoid this. Make a first and lasting good impression.

You need to do your homework, and this includes researching the firm. You should peruse Lexis/Nexis, the World Wide Web, and various retrieval services for information. You should also take a look at *The Wall Street Journal* and the local paper, if there is any chance that events described in it have a bearing on the firm you are courting. Know enough about the business of the firm to recognize issues of the day that may have an impact on the success of the firm, and this includes knowledge of the competitive marketplace.

But don't sound like an overconfident know-it-all. Remember that the person interviewing you already has a job—you need to respect the power play going on. The intelligent recruiter will always try to hire the best person for the job. Sometimes that means hiring someone smarter than he or she is. However, don't forget that many people feel threatened by intelligence surpassing their own. Be a smart job seeker. Watch for the signs of brilliance as well as the signs of the Peter Principle.

The most important advice about an interview is to follow the Boy Scout motto: Be prepared. You should be smart enough to anticipate and respond to every conceivable hostile question. If you already understand the worst-case scenario and you have a well-rehearsed answer addressing the issue, then you have little to worry about. Write out the questions you anticipate and ask a family member or friend to run you through a series of mock interviews. If you can go as far as having these sessions videotaped, you'll be able to see what the recruiters will see. Of course, your answers should not sound well rehearsed. But that is a far cry from your answers sounding well thought out. You might not always get the job, but at least you won't be sweating bullets while you're interviewing.

Your interview starts with the clothes you wear and continues through to the thank-you letter you write the same day of the interview. I've heard of candidates for jobs who thought a power play with the receptionist would indicate their importance, only to find out the receptionist is often one of the savviest and most liked members of any staff. You're being judged by everybody already holding a job at the firm and you are asking to become a member of its club. Treat everyone at the firm with respect if you expect to be given a chance. Start strong and end strong.

Job seekers often express dismay about not getting a job after an interview they thought had gone so well and been so amicable. But you need to know that if you bomb in the first five minutes, the strategies for moving forward typically follow one of two paths. Short of kicking you out of the interview room after the first 5 minutes, the next best strategy to making the following 25 minutes or so as painless as possible *for the recruiter* is to keep it as friendly as possible. Some of the best interviews are the ones where you're pushed to the edge and forced to respond, not the ones that engage in friendly conversation.

Don't let the first five minutes kill your candidacy. Practice your opening salvo and anticipate a variety of questions. Make the right first impression and ride that success until the last few minutes—then end strong. Take the initiative and ask what the next steps are. One student interviewing for a sales position floundered right up until the last question, when the recruiter asked if he had any questions. He won the support of the recruiter because he attempted to close the deal. He asked if the recruiter was willing to support his candidacy for the next steps. It was that simple act of ending with an intelligent question, which many people are unable to ask, that brought him to the next round—where he promptly failed. But at least he advanced to the second step!

Don't ask stupid questions. Yes, there is such a thing as a stupid question. And the craziest questions are the ones you ask at the end of the interview that would require another 30 minutes altogether for the recruiter to respond to. Avoid questions that can be answered simply by reading the company marketing literature or annual report. Avoid questions that are best asked after an offer has been made. Do not talk about money until asked or until the end of the interview cycle.

Don't Make Hasty Decisions

If offered the job, thank the recruiter and express your satisfaction. Ask how much time you have to consider the offer and ask for 48 hours or more if the recruiter suggests anything shorter than that. Any recruiter from a firm who attempts to force you to respond during the interview is probably not a person you'd like to work with anyway, so don't worry too much about asking. The company has offered you a job and indicated its interest in having you. The power has just switched over to your side of the table and you can dictate the terms . . . within reason. Consider the offer and go as far as to inform other employers with whom you already may have interviewed and who are interested in your candidacy about your offer. (They may be willing or able to match or better the offer.)

Most Offers Are Negotiable

Negotiating is a fine art, and volumes have been written explaining and teaching the process. Negotiating is all about providing solutions to conflict, which arises when there is a difference of opinion. That being said, we negotiate every day, whether we know it or not, and a basic understanding of how to negotiate should not only improve your daily lot in life, but will arm you with

The Most Unusual Questions Asked by Job Candidates

- What is it that you people do at this company?
- What is the company motto?
- Why aren't you in a more interesting business?
- What are the zodiac signs of all the board members?
- Why do you want references?
- Do I have to dress for the next interview?
- I know this is off the subject, but will you marry me?
- Will the company pay to relocate my horse?
- Does your health insurance cover pets?
- Would it be a problem if I'm angry most of the time?
- Does your company have a policy regarding concealed weapons?
- Do you think the company would be willing to lower my pay?
- Why am I here?

The Most Interesting Job Search Techniques

- A job applicant challenged the interviewer to an arm wrestle.
- An interviewee wore a Walkman, explaining that she could listen to the interviewer and the music at the same time.
- A candidate announced she hadn't had lunch and proceeded to eat a hamburger and french fries in the interviewer's office.
- A candidate explained that her long-term goal was to replace the interviewer.
- A candidate said he never finished high school because he was kidnapped and kept in a closet in Mexico.
- A balding candidate excused himself and returned to the office a few minutes later wearing a hairpiece.
- An applicant said if he was hired he would demonstrate his loyalty by having the corporate logo tattooed on his forearm.
- An applicant interrupted her interview to phone her therapist for advice on how to answer specific interview questions.
- A candidate brought a large dog to the interview.
- An applicant refused to sit down and insisted on being interviewed standing up.
- A candidate dozed off during the interview.

the skills necessary to optimize your job search. Bear in mind that there are no guarantees when negotiating, but unless you try, you'll never know what you might have accomplished. Len Greenhalgh, professor at the Amos Tuck School of Business Administration at Dartmouth College, lists the eight rules of negotiating:

1. *Be ready to make a commitment.* You cannot negotiate from strength if there is not an offering level at which you would say "Yes, I will take that job." Know what your bottom and top lines are and when you would accept a position.

2. *Emphasize that you really want to work for the firm.* Your candidacy is going to be that much stronger if you express an interest. Some industries and firms are willing to pay more for a candidate who really wants to work there, as there will be less of a turnover risk. But be honest—do not express the same sentiment to *all* firms.

3. *Empathize with the corporate side.* Know that the employer may really want you, but the going rate for a person of your caliber is higher than what the firm is offering. Firms are often constrained by the equity structure of the salaries that are already in place. When negotiating, you are accepting pay in the abstract, but the employer has to live in reality. It's not often the actual money, rather, it's the meaning of the money that causes problems for the employer.

4. *Depersonalize the process of asking for money.* It's OK to ask for a lot of money. Do not make an economic sacrifice to work for the firm because you are afraid to ask for what you believe you are worth.

5. *Negotiate with the right person.* Often the human resources person will make the offer and toe the line on negotiations. However, the line manager may have more wiggle room or the power to influence change. Find allies within the firm and negotiate with people who understand your worth and can make decisions.

6. *Avoid ultimatums.* You don't like to get them, so don't give them. They are counterproductive.

7. *Sign on bonus.* It's a cheap way for a firm to hire you. Consider the time value of money and the benefits of starting at a higher base. Granted, the lure of an extra 20K or more in your pocket is appealing, but taxes will have to be paid on that money and, if the job has a performance bonus (or any kind of increase) based on base salary, wouldn't you rather start from a higher point?

8. *Take the job for the right reasons.* Money alone is usually a bad reason to take a job. Make sure the people, the location, the responsibility, the career path, the product, the industry, the lifestyle are all right for

you. Don't take the job for the wrong reasons because you're currently impoverished or you think there is a bragging benefit to securing a high salary.

USING THE WORLD WIDE WEB

It's hard to deny the importance and power of the World Wide Web (WWW) and the Internet. The advances made every day to this technology render what is listed in this section almost obsolete. The WWW is a fantastic source of information on industries, individual companies, executives, economic trends, and you name it. It's also a link to current job opportunities. Many firms have established home pages that are dedicated to seeking applicants for positions available. Moreover, you have access to this information on a real-time basis through the Internet. A recent poll of 435 human resource professionals, conducted by Lee Hecht Harrison, revealed that 47 percent use the Internet to recruit (31 percent said they use resume banks).[5] While, historically, many of the positions listed on the WWW have focused on job seekers with specific technical skills, more and more firms, from the consumer products industry to the consulting industry, have listed positions and successfully found applicants from a variety of functional areas, including marketing, operations, strategy consulting, and accounting.

Employers like the WWW because it provides greater access to a wider candidacy pool. Job seekers like it because it's fast, it's inexpensive, you make a powerful first impression, and you are accessing and being accessed by a wide group of employers. It also precludes a certain amount of discrimination—potential hirers will initially (at least) be measuring you based on your advertised skills and work history rather than what you look like.

Variations to Web pages range from simple listings of jobs to interactive pages providing resume/skill-matching services—all the way to a level of service that will automatically notify you when a job listing meets your requirements.

It's all a very simple process, even for the most timid surfers. A variety of programs (such as Internet Assistant) exist to translate your word-based resume to a searchable document, so you no longer need to master the intricacies (though they are relatively simple for anybody who wants to try) of programming in HTML.

Tricks to Finding the Right Job on the Web

Key Word Searches
Many search programs scan your resume in search of words that employers select—words they consider rep-

resentative of the type of people they are seeking for specific jobs. What you should avoid are the classic action verbs like "facilitated," "strengthened," and "launched" in favor of nouns that have more meaning to an employer. A financial position might seek references to "CPA," "accounting," "Arthur Andersen," or "Series 7."

The resume you use on the Web is different from one you send through the mail. Web resumes provide links to bodies of work you've created, writing samples, and so on. Web resumes are built in such a way as to make the information highlighting your skills available to the browser in easily accessed form, but they do not dump it on the browser unless the browser initiates the interest.

Web Cautions
Be Wary

Be wary of the hacker. Be wary of the competition. The hacker might alter your resume simply for the fun of it. The competition might alter your resume to eliminate you from the candidacy pool. The ultimate challenge is the hacker competition, who not only has the desire, but also the ability, to sabotage your efforts to find a job online. Check your resume often. If you are paying to have your resume listed in a database, make certain access is secure; make certain there is a reimbursement procedure if your resume is lost or altered. It's not even uncommon for surfers to copy your resume and falsely represent your work experience as their own. A good employer is going to double-check any information found on the Web. You should do the same.

Your Current Employer

Imagine your boss's surprise when your resume shows up on her desk after she performs a search through a job bank. If your current employer does not know you are out looking for a new job, be prepared to do one of two things: (1) roll the dice and hope you are not discovered, or (2) prepare a resume that is blind (i.e., does not include information like your name and address). Blind resumes are often sent to P.O. boxes and might have language like this included:

> *The identity of the person holding the following qualifications and experience is withheld for security reasons until a mutually interesting opportunity exists. If you wish to discuss my employment history and qualifications, please contact me at the address indicated.*

Lack of Information

Avoid any site that does not list a street address, a phone number, or any other way to contact the "owners" of the site. If possible, try to call firms using the service and ask them directly if they have ever hired people off the database you are considering joining. Screen them as much as you expect they will screen you. As much as you want a new job, don't compromise your integrity or your pocketbook to find one.

Avoid Scams

Be careful of sites that charge you to list your resume. While some of them do provide a premium service, there are plenty of sites available that won't cost you any more than the fee to access the WWW. For some job seekers, paying $50 to list their resumes on premium sites is a small tariff to pay for the chance to land an $80,000 job, but others need to watch every cent, especially if they're out of work. In that case, avoid the fees before the service is rendered—if at all.

Perseverance/Follow-through

Ideally, you would like to know who receives the information and be able to contact that person in a few days to ensure that the information was received and try to determine if you have a shot at the job. The last thing you need at this point is more indecision. Knowing you are out of the running is considerably better than thinking you still have a chance for a position. While the news might be bad, the knowledge does free your time to hit the next target. And that's where your persistence pays off.

INTERNET RESOURCES

Best Job Site   http://WWW/itec.sfsu.edu/jobs/
                       bestjobs.html
- Lattice of connections to dozens of sites.
- Good first stop.

Career Magazine   http://www.careermag.com
- Career resource publication in magazine format.
- Key features include Career Forum for networking and Directory of Executive Recruiters.

Career Mosaic   http://www.careermosaic.com
- Comprehensive career service.
- Access to international opportunities in Europe and Asia and site within a site—the Health Care Connection.

Career Net   http://www.careers.org
- Over 11,000 links to employers, federal job opportunities, and career resources.

Career Site   http://www.careersite.com
- Recipient of Creme de la Creme site for August '96.
- Resume matching service—virtual headhunter.

Career Network   http://sgx.com/hg
- Searchable database for information technology professionals.

E-Span   http://www.espan.com
- Links to 1,700 employers and 3,500 job openings.
- Features personalized job search using several criteria to match you with a job opportunity.

Electronic   http://none.coolware.
   Job Guide   com/jobs.html
- Focus on technical but also has listings for financial/marketing positions in San Francisco Bay area.

The Help Wanted   http://www.
   Page   helpwantedpage.com
- Thousands of job listings in marketing, engineering.

High Technology   http://www.
   Career Magazine   hightechcareers.com

Intellimatch   http://www.
     intellimatch.com
- Resume posting service.

JobWeb   http://www.jobweb
- Only site you really need.
- Includes Catapult.
- Links to job listings in *The Chronicle of Higher Education.*

Kiersey Temperament   http://sunsite.unc.edu/
   Sorter   jembin//mb.pl
- Self-assessment tool, derivative of the Myers-Briggs personality type test.

Monster Board   http://www.monster.com
- Searchable database for career opportunities in all fields—mostly East Coast.

NationJob Network   http://www.
     nationjob.com
- Job listings with Midwest focus.

National Business   http://www.occ.com/occ/
   Employment Weekly   NBEW/NBEW01.html
- Tailored to seekers with several years of business experience.
- Parent company is *The Wall Street Journal.*

On-line Career Center   http://www.occ.com
- Enormous Web jobs database.

Recruiter On-line   http://www.ipa.com
- Over 2,000 executive search firms, recruiters.

Riley Guide   http://www.jobtrak.
com/jobguide
- Margaret Riley's acclaimed guide to Internet job searches with lots of great links to job resources, services, and information guides.
- Features international employment information.

Salary Info   http://www.espan.com/
salary/salary.html
- Salary guide for MIS professionals.

Saludos Web   http://www/hooked.net/
saludos
- Great page for Hispanic listings.

Skill Search   http://www/internet-is.com/
skillsearch
- Online employment service creates detailed applicant profile.

Student Center   http://www/StudentCenter.com
- 35,000 firms.
- Internet career planning.
- Recruiting brochures.

Up Software   http://www.upsoftware.com
- Lots o'links to domestic companies.
- Interesting newsletter with up-to-date info on skills and careers in the Information Age.

A Virtual Job Fair   http://www.careerexpo.com
- Magazine, career fair, and technical career resource.
- Lists over 15,000 high-tech career opportunities.

Wet Feet Press   http://www.wetfeet.com
- Great info resource for company comparisons.
- Get the inside scoop before your interview.

Woman's Center   http://amsquare.com/
america/wcenter/center.html
- Great site for 100 best companies for working women.

Workplace   http://galaxy.einet.net/galaxy/
Community/Workplace.html
- Staff/admin positions, universities/arts/government.

Yahoo   http://www.yahoo.com
- What list would be complete without Yahoo? If you couldn't find what you're looking for elsewhere, you'll find it through Yahoo.

NETWORKING

Networking has always been a part of the job search process; it's simply been referred to in different ways over time and never more prominently than in the 1980s when it was considered paramount to finding a job, doing deals, and generally being connected to the power brokers of the time. Networking is a slick way to say nothing more than getting out to alert the market of your availability and discovering potential positions that may not yet be public knowledge. Some will say that the best jobs never make it to the want ads. While that may be true for highly placed executive positions, market notification of which could have a disastrous (or advantageous) effect on stock prices, for most of us, the want ads and other resources for finding a job are still viable opportunities that are strengthened by an extensive networking effort.

The trick to networking is in your preparation, your attitude, and your perseverance. The rules for networking have not changed dramatically over time—regardless of what the promoters of the buzzwords for the day may say. It all comes down to preparation, attitude, and perseverance. This should come as no surprise, but like a good pilot running through a preflight checklist, a job seeker should run through a checklist of events prior to networking. To successfully network, you need to know exactly what you are attempting to achieve. Anybody worth talking to probably has little time for you. Therefore, you need to be direct and focused. Let the people know you're willing to take a chance or even willing to work for free or in a temporary position to get into the right industry.

Even at the MBA level, placement officers have rare and occasional students come into an office, sit down, raise their eyebrows, and say, "Weeeelllll, what are you going to do for me today?" It does not take long to instruct such students that the ball is in their court. That's what a networking visit is about.

Sources of Information

Who do you network with? There's a widely held belief that the higher you go in a firm's hierarchy, the better off you are. This is not always true, and it is partly because employees who are lower on the food chain are also looking for opportunities to move up the food chain. Tap into this group as a resource. The CEO at the top of the corporate food chain has little need to network for a job. Start where you can within the firm, where you consider the source of information the most truthful. Don't worry too much about competition at this stage.

Consider unique sources, such as your neighbor. In an age when many of us barely even know our neighbors, let alone their career experiences, you might consider breaking down that barrier and finding out where your neighbor (or any acquaintance you might not think about speaking to in terms of your career) works or worked before. Your neighbor may have relatives who are well connected to your target industry or firm, or maybe a relative who has conducted his or her own successful job search and has an abundance of leads he or she can no longer use. One student found her job lead for a position in Chicago while riding the chairlift in Colorado. Brief encounters can lead to big results.

The trick to networking is getting over the fear that not having a job (if this is your condition) means you're some sort of failure. Most successful people have been out of work at some time during their careers. Many have even been fired. And many of these people will also tell you that being fired or let go as the result of downsizing was the best thing that could have happened to them because it set them free to do what they always wanted to do. Or it provided clarity of vision so the people finally realized the jobs they had were dead ends and being fired opened up worlds of opportunities. Whatever the circumstances, if you are out of work, you must not consider this a detriment to your success. Rather, it's a chance to use the full workday to discover new opportunities to find a job that's perfect for you.

Consider also that networking should not be a finite activity used only when you are seeking a job. A successful network is a part of your career and requires attention and maintenance—a systemic strategy of contacting people in your network on a regular basis. Taken to an extreme, we are often judged by the quality of the people we consider our peers and those we interact with. Using that credo as a rule requires that you, as a successful networker, cultivate a knowledge base of people who, in a variety of ways, will help you along your career path or provide a resource you can pass on to a person networking with you.

Generosity has significant payback value. The good deeds done today may result in the opportunity of a lifetime for you later. It's rather like buying stock in a start-up firm and just forgetting it's a part of your portfolio—until it turns into the next Microsoft or Netscape. This is not to suggest that we all don't occasionally adopt a mercenary approach and maintain the expectation that we will be compensated in whatever way for our efforts in helping others as they network to success, but let's not disregard the fact that it can and does happen. And be patient throughout. Your time line is your full career—probably close to 40 years of working experiences. Networking requires a long-term view.

If You Don't Get the Job—What Next?

Do it all again! But before doing so, look back and try to figure out what went wrong. Don't expect the employer to tell you (although you might get lucky), for that firm no longer has any vested interest in you. This is where mock interviews can be extremely useful and where the comforting wisdom of people you trust is extremely valuable. It probably will not be your spouse and it would be unkind of you to put your spouse in that position. Often you will be your own best critic, and you simply have to be strong enough to recognize your own faults.

There can be many reasons, or combinations of reasons, you did not get the job. It could be that the competition was simply too intense and it was nothing more than a numbers game. It could be that the recruiter just happened to "like" another candidate. You should try not to despair because it's often not that *you* are rejected. Rather, it's simply your resume the firm rejected. But that doesn't help too much when the crowd down at the local pub hushes when you walk into the room; you still feel like a failure. It may be a few things that went wrong, and the AAA Resume service lists a few in its Web site.[6]

Unprofessional Resume Preparation

There are a lot of bad resumes floating around out there. A professional resume is more than just a well-formatted document. It demands a highly specialized style of writing and incorporates years of knowledge about the finer points of resume dos and don'ts. Computer programs that help you prepare resumes can do a good job of formatting and can help a little with wording. However, such programs simply can't supply the years of acquired knowledge a professional resume writer has. Consider having a professional prepare your resume. The advantage you gain over your competition is worth the investment, but make certain you are fully aware of what is on your resume in case you are asked specific questions.

Lack of Skills and Experience for the Position

You must possess the skills, qualifications, and experience for the position you are applying for. If you don't, be honest about it. You will eventually get caught if you misrepresent your qualifications.

Poor Personal Appearance

Would you hire a poorly dressed applicant? Or one who was poorly groomed or dirty? Shape up.

Inability to Speak Clearly or Express Yourself Correctly

Would you hire a person to meet and greet your customers who abused, defiled, or bastardized the English language? Verbal communication skills are important in the interview as well as on the job.

Expecting Too Much Too Soon

"You have to work your way to the top" is a proven, time-honored philosophy that seems to have disappeared . . . at least in the expectations of a few. If you target a position you are not qualified for, you won't get it.

SUMMARY

We as humans are often measured, not by how we respond to good news, but by how we react to bad news. It is that measure of our characters that establishes how we are perceived and how we should view ourselves. If you got the job, the trick is to keep it and launch from it when you hit another one of those strategic inflection points. If you did not get the job, you just have to revisit the process and keep on trying. Looking for a job is often a job itself and requires the same commitment of time and more. If you're able to step back and look at your life, you'll soon discover that not having a job or not having the perfect job is just one of the rotten things that happens. But you do have to realize that rebounding from a lost job or looking for a new job is exactly one of those things that you *can* do something about. Armed with a core set of skills, it largely boils down to persistence, attitude, patience, and a whole bunch of good luck. *Good luck.*

JOB MARKET

BBS

This stands for *bulletin board systems,* which is a data exchange system used online.

Case Interview

This is a situational problem presented to the candidate with the expectation that the problem will be solved during the course of the interview. A case interview is designed to test paradigms of thought, the ability to structure problems and solutions, and the ability to convey solutions in a convincing manner. All of this is done while interacting with the recruiter to discriminate important issues from nonimportant issues.

Challenge Interview

This aggressive interview behavior is designed to test the resolve of candidates and their ability to maintain composure when faced with hostile tactics (insults, demeaning behavior) that are common in certain industries.

Chronological Resume

This is the most common type of resume. Jobs are listed in reverse chronological order, with the candidate's last job listed at the top of the resume. Descriptions of job experiences can be written in linear or narrative form.

Cover Letter

This letter accompanies the resume, providing the recruiter with an introduction to the candidate. It should be only one page long and should briefly indicate how the candidate learned of the position, two to three reasons why the candidate should be considered for the job, and follow-up steps the candidate will pursue.

Executive Recruiter

This individual is hired by a firm and, acting alone as an agent or on behalf of a candidate, is responsible for facilitating the review, meeting, and selection of candidates seeking employment opportunities. This position is also known as a *headhunter.*

Follow-up

This refers to the process of writing letters, calling, and providing deliverables to determine the success of an interview, as well as the steps necessary to promote further action.

Functional Resume

This is the second most common type of resume. There are two versions: skills-based and function-based. Skill-based resumes identify specific skill sets that the candidate possesses. Functional resumes identify a candidate's capabilities as they relate to specific business functions. The emphasis is *not* on chronological experiences.

Hacker

A hacker is a person who delights in having an intimate understanding of the internal workings of a system, of computers, and of computer networks in particular.

HTML

This stands for *hypertext markup language,* a formatting language most commonly used for Web documents.

HTTP

This stands for *hypertext transfer protocol,* the common protocol or language computers use to "speak" to each other over the Web.

Internet

This is the largest multiprotocol collection of networks interconnected with routers (or gateways) in the world.

Job Banks

These are bulletin boards that receive listings from employers—many of whom pay a fee to have jobs listed—or that are sourced from newspapers and the like. There is a risk of obsolete information with job banks.

Mock Interview

This interview is facilitated by an agreeable party who shares feedback on the candidate's successes and failures during the interview process. It is often facilitated by a coworker, a mentor, a nonhiring firm, family, or a friend.

Networking

This is the process of alerting the market that a candidate is seeking an employment opportunity, through a series of letters and informational interviews that are designed to exponentially broaden a candidate's knowledge of the marketplace. Similar to a pyramid scheme or a chain letter, networking enables the candidate to learn about positions from contacts within the industry, but the candidate also hopes that his availability will be made known to opportunities that are not listed or are not apparent.

Nonverbal Communication

This refers to messages conveyed to and from people without speaking (e.g., crossing arms, looking at one's watch).

Panel Interview

This refers to a situation in which the candidate is interviewed by more than one recruiter at the same time.

Phone Interview

This interview occurs over the telephone.

Resume Banks

These involve posting opportunities to enter your resume into a database that is reviewed by employers. Costs range from free to as high as $100 for a limited run of your resume (anywhere from two weeks to one year).

Sequential Interview

This refers to a situation in which a candidate is progressed from one interviewer to another during the interview cycle. A common approach is for recruiters to try and extract different types of information from the candidate. Information from previous interview sessions is then conveyed to subsequent recruiters.

Server

A server is a provider of resources.

Strategic Inflection Points

These are times in the life of a business or a person when fundamentals are about to change.

Video Interview

This interview occurs through the use of a telephone and videoconferencing equipment.

World Wide Web

This hypertext-based distributed information system was created by researchers at CERN in Switzerland. Users may edit, create, or browse hypertext documents. The clients and servers are freely available.

MORE READINGS
Critical References—Articles

Argenti, Paul A. "Job Search Communication" In *Business Communication Strategy and Skill.* Edited by Mary Munter. Englewood Cliffs, N.J.: Prentice-Hall, 1987.

A good introduction to the entire process of a job search.

Critical References—Books

Beatty, Richard H., and Nicholas C. Burkholder. *The Executive Career Guide for MBAs: Inside Advice on Getting to the Top from Today's Business Leaders.* New York: Wiley, 1996.

This guide is written exclusively for MBAs. Its 12 chapters are meant to provide all of the necessary tools for finding and getting a successful executive job. The first half of the book is based on extensive surveys and interviews with top business executives, including such topics as the changing face of American business, the success absolute, the elements of executive success, and managing a successful career. The second half of the book deals with the executive job search. Topics included in this section are introduction to the executive job search, the executive resume, the chronological resume, the functional resume, how executives find jobs, interview preparation, and winning interview strategies.

Holton, Ed. *The New Professional: Everything You Need to Know for a Great First Year on the Job.* Princeton, N.J.: Peterson's Guides, 1991.

The New Professional is for people who are starting their first full-time professional jobs. It focuses mainly on those people making the transition from student to professional. One hundred newly hired workers and their managers were interviewed to give the reader an accurate account of what to expect during the first year on the job. The book is divided into five parts: (1) the attitude you need as a new employee and what your employers expect of you; (2) the new professional role, the skills you need to build to play that role, and how it differs from student life; (3) how to get along with your boss and the organizational life of the office (company culture, people, politics); (4) the practicalities of going to work, including action steps and timetables; (5) how working affects the personal aspects of your life, including your social life.

Krannich, Caryl Rae and Ronald L. *Interview for Success: A Practical Guide to Increasing Job Interviews, Offers, and Salaries.* 5th ed. Manassas Park, Va.: Impact, 1995.

Interview for Success thoroughly covers all aspects of the interview process. It also includes quizzes and questionnaires that determine what you know, and what you have yet to learn, about the interview process. Some of the interview-related aspects that are covered in the book include managing the interview for success, interview myths and realities, organizing your job search, encountering different interviews, networking for the interview, preparing for the interview, beginning the interview, communicating nonverbally in the interview, managing the verbal interchange, negotiating salaries, and follow-up tactics to use after the interview.

Leape, Martha P., and Susan M. Vacca. *The Harvard Guide to Careers.* 5th ed. Cambridge, Mass.: Harvard University Press, 1995.

This guide is intended to teach students the skills necessary for career exploration and decision making. It also discusses how today's global marketplace affects certain issues of career development. The book's broader topics include the changing nature of careers, career exploration, career decision making, job search, transition, and career development skills.

Sturman, Gerald M. *If You Knew Who You Were, You Could Be Who You Are: Your Personal Career Profile.* Bedford, N.Y.: Bierman House, 1992.

This is a workbook-style text that is meant to help individuals figure out what type of occupation is best for them. There are quizzes, charts, and questionnaires to assist the reader with the self-discovery process. By analyzing the reader's style, career type, motivation, skills, and internal barriers, the book helps to create and apply a personal career profile.

NOTES

CHAPTER 2

1. Mary Munter, *Guide to Managerial Communication,* 4th ed. (Upper Saddle River, N.J.: Prentice-Hall, 1997).

CHAPTER 4

1. William D. Bygrave, *The Portable MBA in Entrepreneurship* (New York: Wiley, 1994), p. 1.
2. Ibid., p. 2.

CHAPTER 6

1. Christopher Bartlett and Sumantra Ghoshal, *Managing Across Borders: The Transnational Solution* (Cambridge, Mass.: Harvard Business School Press, 1989).

CHAPTER 7

1. Paul A. Argenti, *The Portable MBA Desk Reference* (New York: Wiley, 1994), p. 109.
2. Ibid.
3. J. Paul Peter and James Donnelly, *A Preface to Marketing Management,* 6th ed. (Burr Ridge, Ill.: Irwin, 1994), pp. 56–73.
4. Ajay K. Kohli and Bernard J. Jaworski, "Market Orientation: The Construct, Research Propositions and Managerial Implications," *Journal of Marketing,* Vol. 54 (April 1990), pp. 1–18.
5. John Hampton, ed., *American Management Association Management Handbook* (New York: ANACOM, 1994).

CHAPTER 8

1. Irving Lester Janis, *Victims of Groupthink: A Psychological Study of Foreign Policy Decisions and Fiascoes* (Boston: Houghton Mifflin, 1972).

CHAPTER 9

1. Thomas J. Peters and Robert H. Waterman, *In Search of Excellence* (New York: Harper & Row, 1982), p. 5.

2. Gary Hamel and C. K. Prahalad, "Strategic Intent," *Harvard Business Review* (May-June 1989).

3. C. K. Prahalad and Gary Hamel, "The Core Competence of the Corporation," *Harvard Business Review* (May-June 1990).

4. Ibid., p. 80.

5. Ibid., p. 84.

CHAPTER 10

1. Lee Dyer and Donna Blancero, "Workplace 2000," Working Paper 92-10, Center for the Advanced Human Resources Studies, Cornell University (February 1992).

2. Andy Grove, interview in *Newsweek* (September 26, 1996), p. 63.

3. "Saving the World," *Fortune* (September 9, 1996), pp. 44–46.

4. Alfred Mauer, "From My Perspective," *National Business Employment Weekly* (July 21–27, 1996), p. 4.

5. Cassandra Hayes and Nadirah Z. Sabi'r, "Taking Your Job Search On-Line," *Black Enterprise* (January 1996), pp. 70–74.

6. AAA RESUME http://www.infi.net/ resume/

Electronic References

With the development of the World Wide Web, you can now find additional information about each of the topics presented in this book. Here is a brief overview of the Internet and addresses from which to start your search.

The Internet consists of a global collection of computer-mediated networks, including e-mail, the World Wide Web (WWW), Usenet newsgroups, Listserv's mailing lists, Telnet sites, FTP file libraries, and Gopher sites.

E-mail enables users to send messages to anyone else with an e-mail address. The format is generally structured: *myname@mylocation.com.*

Usenet Newsgroups and *Listserv* are discussion groups where people from around the globe can share views on a specific topic.

Telnet sites are computer data banks of libraries and universities that can be accessed from a distance via computers.

FTP file libraries and *Gopher* sites are computer library links that contain not only documents, but also software, which you can download onto your own computer.

The *World Wide Web* (*WWW*) is a form of computer-mediated communication that uses graphical interfaces of colorful images and sounds and offers links to a wealth of information on just about any conceivable topic. Companies, institutions, and individuals have created Web sites consisting of home pages and links to subdivisions of information. WWW's assets include the ability to access information about a specific company or theme, to keep up to date with news from around the world, and also to purchase services or products.

The network is vast and the sheer volume of information can be overwhelming. To facilitate manageable usage of the multitude of information that the WWW offers, dedicated Web sites have been created that effectively navigate through the WWW to find specific topics of interest. The most popular of these information-finding Web sites include Infoseek, Lycos, and Yahoo!, and the best is Digital's Alta Vista. These Web sites all offer the feature of searching a specific subject, topic, or company name. Despite this commonality, these sites have different features. Each is an effective information-finding tool and the site that you select to frequent depends on your personal preference and your specific needs. The following is a list of information-finding Web sites as well as some of their subdirectory features:

Digital's Alta Vista
http://altavista.digital.com/
The largest Web index with the fastest search capabilities to locate topics, people, and information. At the time of publication, Alta Vista offered access to over 11 billion words found in 22 million Web pages. Alta Vista also offers over 13,000 newsgroups with access not only to headlines, but the full text of the articles.

Alta Vista Help
http://altavista.digital.com/cgi-bin/query?pg=h&what=web
Detailed explanations on how to notate a simple query and an advanced query, as well as general information about the use of Alta Vista.

Alta Vista Simple Query
http://altavista.digital.com/cgi-bin/query?pg=q&what=web
Search capabilities of broad topics on the Web and in Usenet.

Alta Vista Advanced Query
http://altavista.digital.com/cgi-bin/query?pg=aq&what=web
With the immense volume of information on the Web and Usenet, this is a very useful feature to search a collection of themes with criteria in a ranked order. The advanced query is particularly useful to add greater specifications to a broad topic.

Alta Vista Surprise
http://altavista.digital.com/cgi-bin/query?pg=s&what=web
Categorical divisions to initiate surfing the Web or Usenet for a specific theme, such as art, sports, museums, interviews, universities, sports, movies, or home pages.

Infoseek
http://www.infoseek.com/
Directory to facilitate browsing the Web. It offers directions and insights about searching through the Web that may prove helpful for novice users. Comprehensive directory with topical areas of interest to browse, as well as means of accessing specific topics.

Infoseek World News
http://guide.infoseek.com/Ticker?pg=DCticker.html&sv=IS&lk=noframes
Easy access to world news headlines from infoseek home page. Ability to access specific news topics of interest.

Infoseek Fast Facts
http://guide.infoseek.com/Ticker?pg=DCticker.html&sv=IS&lk=noframes
Infoseek subdirectory with the capability of accessing e-mail addresses, stock quotes, phone numbers, dictionaries, thesauruses, U.S. historical documents, national archives and records, conversion table, world factbooks, and zip codes.

Corporate Communications
http://www.corpcomm.net/
Provides a full range of Internet connections and offers consultation services to help integrate existing networks with connectivity to the Internet.

Lycos
http://www.lycos.com/
Comprehensive Web directory that offers search features and organization of Web pages into exploration categories.

Point Communication
http://www.pointcom.com/now/news.htm
Newspaper headlines continually updated from the array of newspapers that span the Web. If a headline strikes your interest, you have direct access to the article.

Four 11 Directory Services
http://www.four11.com/
Internet's largest white-page directory with over 6.5 million listings. The best way to search for someone's e-mail address or Web page.

Yahoo!
http://www.yahoo.com/
Search capabilities and easy access to category divisions such as business and the economy, computers and the Internet, and education.

New Yahoo!
http://www.yahoo.com/new/
Insight on all the new Web sites from the past week. The number of new sites can be accessed by category

or complete listings. Great for following new trends on the Web, as well as accessing the newest sites online.

News Yahoo!
http://www.yahoo.com/headlines/
Daily news headlines with categorical divisions based on information topic. Ability to easily access headlines and summaries. An additional asset is that the date of the most recent site update is listed. Accesses the previous day's top stories.